MODERN HUMANITIES RESEARCH ASSOCIATION
TEXTS AND DISSERTATIONS
VOLUME 95

NARRATIVE STRUCTURE AND PHILOSOPHICAL DEBATES IN
TRISTRAM SHANDY AND *JACQUES LE FATALISTE*

MODERN HUMANITIES RESEARCH ASSOCIATION
TEXTS AND DISSERTATIONS

Established in 1970, the series promotes important work by younger scholars by making the most accomplished doctoral research available to a wider readership. Titles are selected and edited by a Board of distinguished experts from across the modern Humanities.

Editorial Board

English: Professor Catherine Maxwell, Queen Mary, University of London
French: Professor William Brooks, University of Bath
Germanic: Professor Ritchie Robertson, University of Oxford
Hispanic: Professor Derek Flitter, University of Exeter
Italian: Professor Brian Richardson, University of Leeds
Latin American: Professor Catherine Davies, University of Nottingham
Portuguese: Professor Thomas Earle, University of Oxford
Slavonic: Professor David Gillespie, University of Bath

Narrative Structure and Philosophical Debates in *Tristram Shandy* and *Jacques le fataliste*

by
Margaux Elizabeth Whiskin

Modern Humanities Research Association
2014

Published by

The Modern Humanities Research Association,
1 Carlton House Terrace
London SW1Y 5AF
United Kingdom

© The Modern Humanities Research Association, 2014

Margaux Elizabeth Whiskin has asserted her right under the Copyright, Designs and Patents Act 1988 to be identified as the author of this work. Parts of this work may be reproduced as permitted under legal provisions for fair dealing (or fair use) for the purposes of research, private study, criticism, or review, or when a relevant collective licensing agreement is in place. All other reproduction requires the written permission of the copyright holder who may be contacted at rights@mhra.org.uk.

First published 2014

ISBN 978-1-78188-016-6 (hardback)
ISBN 978-1-78188-017-3 (paperback)
ISSN (MHRA Texts and Dissertations) 0957-0322

www.texts.mhra.org.uk

CONTENTS

	Acknowledgements	vi
	Abbreviations	vii
	Introduction	1
1.	Ludic Narrative	12
2.	Ideas and Examples	42
3.	Mindscapes: Descriptions and Spatial Representations	79
4.	Sentimentalism and the Grotesque	123
	Conclusion	158
	Bibliography	163

ACKNOWLEDGEMENTS

My warmest thanks go to Dr Tom Jones and Dr David Culpin who have supervised my work jointly. I am most grateful to them for having helped me to develop my ideas and to give them structure. If I have even but partly partaken in their intellectual rigour and elegance, this would be the greatest reward of my doctorate. I am grateful to the School of English and the School of Modern Languages of the University of St Andrews for the financial support they have provided. Dr Christopher MacLachlan from the University of St Andrews and Prof. Derek Connon from Swansea University have provided very useful corrections and have been most helpful in their criticism and guidance as to how to further my ideas and improve my work. I am indebted to my parents, Keith Whiskin and Sophie Marsaudon. They have encouraged me unwaveringly in the course of this project and have been its main financial source. They have also taken the time to engage with my work, and through conversations have furthered my reflection. I wish to thank my sister Solène Whiskin for her gracious support. My husband, David Bagot, has been an unfaltering and most precious source of encouragement and guidance on both academic and practical matters. Last but not least, I include Antioch to whom this work is dedicated:

'Thoughts come clearly while one walks.' (Thomas Mann)

ABBREVIATIONS

JF: *Jacques le fataliste* in Diderot, Denis, *Contes et romans*, ed. Michel Delon (Paris: Gallimard, 2004)
TS: *Tristram Shandy* in Sterne, Laurence, *The Life and Opinions of Tristram Shandy, Gentleman*, ed. Melvyn New and Joan New (London: Penguin Classics, 1997)
ECS: *Eighteenth-Century Studies*
ELH: *English Literary History*
MLN: *Modern Language Notes*
MLS: *Modern Language Studies*
OED: *Oxford English Dictionary*
PMLA: *Publication of Modern Language Association of America*
SEL: *Studies in English Literature*

To Antioch

INTRODUCTION

In his study entitled *Comparative Literature*, Henry Gifford suggests that the most useful comparisons

> [...] are those that writers themselves have accepted or challenged their readers to make — those that spring from the 'shock of recognition' where one writer has become conscious that an affinity exists between another and himself. Henry James felt this about Turgenev, Pound felt it about Propertius, Pushkin about Byron.[1]

To Gifford's list of examples I wish to add the case of Diderot and Sterne. In the closing pages of *Jacques le fataliste*, Diderot does indeed challenge the reader, in a rather ambiguous way, to draw a two-way affinity between Sterne and himself. This passage probably constitutes the starting point of all comparative studies on *Tristram Shandy* and *Jacques le fataliste*. Diderot's particular bond with Sterne was indeed noted as early as 1913 by Loyalty Cru who recognised it as a perfect case study for comparative literature. For Cru, '[there] is, to our knowledge, no instance in comparative literature of an apparently more obvious "influence" than this'.[2] The affiliation between Sterne and Diderot appears explicitly in the concluding pages of *Jacques le fataliste*.

> Voici le second paragraphe copié de la vie de *Tristram Shandy*, à moins que l'entretien de Jacques le fataliste et de son maître ne soit antérieur à cet ouvrage, et que le ministre Sterne ne soit le plagiaire, ce que je ne crois pas, mais par une estime toute particulière de M. Sterne que je distingue de la plupart des littérateurs de sa nation dont l'usage assez fréquent est de nous voler et de nous dire des injures.[3]

This paragraph is at the origin of the critics' interest in the connection between Diderot's novel and Sterne's *The Life and Opinions of Tristram Shandy, Gentleman*. The excerpt is circumvoluted; the meaning is unclear. Diderot's narrator hesitates: the following scene in which Denise rubs Jacques's leg could be a plagiarised version of Sterne's description of the 'fair Beguine' tending to Trim's wound.[4] However, the narrator does not rule out the possibility that Sterne might have been the plagiarist, despite having some reservations as to this second possibility. To this hesitation concerning the identity of the plagiarist, and the originality of *Jacques le fataliste* and *Tristram Shandy*, the narrator adds the problem of an ambiguous relationship between French and English authors. The narrator esteems Sterne, but is critical of English writers generally. The mist surrounding this perplexing paragraph and Diderot's intentions in writing it acts as an invitation to compare *Jacques le fataliste* and *Tristram Shandy*.

At the first publication of *Jacques le fataliste* in 1796, the critics sought traces of influence from *Tristram Shandy*, which was already enjoying great fame in France.[5] Diderot's own suggestions of plagiarism gave the cue. In the 31 October 1796 issue of the *Décade philosophique*, Andrieux offers a disparaging review of *Jacques le fataliste*:

> Vous connaissez *Rabelais*? vous connaissez *Sterne*? Si vous ne les connaissez pas, je vous conseille de les lire, sur-tout le dernier. Mais si vous voulez connaître une très-faible imitation du *Tristram-Shandy*, vous n'avez qu'à lire Jacques le Fataliste . . .
>
> Vous y trouverez encore moins tout ce qui fait le charme des écrits du ministre anglais, cette aimable naïveté, cette finesse d'observation, cette délicatesse de sentimens, cette abondance d'idées justes, plaisantes, profondes; l'érudition, la morale, le bouffon et le pathétique traités avec la même supériorité; il n'appartient qu'à Sterne de vous faire ainsi rire d'un œil et pleurer de l'autre.
>
> Diderot n'a de son modèle que le décousu et le défaut de liaison.[6]

On the other side of the spectrum, a critic from the *Gazette nationale ou le Moniteur universel*, far more complimentary to Diderot's novel, nuances the accusations of plagiarism. He recognises Sterne's influence on *Jacques le fataliste* whilst at the same time acknowledging its originality:

> Il est impossible dans un court extrait de donner une idée satisfaisante, d'un ouvrage qui présente à chaque instant des traits de gaieté et d'originalité, qu'on lit avec plaisir d'un bout à l'autre, et qu'on regrette de voir finir sitôt. Tout le monde connaît la vie et les opinions de Tristram-Shandy de l'anglais Sterne; je pense que Diderot a eu cet ouvrage en vue en écrivant son Fataliste. Il le laisse même entrevoir dans un endroit; mais c'est un original tracé d'après un autre. Le roman de Sterne ne ressemble à rien, tout y est neuf; mais il est bisarre [sic] et obscur à force d'être original.[7]

These two reviews are representative of the approach many critics have taken when studying jointly *Jacques le fataliste* and *Tristram Shandy*.

The question of who has plagiarised whom, opened by Diderot, can be very easily resolved by looking at a few key dates necessary to clarify Diderot's connection to Sterne. In a letter addressed to Sophie Volland, we find Diderot's first impressions of *Tristram Shandy*:

> Ce livre si fou, si sage et si gai est le Rabelais des Anglais. Il est intitulé *La Vie, les mémoires et les opinions de Tristram Shandy*. Il est impossible de vous en donner une autre idée que celle d'une satire universelle. M. Sterne qui en est l'auteur est aussi un prêtre.[8]

Indeed, we know from a letter dating from 22 April 1762 that Sterne wanted to offer to Diderot the complete works of Pope, Cibber, Locke, Tillotson's Sermons,

Chaucer, and the first six volumes of *Tristram Shandy*.[9] Diderot would have read Sterne's work in the original. Indeed, the first four volumes of *Tristram Shandy* were translated for the first time into French in 1776 by Frénais. Sterne had also read one of Diderot's works, *Le Fils naturel, ou Les épreuves de la vertu*, but he did not seem to reciprocate the latter's admiration.[10] In June 1765 Baron d'Holbach had in his possession volumes 7 and 8 of *Tristram Shandy*, which contain the episode of Trim and the Beguine alluded to in *Jacques le fataliste*. We may speculate that d'Holbach lent these volumes to his close friend Diderot.[11] In September 1771, *Jacques le fataliste* was well under way.[12] These dates shift the attention from plagiarism to that of the circulation of ideas and texts. The notion of circulation is itself present in *Jacques le fataliste* and draws another connection to Sterne, though in a much more discreet way.

In *A Sentimental Journey*, Sterne illustrates the notion of circulation with the image of a coin passing from hand to hand. In the course of his visit to Paris, Yorick uses shillings to explain the reason for the politeness of the French as opposed to the originality of the English:

> I had a few king William's shillings as smooth as glass in my pocket; and foreseeing they would be of use in the illustration of my hypothesis, I had got them into my hand, when I had proceeded so far —
> See, Mons. Le Compte, said I rising up, and laying them before him upon the table — by jingling and rubbing one against another for seventy years together in one body's pocket or another's, they are become so much alike, you can scarce distinguish one shilling from another.
> The English, like antient medals, kept more apart, and passing but few peoples hands, preserve the first sharpness which the fine hand of nature has given them — they are not so pleasant to feel — but in return, the legend is so visible, that at the first look you see whose image and superscription they bear.[13]

The image of the circulation of the coin reappears in *Jacques le fataliste* where it is also used to represent originality, as Jacques is described as 'un franc original, ce qui arriverait plus souvent parmi les hommes, si l'éducation d'abord, ensuite le grand usage du monde ne les usaient pas comme ces pièces d'argent qui à force de circuler perdent leur empreinte' (*JF*, p. 813). The illustration of originality through the image of the circulating coin is problematical in more than one way and for both novels. As we will see in the course of this work, more often than not examples in *Jacques le fataliste* and *Tristram Shandy* contradict the ideas they are supposed to illustrate. The fact that Yorick illustrates French politeness with 'king William's shillings' seems to be an awkward choice. The logical equation would have been that unused English coins should stand for English originality, and French polished coins for French politeness. The comparison fails at a second level. By embarking on the Grand Tour, Yorick leaves his retired parsonage and circulates in foreign polite circles. Yet, instead of losing his mint, his originality becomes all the more visible. In the case of *Jacques le fataliste*, the comparison is also flawed as Jacques has a long history of circulation. He has an impressive genealogy of masters, having passed, like a coin, from the hands of Desglands to those of de La Boulaye, to de La Boulaye's older brother, to his younger brother, M. Pascal, to de Tourville, to the Marquise du Belloy, to one of her cousins, to M. Hérissant, to M. de Rusai, to Mlle Isselin, to his current master (see *JF*, pp. 793-94). Here, Jacques stands for the circulation of the servant, of Diderot's actual book, *Jacques le fataliste*, and for the circulation of intertextuality.

Such literary circulations, exemplified by the image of the coin from *A Sentimental Journey* or variations on certain scenes of *Tristram Shandy*, create connections, or, to use Diderot's own expression, 'rapports', with *Jacques le fataliste*. For Diderot, any form of rapport takes on an aesthetical dimension. In his article on 'Le Beau' in the *Encyclopédie*, Diderot argues that the concept of beauty depends on the perception of relations. These relations may be contained within the object itself, but may also be formed with regard to other objects: 'J'appelle donc beau hors de moi, tout ce qui contient en soi de quoi réveiller dans mon entendement l'idée de rapports; & beau par rapport à moi, tout ce qui réveille cette idée.' From this follows that the connection to Sterne contributes to *Jacques le fataliste*'s aesthetical quality; and as the contradictions and ambiguities of the references to Sterne indicate, there is more to those rapports than simply a question of plagiarism.

The problem of originality and plagiarism has very often been taken seriously. The comparisons Diderot invites us to draw have started by the identification of passages the French author copied from Sterne. J. Robert Loy has methodically listed those passages and comes to the conclusion that the 'actual copied passages in question are rather unimportant when brought to light'.[14] Diderot has mainly borrowed from Sterne traits and episodes relating to Trim for the creation of his main character. Jacques and Trim are retired soldiers now acting as servants, and who take great delight in talking. Jacques's brother Jean and Trim's brother Tom both went to Lisbon where it is feared they met a sad end. Jacques and Trim trust in the saying that every bullet has its billet. They both attribute their falling in love to the shot they received in the knee during action. They are put on a cart, and unable to do the whole journey in such a bad state, they receive hospitality and care in the house of charitable peasants. Trim meets there the fair Beguine, whilst Jacques is transferred to a castle where Denise lives as a maid. Their respective paramours ease the itching of the soldiers' wounded knees by rubbing them, thus arousing their passion. In terms of actual story content, the passages plagiarised are inconsequential and their interest probably mainly lies in the fact they obviously draw a connection with *Tristram Shandy*. Trim's love story is contained and constitutes but one amongst many amusing episodes in Sterne's novel. The importance of Jacques's love story however has been inflated to the point of focusing the reader's attention throughout the novel. Diderot has indeed copied elements from *Tristram Shandy* but has adapted them for his own purpose. As Derek Connon says of Diderot, 'even when he is quoting almost verbatim, he is constantly adapting the original material to his own ends.'[15]

Agnès Raymond's monograph on the genesis of *Jacques le fataliste* proposes a more detailed account of the story of the connection between Sterne and Diderot. Raymond suggests that the connection is not a direct one, and that the missing link is a series of fragments written by Mlle de Lespinasse who wanted to imitate the sentimentalism in Sterne's *Sentimental Journey*. Those fragments narrate incidents which happened to Mme Geoffrin, involving Sterne during his trip to Paris, and a handyman called Jacques who risks serious reprimand from his master but whom Sterne helps. Raymond mentions a second fragment reminiscent of the episode when Jacques offers his money to an indigent woman who has accidentally broken her master's oil jar. Raymond's argument is that Mlle de Lespinasse's fragments are at the origin of *Jacques le fataliste* and not *Tristram Shandy*. Through her study, Raymond sheds light on the story of the writing process of *Jacques le fataliste*. Far from negating the essential connection between *Jacques le fataliste* and *Tristram Shandy*, Raymond reasserts it: 'En vérité, il serait plus logique d'interpréter le plagiat avoué de *Tristram Shandy* dans le roman de Diderot comme un hommage à un grand maître du genre romanesque'.[16] She suggests that Diderot's novel started as 'une critique discrète du mauvais pastiche de Sterne par Mlle de Lespinasse'.[17] Diderot thus offered his own pastiche of Sterne to correct Mlle de Lespinasse's misunderstanding of the English author, and by doing so wrote a eulogy far more powerful than his *Eloge de Richardson*: 'En faisant un pastiche digne de cet auteur, Diderot a fait un chef d'œuvre. Il a érigé un monument à la mémoire de Sterne plus durable que le marbre et plus éloquent que la rhétorique des éloges traditionnels.'[18] Raymond's position approaches that of the critic from the *Gazette nationale*: *Jacques le fataliste* has indeed been influenced by *Tristram Shandy* but this does not prevent it from being an original and brilliant piece of literature in its own right.

Twentieth-century studies on the connection between Sterne and Diderot may be said to have seriously started with Cru's *Diderot as a Disciple of English Thought*. Sterne's influence on Diderot is but one of the facets Cru explored, as his study more generally looks at the French philosopher's fascination with the ideas and works taking shape on the other side of the Channel. Though Diderot never travelled to Great Britain, he had read many British contemporary philosophical and literary works, translated some of them, and in certain cases engaged in correspondence with, or even met British intellectuals.[19] Francis B. Barton's study and Charles Sears Baldwin's article complement Cru's research, as they explore the intellectual legacy Sterne left in France.[20] Alice Green Fredman continues the work of these authors, as she furthers the discussion on circulation of ideas but strictly focuses on Sterne and Diderot. In *Diderot and*

Sterne, Fredman defines the directing line of her work as a study of these two authors' 'efforts [...] to break with vestiges of the neoclassical spirit and to arrive at modes of literary creation and expression that led to romanticism and the modern era.'[21] Focusing on sensibility, humour, and literary style, Fredman compares and contrasts the impact of intellectual currents of the time on Sterne's and Diderot's works. Frédéric Ogée and Lana Asfour have pursued and up-dated the study of cultural exchanges between France and Britain during the eighteenth century.[22] Though *Better in France?*, edited by Ogée, does not contain any article concentrating specifically on either Sterne or Diderot, its contributions examine cultural exchanges and the translatability of ideas from one country to another. This work brings to light the Franco-British intellectual dynamism Diderot and Sterne were contemporary and familiar with, and which, in certain cases, influenced their own work. Asfour's angle is much narrower as she focuses on the reception of Sterne's work in eighteenth-century France and how it participated in the discussion of the novelistic genre generally. The connections between Sterne and Diderot have been studied through the broader perspective of European intellectual interchange, but comprehensive comparative studies of *Jacques le fataliste* and *Tristram Shandy* remain scarce. Though focusing on Sterne and Diderot, Fredman is not interested in confronting the two novels. Since Fredman, there has been no work in French or English solely focusing on Sterne and Diderot.[23] *Jacques le fataliste* and *Tristram Shandy* have appeared in thematic works, but without being studied jointly.[24]

At the origin of my work is the belief that the study of Sterne and Diderot as intellectuals participating in, and influenced by, the circulation of ideas at home and across the Channel sheds some light on the *rapports* between *Tristram Shandy* and *Jacques le fataliste*, but does not explain them. As for the accusation of plagiarism, it explicitly pointed to the existence of those *rapports* but at the same time sent the reader on a false track as to their exact nature. Mikhail Bakhtin suggested another angle as to how to understand the affiliation between the two texts. Amongst the works Bakhtin referred to so as to illustrate his concepts, Sterne and Diderot, *Tristram Shandy* and *Jacques le fataliste*, regularly came up, and often together. Rather provokingly, Shklovsky had declared *Tristram Shandy* to be 'the most typical novel in world literature'.[25] As *Jacques le fataliste* shared many of the Shandean modes of writing, it seemed appropriate to study comparatively those two texts in the light of the concepts of one of the greatest theorists of the novel as a genre. This study is very obviously a Bakhtinian reading of *Tristram Shandy* and *Jacques le fataliste*. Bakhtin's theories on the novel have given coherence to the interplay of the narrative structure and the philosophical debates, of the aesthetics and the ideas in both novels. By offering a comparative study, I wished to demonstrate that what Diderot retained from Sterne was less the knee-rubbing scene or the garrulous soldier-servant than the philosophical and aesthetical open-endedness. The directing argument of this work is to explore how the narrative structure alters and renews the meaning of the philosophical debates between the characters, or between the narrator and reader. My argument hinges on Bakhtinian dialogism, which can be defined as the presence of interacting voices and views. In *Tristram Shandy* and *Jacques le fataliste*, dialogism occurs through the narrative structure allowing for the confrontation of the contradictory discourses in the philosophical debates, and enabling them to dialogue, instead of establishing the authorial voice as the sole valid discourse in the text.

One would expect that a novel with a philosophical content would naturally attempt to convince the reader of the truth of its author's views by defending and corroborating them. In *Jacques le fataliste* and *Tristram Shandy*, the narrative structure serves this end by making the reader experience associationism, sympathy and determinism for example. However, this same narrative structure may also contradict and refute those same concepts. The apparent philosophical stance of those texts is thus made untenable. The reader is left to hesitate constantly between accepting and rejecting the ideas expressed, as they work in some cases but not in all. Through those contradictions, the philosophical content takes on a different form, that of a refusal of systematic thinking which is at the heart of *Tristram Shandy* and *Jacques le fataliste*. No philosophical system is imposed: the reader is left to experience its truth and limits for himself, without having the author trying to convince him didactically one way or the other. This allows for an intricate interplay of voices freely expressing and contradicting ideas, in constant dialogue. The balance between these voices is achieved by preventing one particular stable voice from dominating the text. If Sterne's and Diderot's position within their own novels were to be pinpointed, then it could be said to be dialogism as it embraces all voices and allows them to converse whilst refusing systematic thinking often brought about by conclusions. To use Diderot's own words, dialogism opens and creates *rapports* between the various voices of the novels, whether conflicting or not. It does not bring them to a close and consequently the incompletion of philosophical debates impedes the dominance of an authoritative system. Paradoxically, dialogism may be seen as the ruling principle of *Jacques le fataliste* and *Tristram Shandy* in that it prevents a dogmatic view from forcing itself upon the texts. It is interesting to note that the affiliation between *Jacques le fataliste* and *Tristram Shandy* offers an example of dialogism by introducing the external voice of Sterne's novel (the hypotext) into Diderot's (the hypertext). Thus a *rapport* is created, connecting the two texts, though it is left to the reader to decide for himself exactly what this *rapport* consists of. More than a philosophical method, dialogism also represents an aesthetical approach through its open-endedness. Indeed, if dialogism is at the origin of the *rapports* of the two texts, then, following Diderot's definition of 'Le Beau', it is also at the source of the texts' beauty. In both novels, the philosophical content and the aesthetic quality serve and complement each other. The structure of the narrative and the philosophical debates are closely connected. Jacques's core belief that everything is written on the Great Scroll of the heavens points to the interdependence between narrative and philosophy.

In order to argue that the narrative structure alters and renews the significance of the philosophical debates, I explore in the first chapter the ludic nature of *Tristram Shandy* and *Jacques le fataliste,* and how Diderot and Sterne use game within their novels as a narrative mode so as to redefine the reader's approach to the text. Indeed, dialogism first takes the form of play as the reader is gradually brought to embrace conflicting views and reject systematic thinking in the context of the text as game. The first chapter focuses on the self-referentiality of the two narratives and how the removal of certain elements in a logical argument transforms the text into a game. Games occupy in *Tristram Shandy* and *Jacques le fataliste* a specific purpose. They replace didactic explanations by practical demonstrations where a character or the reader experiences for himself the truth of a particular view instead of simply receiving from another an abstract reasoning. Games in Sterne's and Diderot's novels are accompanied by a certain amount of tension between reader and narrator. Indeed, the rules appear to be changing constantly, taking the reader unawares. I argue that this looseness in the game, the fact that there are no fixed rules, corresponds to the authors' rejection of any form of authoritative system. The textual games, like the debates, are left open; no ending has been imposed upon the reader.

In the first chapter, philosophical demonstrations are shown to take the guise of games. The second chapter focuses more specifically on the relation between ideas and examples in *Tristram Shandy* and *Jacques le fataliste*. Concrete illustrations, which can take the form of an explanatory anecdote or even a practical demonstration, usually serve to help the understanding of an abstract concept. This is not however always the case, as there are instances when the example contradicts and thus invalidates the idea it is supposed to illustrate. Such ruptures occur when an idea goes against common sense, when a character's actions are inconsistent with his beliefs, or when the example chosen proves itself to be the exception to the rule. The contradictions between ideas and examples prevent debates from reaching a conclusion as long as they are left unresolved. Bringing into play Bakhtin's concept of heteroglossia, I argue that avoiding a conclusion is exactly Sterne's and Diderot's aim. The incomprehension resulting from an unresolved juxtaposition of diverging views furthers the dialogue, whilst the absence of conclusion to the debate prevents one voice from asserting itself as the dominant position in the novel.

The third chapter concentrates on how the characters and the reader try to use space as a visual illustration of ideas, but fail. This chapter studies how the fragmentary nature of the descriptions of the characters and their surroundings parallels that of their philosophical debates. My argument hinges on the absence of outsideness, which Bakhtin presents as the external gaze of the author embracing the entire existence of his character so as to offer him to the reader as a complete, perfect entity. Sterne and Diderot offer no such outside reconstruction. The characters attempt to reconstruct the missing authorial external gaze. Indeed, outsideness would enable them to gain an overall view of themselves and the beliefs they stand for. However, they fail in disentangling their thoughts, consequently making their contradictions even more noticeable. The reader is placed in a similar situation. Engaged in the complex game of the text, he too desires an overall view of the progression of the narrative, of the characters and their surroundings, so as to simplify his reading. Yet this is also denied, as the author does not provide a coherent and comprehensive description. I argue that Sterne's and Diderot's refusal to provide a unifying perspective in descriptions correlates with their decision to leave the philosophical debates as fragments of conversations without conclusion. The voluntary absence of outsideness corresponds to the rejection of an authoritative perspective on the characters just as the fragmentary and open-ended philosophical debates oppose the dominance of a dogmatic stance.

The fourth chapter analyses how social interaction is at the heart of certain philosophical debates. In *Tristram Shandy* and *Jacques le fataliste*, the surroundings of the characters usually constitute spaces of sociability, inviting the characters, the narrator and the reader to engage with others. Social interaction also crystallises one of the major contradictions of both texts, that of the paradoxical juxtaposition of sentimentalism and the grotesque. I look at how Sterne and Diderot shared the interest in sensibility as an approach to further their understanding of the nature of society and morality. Though including discussions on sensibility and sentimental scenes in their novels, Sterne and Diderot also challenge this approach by juxtaposing it with its opposite, the grotesque. I argue that Bakhtin's notion of the carnivalesque offers a key to resolve such a problematical coincidence of contraries. Sentimentalism and the grotesque should not be dissociated as they complement each other to offer a carnivalesque dimension to both texts. The carnivalesque laughs at any form of authoritative discourse and so prevents a dominant system from imposing itself. Through the carnivalesque, Sterne and Diderot are not invalidating sentimentalism, but they are preventing it from becoming the only mode of reading.

As dialogic novels, *Tristram Shandy* and *Jacques le fataliste* offer a plurality of contradictory voices. As the present study will demonstrate, the narrative structures of the two novels prevent an authoritative voice from emerging and invalidating all other forms of discourse. This allows Sterne and Diderot to maintain the dialogue they have initiated through their works with the reader, whose voice is but one amongst many others.

Notes to the Introduction

1. Henry Gifford, *Comparative Literature* (London: Routledge & Kegan Paul, 1969), p. 73.
2. R. Loyalty Cru, *Diderot as a Disciple of English Thought* (New York: AMS Press, 1966), p. 373.
3. Denis Diderot, *Jacques le fataliste et son maître*, in *Contes et romans*, ed. by Michel Delon (Paris: Gallimard, 2004), p. 883 (hereafter *JF*).
4. Laurence Sterne, *The Life and Opinions of Tristram Shandy, Gentleman*, ed. by Melvyn New and Joan New (London: Penguin Classics, 1997), VIII, xxii, p. 522 (hereafter *TS*).
5. *Jacques le fataliste* had been published first as a serial in the *Correspondance littéraire* from 1778 to 1780.
6. Section 'Littérature', *La Décade philosophique, littéraire et politique, par une société de républicains*, 31 Octobre 1796, p. 224–25.
7. Section 'Littérature', *Gazette nationale ou le Moniteur universel*, 16 novembre 1796, p. 222. Both reviews are mentioned by J. Robert Loy, *Diderot's Determined Fatalist, a critical appreciation of* Jacques le fataliste (New York: King's Crown Press, Columbia University, 1950), p. 3.
8. This letter was written on Thursday 7 October 1762. *Correspondance de Diderot*, ed. by Laurent Versini (Paris: Robert Laffont, 1997), p. 456.
9. See Cru, p. 95.
10. 'It has too much sentiment in it (at least for me), the speeches too long, and savour too much of preaching — this may be a second reason, it is not to my taste'. Quoted by Cru, p. 96.
11. See A. G. Raymond, *La Genèse de* Jacques le fataliste *de Diderot, quelques clefs nouvelles* (Paris: Archives des Lettres Modernes, 1977), p. 5.
12. A letter from Johann Heinrich Meister to Johann Jakob Bodmer from 12th September 1771 helps us to establish an approximate date for *Jacques le fataliste*: 'Diderot n'a pas encore commencé son traité *De vita bona et beata*, mais il a fait un conte charmant, *Jacques le fataliste*. L'auteur en a lu à notre homme pendant deux heures.' in *Lettres inédites de Mme de Staël à Henri Meister*, ed. by Paul Usteri and Eugène Ritter (Paris: Hachette, 1903), p. 24.
13. Laurence Sterne, *A Sentimental Journey through France and Italy by Mr. Yorick*, ed. Paul Goring (London: Penguin Books, 2001), p. 87.
14. Loy, p. 32. The passages are listed in pp. 32–41.
15. Derek Connon, *Diderot's Endgames* (Berne: Peter Lang, 2002), p. 303. On Diderot's borrowings from Sterne, see pp 299–304.
16. Raymond p. 17.
17. Ibid., p. 19.
18. Ibid., p. 20.
19. Though there is no need to repeat them here, it is still interesting to point out that Diderot's attraction to British thought marks the starting point of his own intellectual development. Diderot's career began with translations of English works. In 1743, he started by translating a minor text, *The Grecian history* by Temple Stanyan. In 1745, he translated Shaftesbury's *Inquiry concerning Virtue or Merit* under the title *Essai sur le mérite et la vertu*. More than just a translation, the *Essai* constitutes a commentary on the *Inquiry*, allowing Diderot to engage with Shaftesbury's ideas.
20. See Francis B. Barton, *Etude sur l'influence de Laurence Sterne en France au dix-huitième siècle* (Paris: Hachette, 1911), and Charles Sears Baldwin, 'The Literary Influence of Sterne in France', *PMLA*, 17 (1902), 221–36.
21. Alice Green Fredman, *Diderot and Sterne* (New York: Columbia University Press, 1955), p. 15

22. See *"Better in France?" The circulation of ideas across the Channel in the eighteenth century*, ed. by Frédéric Ogée (Lewisburg: Bucknell University Press, 2005), and Lana Asfour, *Laurence Sterne in France* (London: Continuum, 2008).
23. I must however specify that a German study on *Tristram Shandy* and *Jacques le fataliste* was published ten years after Fredman's book. See Rainer Warning, *Illusion und Wirklichkeit in "Tristram Shandy" und "Jacques le Fataliste"* (Munich: Wilhelm Fink Verlag, 1965).
24. One of the more recent examples of this is Will McMorran's *The Inn and the Traveller: Digressive Topographies in the Early Modern European Novel* (Oxford: Legenda, 2002).
25. Victor Shklovsky, 'Art as Technique', in *Russian Formalist Criticism, Four Essays*, trans. by Lee T. Lemon and Marion J. Reis (Lincoln, London: University of Nebraska Press, 1965), p. 57.

CHAPTER 1

~

Ludic Narrative

At the origin of the comparison between *Jacques le fataliste* and *Tristram Shandy* lies a puzzle set by Diderot. In the paragraph from *Jacques le fataliste* quoted in the introduction, the narrator suggests that one text is authentic and the other a copy, without specifying which one. The narrator thus puts a cloud over the nature of two already very puzzling novels. The chronology however leaves no doubt as to which work precedes the other.[1] This begs the question: why should an author thus denounce his own work? Jean Catrysse's claim might contain the clue to the riddle: 'à la base de toute création romanesque de Diderot: la *mystification*'.[2] As Catrysse mentions, this would certainly not have been the first time that Diderot had misled his audience.[3] We cannot however wave off the connection drawn by Diderot between Sterne and himself as mere tomfoolery. The sensational suspicion of plagiarism acts as a diversion from a more essential analogy: the ludic nature of both novels.

When introduced to *Tristram Shandy* and *Jacques le fataliste*, one is first struck by the two novels' exhibition of their own artificiality and by their demands for the reader's involvement. The unconventionality of Sterne's work has even led Samuel Weber to question its literary categorisation: 'By referring to *Tristram Shandy* here as a *text*, rather than as a *novel*, I want to express a certain scepticism concerning the status of this book'.[4] The term *novel* has of course prevailed over the hazy *text*, yet Weber's doubts remain pertinent. *Tristram Shandy* and *Jacques le fataliste* are novels but play with the genre by exaggerating and unconventionally applying its characteristics, in the same way that games play with and distort reality. The study of the ludic nature of these two novels provides us with another 'handle' — a well-loved Shandean image — to grasp Sterne's and Diderot's work. Not only is play at the origin of the connection between the two novels, it is also the basis of their narrative mode. The purpose of this chapter is to establish that the ludic narrative redefines the reader's approach to the text as it is used for philosophical demonstrations, the most crucial being the rejection of dogma.

Sterne's and Diderot's nonconformism and their refusal of systematic thinking appear more clearly linked through Diderot's definition of the paradoxical author in his *Réflexions sur le livre de l'Esprit*:

Un auteur paradoxal ne doit jamais dire son mot, mais toujours ses preuves: il doit entrer furtivement dans l'âme de son lecteur, et non de vive force. C'est le grand art de Montaigne, qui ne veut jamais prouver, et qui va toujours prouvant, et me ballottant du blanc au noir, et du noir au blanc. D'ailleurs l'appareil de la méthode ressemble à l'échafaud qu'on laisserait toujours subsister après que le bâtiment est élevé. C'est une chose nécessaire pour travailler, mais qu'on ne doit plus apercevoir quand l'ouvrage est fini. L'esprit d'invention s'agite, se meut, se remue d'une manière déréglée; il cherche. L'esprit de méthode arrange, ordonne, et suppose que tout est trouvé . . .[5]

The spirit of invention animates the paradoxical author's work and its unruliness is opposed to the ordering of the methodical spirit. Yet this unruliness allows the paradoxical author to move from one idea to its contrary, to invite his reader to share his intellectual dynamic. On the contrary, the methodical author supposes that everything has already been found; he imposes a system. We may suppose here that Diderot is mostly talking of a distinction between authors of philosophical works. However, the analogy with Montaigne invites us to apply this definition to texts combining philosophy and literature. More significantly, Diderot associates an intellectual dynamic to a style of writing.

Tristram Shandy and *Jacques le fataliste* correspond to Diderot's definition of the paradoxical author and his spirit of invention. Their narrative structure allows Sterne and Diderot to 'ever point out to the curious, different tracts of investigation, . . . not with a pedantic *Fescue*' but with an intellectual humility solely motivated by inquisitiveness (*TS*, I, xxi, p. 59). As we will see in the course of this chapter, the narrative structure of our two novels rests on the principle of play. This at first appears to contradict Diderot's definition of the spirit of invention. In literary play, the scaffolding of the narrative is left apparent and even amplified. This brings us close to the functioning of methodical writing described by Diderot, which maintains the scaffolding once the argument has been made. The scaffolding Diderot is referring to consists in the development of an idea and its various logical phases. The first chapter demonstrates how the scaffoldings of play have deconstructed and replaced those of logic. The effect of this appears in the contradictions between ideas and their illustrations in Sterne's and Diderot's novels, and is analysed in the second chapter.

To explore how the ludic narrative of *Tristram Shandy* and *Jacques le fataliste* participates in the inquisitive embrace of conflicting notions and the rejection of systematic thinking, it is necessary to understand how the scaffoldings of play actually appear in the two novels. I will first study the ludic nature of the texts by concentrating on their self-referentiality and the exhibition of their narrative structure. Withdrawal of information is one of the most common features in games and it also appears in *Tristram Shandy* and *Jacques le fataliste*. Whilst contributing to their ludic nature by engaging with the reader, withdrawal of information corresponds to the removal of certain parts of the logical argument, which are left missing. The scaffoldings of the argument having been withdrawn, play can stand in and become the means of a demonstration which does not declare its view, but makes the reader feel its truth. Neither novel claims to provide the reader with the single right answer to every question raised. On the contrary, they both suggest that there may be multiple and contradictory answers to any one question, thus 'ballotant [le lecteur] du blanc au noir, et du noir au blanc'. The open-endedness of the questions is accompanied by the unfixed nature of the rules, which are constantly changing. This looseness in the play, this free space, equivalent to a tolerance, allowing the literary mechanism to move, implies a certain degree of flexibility in the scaffolding of the narrative. The novelistic genre is not a rigid structure governed by imposed rules. Going back to Diderot's association between an intellectual dynamic and a style of writing, this play in the narrative, in terms of both game and looseness, is consistent with the authors' refusal of dogma. The game is left open, and not trapped into a predetermined ending. Similarly, the spirit of invention 'cherche' and does not 'suppose que tout est trouvé'.

In this chapter I first look at how *Tristram Shandy* and *Jacques le fataliste* make manifest the ludic nature of their narratives by making the artificiality of the text visible to the reader. The obvious presence of the narrator and implied reader enables the historical reader to recognise the self-referentiality of the text. This self-referentiality will set the grounds necessary for the construction and signalisation of textual games, for example, the repetition of patterns. As in any game, there are stakes in ludic narratives; and these are the stories themselves.

Once the ludic nature of Sterne's and Diderot's novels has been established, and the stakes of their textual games identified, we must turn to the mechanics of these games. The narrator challenges the reader by withdrawing information or by introducing noise which clutters the story with unnecessary information and consequently obscures it. Clues are scattered throughout the text whilst other elements have been removed. The narrator thus plays with the curiosity of the reader who will want to reconstruct the story in its entirety by using the clues to supply the missing information. It is necessary that the reader first identifies the ludic nature of the two novels, and understands how their textual games actually work, to allow Sterne and Diderot to use these games for a specific purpose.

Games are used as demonstrations of certain philosophical points discussed in the texts. This function is first used by Jacques who plays a trick on his master, thus forcing him to experience determinism, an idea he had fundamentally rejected. The narrator submits the reader to a similar treatment. Indeed, associationism, determinism and cause and effect are demonstrated to the historical reader through textual games accompanying the philosophical discussions between the characters and the narrator and implied reader. This method enables Sterne and Diderot to avoid imposing on the reader ideas the truthfulness of which he must take for granted. Here, the historical reader is left free to agree or disagree with the ideas expressed, as all positions are represented. For example, the master defends free will whilst his servant believes in fatalism. The reader is also given the opportunity to experience for himself the truthfulness of these ideas through textual games. The function of the ludic narrative as a practical demonstration to the reader of a philosophical point has not been announced. The device of a game has only been explicitly used as a demonstration in the trick Jacques played on his master, so between characters. This means that the reader is given the freedom to interpret the textual games as serving exclusively a ludic purpose, or to consider their meaning in relation to the philosophical discussions. The reader is free to draw his own conclusions. This refusal to impose on the reader a dominant view is particularly visible in certain types of textual games and from the principles by which the ludic narratives are generally constructed.

If rules do indeed exist, they are not strictly followed nor rigidly set. They may change in the course of the novel; they may be broken and even rejected. Such play with the rules signals Diderot's and Sterne's refusal to confine their narratives in a fixed system. This refusal is expressed at another level. In both novels, there exist riddles which cannot be answered by a single response. There is no right answer, but instead a multitude of possibilities. Such riddles defeat the purpose of the systematic thinker who can only admit one single answer, his own. These riddles do not reject the systematic thinker's answer, but offer the space for other solutions to be just as valid. It is through their ludic narratives that Sterne and Diderot introduce a polysemic dimension to their novels.

This chapter demonstrates that philosophical and aesthetical open-endedness can be achieved through ludic narrative. Practical and textual games accompany the various philosophical discussions between the characters, and between the narrator and reader. The truthfulness of certain notions is experienced by the reader, and not imposed upon him. The ludic narrative also offers an open space for dialogism and polysemy. There is no unique answer to a set question. Sterne and Diderot offer multiple and contradictory solutions: the point of their textual games is not for the reader to pick the right answer, but to understand that each is a valid possibility.

Bakhtin was interested in the use of games in Rabelais' work, and urges the reader not to dismiss them:

> The peculiar interpretation of games in Rabelais' time must be carefully considered. Games were not as yet thought of as a part of ordinary life and even less of its frivolous aspect. Instead they had preserved their philosophical meaning. Like all humanists, Rabelais was familiar with the ancient conception of games which held them to be far better than ordinary idle pastimes.[6]

With Rabelais still in mind, Bakhtin continues by tying literary games to his notion of the carnivalesque. Games offer an antithetical version of certain set truths;

they participate in the de-hierarchising of ideas and the deposing of dominant and authoritative discourses without invalidating or attacking the idea itself.

> The basic artistic purpose of the parodied and travestied prophecies and riddles is to uncrown gloomy eschatological time, that is, the medieval concept of the world. The parodies renew time on the material bodily level, transforming it into a propitious and merry notion. The images of games, also, are usually subjected to this purpose. In the Bridlegoose episode games have an additional function: they offer a gay parody of the legal methods of establishing truth.[7]

Though Bakhtin recognised the importance of games and how they could corroborate and refine his own key notions, especially the carnivalesque (which I will analyse in the fourth chapter), he did not develop the notion of play.[8] For this reason, the first chapter is the only one not directly centred on the ideas of Bakhtin, though it does stay faithful to his line of thought. In the current chapter, I argue that the function of play described by Bakhtin in Rabelais' work may be found in *Tristram Shandy* and *Jacques le fataliste*.

Text as Game

This study starts by considering a dissimilarity between the two novels. References to games abound in diversity and number in *Jacques le fataliste*, whereas in *Tristram Shandy*, they are extremely scarce and hardly developed.[9] The word 'play' and its derivatives occur very regularly in the text of *Tristram Shandy*, and yet the only characters engaged in playing at a specific game are Trim and Toby. Here are two obsessive wargamers who take their hobby extremely seriously and think nothing of spending their income, filching lead from sash windows and destroying a bowling green and family heirlooms to produce the right setting for their recreated battles. For Trim and Toby, wargaming is far too serious to be mistaken for mere play: ''tis for the good of the nation' (*TS*, III, xxii, p. 185). Except with Trim and Toby, there are no actual scenes of characters playing at a specific game. It seems that play inside *Tristram Shandy* appears mainly through figurative language.

In *Jacques le fataliste*, play takes a much more concrete and obvious form as the descriptions of actual games abound. Scenes in which games are played are often provided with detailed settings, and are enriched with very technical vocabulary specific to the rules of that particular game. This is particularly striking in the gaming story Jacques tells his master. It is set 'aux foires de Saint-Germain et de Saint-Laurent', a location in Paris where 'jeux de hasard' were authorised.[10] Diderot provides us with the precise terms of the game of 'passe-dix', where the dice are put in a 'cornet', or small goblet, and the players have to achieve 'le tout, le tout du tout, les petites moitiés, les grandes moitiés, le grand tout, le grand tout du tout' (*JF*, 756).[11] Games appear mostly in digressive stories as in the case of the story of M. de Guerchy and Desglands. They also appear very briefly in the story of Mme de La Pommeraye and in that of the master's unfortunate love affair, two major embedded narratives.[12] Games were of course one of the most popular forms of entertainment and the eighteenth-century reader would have been familiar with the very specific and technical terms used, such as 'passe-dix', 'brelan', 'bouillotte'. Yet Diderot's intentions go deeper than simply creating the illusion of *vraisemblance*. By describing characters playing, the narrator gives the cue to the reader who, in the course of the novel, will also engage in a game, but this time at a textual level.

One of the reader's challenges is to recognise the repetition of certain patterns wilfully created as part of the textual game. While Jacques is sent looking for his master's watch and wallet, the narrator takes the opportunity to draw a brief portrait of the master waiting for the return of his servant:

> Puis il cherchait sa montre à son gousset où elle n'était pas et il achevait de se désoler, car il ne savait que devenir sans sa montre, sans sa tabatière et sans Jacques, c'étaient les trois grandes ressources de sa vie qui se passait à prendre du tabac, à regarder l'heure qu'il était, à questionner Jacques, et cela dans toutes les combinaisons. (*JF*, 687)

This passage is not sufficient in itself to signal the ludic nature of *Jacques le fataliste*. However, it is followed by brief passages where the master is described performing these three actions, that is to say taking tobacco, looking at his watch and asking Jacques questions. The frequency of such descriptions, seemingly rather gratuitous, as they do not add anything to the progress of the narrative, becomes conspicuous. It invites the reader to go back to the first description here quoted, and realise that the purpose of those passages is not narratological but ludic. The first description provides a sequence-pattern for the master, which will be repeated throughout the novel and, as the narrator indicated, only varying in order.[13] Such repetitions would have seemed tedious if they had not been part of an implicit game. All these recurrences may only be understood if the reader is attentive enough to the text and looks back retrospectively to the original instance. This often forces the narrator to signal much more forcibly and explicitly to the reader the ludic nature of his text.

The presence of play and games amongst the characters enables the reader to be more attentive to play taking place at the extradiegetic level.[14] In the same way as a game can be played only once its rules have been stated, a literary work needs to establish a *pacte de lecture*, that is to say a series of conventions set out within the text and outlining the specific terms on which it should be approached. As David Gascoigne points out, the *pacte de lecture* constitutes a common feature shared by all narratives, to the point of being naturalised. It becomes an automatism in the reader who is then no longer able to recognise that particular feature as an artificial device. So that a narrative may be recognised as ludic, its *pacte de lecture* must be exacerbated so that it becomes visible once again to the reader.

Gascoigne uses this notion of *pacte de lecture* to define ludic narrative. A narrative may be considered as ludic once the rules of the literary game can no longer be taken for granted, and so constitute a 'substantial — perhaps even the principal — challenge to the reader'.[15]

As previously mentioned, the particular rules of ludic narratives cannot follow literary conventions as these have been completely assimilated to the point of passing unnoticed. The text needs to signal its own mechanisms so that its specific rules may be recognised. According to Peter Hutchinson, this accounts for the particular use of the implied reader whose role is to act as mediator between the text and the historical reader:

> Another characteristic of literary play is its self-conscious nature: in order to function as game, play must draw attention to itself. Clearly, some literary games may remain hidden to all but the most sensitive of readers, but they will at least be visible to what has been called the 'implied' reader [...].[16]

For such a mediation to be successful, the implied reader, whose presence is normally discreet, is hypertrophied in ludic narratives.

Tristram continually addresses his reader whose identity keeps varying. Diderot portrays the implied reader as a very turbulent audience responsible for many of the text's digressions. He is so disruptive that the narrator is obliged to remind him of the rules, or conditions to the progress of the narrative:

> Je vous entends, vous en avez assez, et votre avis serait que nous allassions rejoindre nos deux voyageurs. Lecteur, vous me traitez comme un automate, cela n'est pas poli; dites les amours de Jacques; ne dites pas les amours de Jacques; je veux que vous me parliez de Gousse; j'en ai assez ... Il faut sans doute que j'aille quelquefois à votre fantaisie; mais il faut que j'aille quelquefois à la mienne, sans compter que tout auditeur qui me permet de commencer un récit s'engage d'en entendre la fin. (*JF*, 718)

The narrator here signals the terms of the cooperation and prompts the necessity for mutual agreement and for concessions made on each side. Since the rules of the ludic narrative must be known to the reader for the literary game to be played, the text cannot avoid self-referentiality, thus exhibiting mechanisms responsible for the progress of the narrative.[17]

The intrusion of the implied reader naturally calls for that of the narrator: metalepsis of the author constitutes another facet of ludic self-referentiality. Illustrating his comments by examples from *Tristram Shandy* and *Jacques le fataliste*, Genette calls such 'transgressions' *métalepse de l'auteur* 'qui consiste à feindre que le poète "opère lui-même les effets qu'il chante"'. He offers a more complete definition:

> [...] toute intrusion du narrateur ou du narrataire extradiégétique dans l'univers diégétique (ou de personnages diégétiques dans un univers métadiégétique, etc.), ou inversement [...], produit un effet de bizarrerie soit

bouffonne (quand on la présente comme Sterne ou Diderot, sur le ton de la plaisanterie) soit fantastique.[18]

The strangeness of authorial metalepsis may be accounted for by the fact that it participates in the unconventional self-referentiality by announcing the rules specific to *Tristram Shandy* and *Jacques le fataliste*.[19]

One of the purposes of the intrusive narrator and fictional reader is to state what the rules of Sterne's and Diderot's work are. These rules establish the nature of the relationship between the narrator and the reader, in the same way as the rules of a game set the parameters for the interaction between the players. The French expression *jeux de société* clarifies this function. *Jeux de société*, games requiring two or more players, employ pastime as a pretext momentarily to redefine social rules at a microcosmic scale. When a narrative is constructed as a game, then the novel itself becomes a *jeu de société* played between the narrator and the reader, whose relationship it has delineated. Rules are necessary to govern the relationship between players as games introduce a dynamic of conflict and competition. As opposed to solitary games where the progression exclusively depends on a single player, *jeux de société* progress in a more complex way since each contestant tries to impede the advance of others, and attempts to force them to recede. The flow of game thus naturally follows a backward and forward progression. According to Gadamer, this progression constitutes the *sine qua non* condition of game:

> [...] there arises through the contest the tense movement to-and-fro from which the victor emerges, thus showing the whole to be a game. The movement to-and-fro obviously belongs so essentially to the game that there is an ultimate sense in which you cannot have a game by yourself. In order for there to be a game, there always has to be, not necessarily literally another player, but something else with which the player plays and which automatically responds to his move with a counter-move.[20]

Backwards and forwards is the elected movement of choice in *Tristram Shandy*.[21] For example, it is used to explain how a 'blow' was the cause of Toby's modesty (*TS*, I, xxi, p. 60). To clarify the connection, Tristram is forced to interrupt his progress and go back in his autobiography to offer 'an exact account of the road which led to' Toby's modesty (*TS*, III, xxiii, p. 186). The meandering narrative between when the misunderstanding first happens and its explanation offers a resistance, a 'counter-move' to the player. The structure of the narrative constitutes a puzzle where the reader has to make an effort of memory to reconstitute the narrative in a chronological order. The backward and forward movement constitutes the main mode of progression in *Tristram Shandy*; and for this reason, examples of its occurrence are numerous.

The backward and forward movement corresponds to the difficulty of the game preventing the player from making easy linear progress. What motivates this movement are the stakes of the game. In ludic works, the nature of what is to be won or lost is slightly different. To wile away the tediousness of travelling, Jacques and his master entertain each other with stories. As Jacques was 'né bavard' (*JF*, 794), his master lets him indulge in his passion for talking and contents himself with the role of listener. But when his servant is no longer able to speak because of a sore throat, it is the master's turn to provide a good story. However, this collaboration is not always so amicable. Jacques will spitefully take his revenge by paying his master back for a lengthy and tedious description with an equally prolix and dull story: 'Vous avez sur le coeur le long et ennuyeux portrait de la veuve, mais vous m'avez, je crois, bien rendu cet ennui par la longue et ennuyeuse histoire de la fantaisie de son enfant' (*JF*, 863). Stories are presented here as goods to be exchanged, each with its own value. The portrait of the master, not being worth much, is paid back with a story of equivalent value, as the repetition of the two adjectives 'long et ennuyeux' signals. The relation between storyteller and listener, or in other words between narrator and reader, rests on a balance of give and take: the narrator makes the reader pay the price for his story. This perfectly applies to the notion of story as merchandise developed by Barthes:

> Le Récit: monnaie d'échange, objet de contrat, enjeu économique, en un mot *marchandise* [...] on ne raconte pas pour 'distraire', pour 'instruire' ou pour satisfaire un certain exercice anthropologique du sens; on raconte pour obtenir en échangeant; et c'est cet échange qui est figuré dans le récit lui-même: le récit est à la fois produit et production, marchandise et commerce, enjeu et porteur de cet enjeu.[22]

The story has become the stake of Sterne's and Diderot's textual games.

The ludic nature of the narratives has been established in both novels, together with the way they signal themselves as such to the reader. I have also shown that the stakes to be won by the reader are the stories themselves. The chapter will now turn to the mechanics of the ludic narratives, that is to say how the author has transformed the stories into stakes and how the reader may try to win them.

Withdrawal of Information

The analogy between games and ludic literary works is useful, as the devices of play used are similar. Competition between players often works on a principle based on alternately obscuring and revealing information. Those are the strings on which the narrator pulls to maintain the reader's attention by providing him with clues whilst keeping information away. Withdrawal of information is systematic in *Tristram Shandy* and accounts for much of the digressive mode of writing. In the first volume, Tristram interrupts his uncle in the middle of a sentence eventually completed in the second volume. Such a lengthy interruption puts a stress on that particular sentence and artificially draws the reader's attention to it. This heightened sense of expectation suddenly is deflated once the sentence is completed. 'I think, says he' appears in the first volume (*TS*, I, xxi, p. 56) and the sentence is only completed in the second: 'I think, replied he, — it would not be amiss, brother, if we rung the bell' (*TS*, II, vi, p. 88). The reader's anticipation is disappointed and left unrewarded, as his attention was focused on something which was in reality completely trivial whereas the narrator's frustrating interruption seemed to promise something far more consequential. In *Jacques le fataliste*, stories are constantly interrupted, replaced by others from a different narrative level, then are continued later on, only to be interrupted again. The reader is left with the impossible task of trying to keep simultaneously in mind a number of unfinished stories which are as many gaps in the narrative.[23]

Withdrawal of information may take the form of explicit riddles the narrator sets for the reader. Riddles abound in *Tristram Shandy*, and most of them contain sexual innuendo. The moral need to conceal these innuendos serves as a pretext to transform the riddles in a literary game. The use of Latin in the play on words seems at first to make them even more obscure. However, the reader rapidly finds out that the Latin is very accessible. Latin pretends to hide when in fact it is allowing the narrator to be more explicit. '*De re concubinariâ*' in which Phutatorius is about to put his injured body-part is an example of this (*TS*, IV, xxviii, p. 293). If some riddles are to be guessed, others are obviously not. Those riddles are often completely improbable. Though the narrator might be shocked that they are not solved immediately, it is most likely that the author was expecting only complete bewilderment from the reader. Tristram severely rebukes his female reader for her inattentiveness in not heeding the allusion to the fact that his '*mother was not a papist*' (*TS*, I, xix, p. 51). The answer to the riddle comes a page later where he repeats the allusion: '"It was *necessary* I should be born before I was christen'd." Had my mother, Madam, been a Papist, that consequence did not follow' (*TS*, I, xx, p. 52). Though the logic of the riddle is correct, it is so far-fetched that Sterne expected his reader to be unable to solve it.

The most famous example of riddle in *Jacques le fataliste* occurs during the protagonists' first evening at the inn of the Grand-Cerf. Hearing a great commotion, Jacques asks the landlady the reason why she is so upset with two gentlemen customers. They have maltreated Nicole to the point that she might be crippled for life. After the landlady's explanations, Nicole's misfortunes are put aside immediately, and the return to Jacques's love story around the dinner table literally acts as an interlude to distract the reader from the riddle. The first clue is given shortly afterwards: the landlady calls out for Nanon to bring the dessert. Jacques, confusing her with the bedridden Nicole, is shocked that after suffering such injuries she should be called back to work so quickly. Indeed, Jacques believes that Nicole is a maid, the most logical assumption shared by the reader. This however is inconsistent with the fact that the landlady is still scandalised and railing against the cruelty of the two men. The inconsistency is made even more obvious by what follows:

> LE MAÎTRE: Y a-t-il longtemps que vous l'avez?
> L'HÔTESSE: Une quinzaine au plus. Elle avait été abandonnée à la poste voisine.
> LE MAÎTRE: Comment abandonnée!

Here the most logical guess as to Nicole's identity is that she is a young girl abandoned by her parents and taken care of by the landlady out of charity. But still this assumption only half fits in with the rest of the account.

> L'HÔTESSE: Eh, mon Dieu, oui. C'est qu'il y a des gens qui sont plus durs que des pierres. Elle a pensé être noyée en passant la rivière qui coule ici près, elle est arrivée ici comme par miracle et je l'ai reçue par charité.
> LE MAÎTRE: Quel âge a-t-elle?
> L'HÔTESSE: Je lui crois plus d'un an et demi.

This provides us with the final clue to the riddle, which Jacques is able to answer, while the master and probably also the reader are left perplexed.

> A ce mot Jacques part d'un éclat de rire et s'écrie: 'C'est une chienne?'
> L'HÔTESSE: La plus belle bête du monde; je ne donnerais pas ma Nicole pour dix louis. Ma pauvre Nicole! (*JF*, 735–36)

The example of Nicole shows us how Diderot plays with the reader by putting him on a false track while scattering clues leading to the right answer. The human name Nicole, the landlady's shock at her treatment, the fact that she has been put to bed and that a surgeon has been called, her cries (and not barks), all naturally lead the reader to share Jacques's and his master's belief that Nicole is a maid. But Diderot interweaves in this misleading information some clues which cannot fit in with this first guess: the confusion between Nicole and Nanon, Nicole being abandoned and then escaping drowning, and finally her age. The game acts here as a prelude to the discussion on misplaced sympathy, first whetting the reader's interest for the subject. The riddle also provides a concrete illustration making the discussion between Jacques and the master easier to follow.

Misleading information in a character's discourse slows down and impedes the reader's discovery of the answer to the set clue. Noise constitutes another form of obstruction to the reader's curiosity by hindering the progress of the narrative. Noises should be understood here in the sense of 'random or irregular fluctuations or disturbances which are not part of a signal (whether the result is audible or not), or which interfere with or obscure a signal' (*OED*). In 'Information Theory and the Style of *Tristram Shandy*', Louis T. Milic works on the concept of noise which he defines thus:

> Because messages are subject to the vagaries of communication channels, which involve encoding, transmission and decoding, their formal characteristics are frequently altered by what is called *noise*. Noise is simply an

interference with the communication process which causes the symbols of the message sent to differ from those of the message received. [...] In a sense, noise increases the information content of a message in an undesirable way, by making it unintelligible or misleading.[24]

In *Tristram Shandy*, noise more often than not takes the form of irrelevant digression, as is the case with Tristram's interruption of Toby's sentence, previously mentioned. In *Jacques le fataliste*, the landlady's inappropriate way of talking of her dog fits into Milic's definition of noise as it 'increases the information content of a message in an undesirable way' and misleads the reader.

There is a second instance in *Jacques le fataliste* where noise interferes with the message by making it unintelligible. In the first example, the landlady was responsible for the noise; this time, she is its victim. Noise disturbs the landlady's story of Mme de La Pommeraye and le Marquis des Arcis by introducing matters belonging to the logistics of running an inn. This is doubly troublesome since the landlady 'raconte beaucoup mieux qu'il ne convient à une femme d'auberge' (*JF*, 753). The noise also jars with the story set in Paris and involving members of the French nobility. To translate the maddening incessancy of the interruptions, but also to make their pattern apparent, it is necessary to quote the interferences in full:

> (— Madame? — Qu'est-ce? — La carte du numéro cinq. — Voyez sur le coin de la cheminée.) [...] (— Madame? — Qu'est-ce? — La clef du coffre à l'avoine. — Voyez au clou, et si elle n'y est pas, voyez au coffre.) [...] (— Madame? — Qu'est-ce? — C'est le courrier. — Mettez-le à la chambre verte et servez-le à l'ordinaire) [...] (— Madame? — Qu'est-ce? — Le frère quêteur. — Donnez-lui douze sous pour ces messieurs qui sont ici, six sous pour moi, et qu'il aille dans les autres chambres.) [...] (— Madame? — Qu'est-ce? — Le tonnelier. — Qu'il descende à la cave et qu'il visite les deux pièces du coin.) [...] (— Madame? — J'y vais, j'y vais.)
> L'hôtesse fatiguée de ces interruptions, descendit et prit apparemment les moyens de les faire cesser.
> [...] (— Madame? Madame? Madame? — Pour qui et pour quoi que ce soit je vous ai défendu de m'appeler, appelez mon mari — Il est absent.) Messieurs, je vous demande pardon, je suis à vous dans un moment.
> Voilà l'hôtesse descendue, remontée et reprenant son récit.
> [...] (— Ma femme? — Qu'est-ce? — Rien.) On n'a pas un moment de repos dans cette maison, même les jours qu'on n'a presque point de monde et que l'on croit n'avoir rien à faire. Qu'une femme de mon état est à plaindre, surtout avec une bête de mari! ... [...] (— Ma femme? — Qu'est-ce? — Le marchand de paille. — Vois sur le registre. — Et le registre? — Reste, reste, je l'ai.) [...] (— Madame? — Qu'est-ce? — Le coche.) 'Messieurs, dit l'hôtesse, il faut que je vous quitte. Ce soir, lorsque toutes mes affaires seront faites, je reviendrai et je vous achèverai cette aventure, si vous en êtes curieux ...' ('Madame? — Ma femme? — Notre hôtesse? — On y va, on y va.') (*JF*, 747, 748, 749, 750, 751, 752)

The sentences are constructed on the same model. The repetition of sentence-pattern increases the monotony of the noise. The only variations depend on whether the landlady is called by the servants, her husband, or her customers. Thrice Diderot seems to promise to put an end to the interruptions, becoming increasingly pressing and gratuitous. However, the landlady's travels downstairs are to no avail, and her own complaints about the situation only add to the story's disturbance. The reader, placed in the same situation as Jacques and his master, has to make the effort not to be distracted and keep the story's progress in mind. The final interruption, much longer than its long line of predecessors, threatens to be more challenging to the reader. The landlady's last trip downstairs leaves enough time for Jacques to tell 'la fable de la Gaine et du Coutelet' (*JF*, p. 753), the story of his grandfather, but not to finish that of his captain and M. de Guerchy, which is interrupted by the landlady's return. What starts as a realistic depiction of an inn rapidly becomes, through the exaggerated frequency of the interruptions, a manifestation of the artificiality of the novel and of the narrator's meddling.

Riddles and interruptions correspond to different types of noise. Yet both illustrate how ludic narrative introduces noise to withhold information. The interference of noise is often counterbalanced by clues provided to the reader to help him guess what is being hidden from him. The narrator plays on the reader's curiosity and holds him in a state of suspense long enough to make him impatient and want to discover the hidden information. The clues leading to this information must be obscure enough so as to delay the climax and make the game more challenging. For Johan Huizinga, whose *Homo Ludens* served as a starting point for game theory, the feeling of competition and the pleasure of being challenged and succeeding on one's own, increase the enjoyment of the game.[25] The narrator is betting on man's desire to know what is hidden from him, to egg the reader on in the text in which he has scattered clues along the way.[26] Barthes compares the narrator-reader relationship to bullfighting. In the same way as the torero with the bull, the narrator pricks the reader's impatience by teasing him with clues, or references to the seme, without providing the final answer, the seme itself.

> Le sème est ainsi plusieurs fois "cité"; on voudrait donner à ce mot son sens tauromachique: *citar*, c'est ce coup de talon, cette cambrure du torero, qui appellent la bête aux banderilles. De la même façon, on cite le signifié (la richesse) à comparaître, tout en l'esquivant au fil du discours.[27]

The landlady of the Grand-Cerf thus 'quotes' the seme through Nicole's abandonment, her escape from drowning and her age, without actually referring to the seme itself: the dog.

Jacques le fataliste and *Tristram Shandy* are ludic novels using their stories as stakes of a game. Scenes are interrupted, episodes are missing, but clues are also provided, inviting the reader to change his approach to the text by actively engaging with it. Yet, for Sterne and Diderot, play is not an end in itself. Play has prepared the reader for being receptive to the philosophical content in both novels. It is used as a heuristic method for replacing didactic explanations with practical demonstrations. The pertinence of a certain philosophical point is verified through experimentation rather than through persuasion.

Games as demonstration

Tricks are based on the principle of exclusion and inclusion: they exclude those whom they choose as victims, and include the spectators who understand the joke and laugh at its object. The appreciation of an enigma depends on its discovery by an audience. The mystery around Nicole's identity would have been pointless if the master and the reader had not understood it. Most of the time, the master is the spectator to Jacques's tricks, and heartily laughs at them. However, this may have lulled the master into a false sense of security. Jacques will hoax his master in the same way as he has hoaxed others. Indeed, Jacques plays a trick on his master by not harnessing his horse properly, so that the stirrups, instead of providing support, in fact give way. Thus, as soon as the master attempts to dismount, he ends up falling off his horse and into his servant's arms. Jacques had planned the whole stratagem with the intention of making a practical joke, not an injury. The trick needing an audience to be appreciated, Jacques cannot resist telling his master the elaboration of his ploy:

> LE MAÎTRE: Quoi ! c'était un jeu?
> JACQUES: Un jeu.
> LE MAÎTRE: Et tu t'attendais à la rupture des courroies?
> JACQUES: Je l'avais préparée.
> LE MAÎTRE: Et ta réponse impertinente était préméditée?
> JACQUES: Préméditée.
> LE MAÎTRE: Et c'était le fil d'archal que tu attachais au-dessus de ma tête pour me démener à ta fantaisie? (*JF*, 880)

Far from being a mere *fantaisie*, this horseplay serves as a concrete demonstration of a philosophical argument Jacques was making earlier. Jacques does not believe that man ever acts by free will, as there is always a cause to an action. The master on the other hand, disagrees and opposes to Jacques the fact that he feels he is free in his actions: 'il me semble au-dedans de moi-même que je suis libre' (*JF*, p. 867). Jacques, to prove his point, sets his master a conundrum. Would he voluntarily fall from his horse, without any reason, to prove that he is free?[28] By affirming he would, the master falls into the trap of the question, as the proof of his freedom is the cause of his action:

> JACQUES: Mon capitaine disait: 'Quoi! vous ne voyez pas que sans ma contradiction il ne vous serait jamais venu en fantaisie de vous rompre le cou? C'est donc moi qui vous prends par le pied et qui vous jette hors de la

> selle. Si votre chute prouve quelque chose, ce n'est donc pas que vous soyez libre, mais que vous êtes fou.' (*JF*, p. 868)

The hypothetical fall described by the captain will be put into practice. Jacques has just rhetorically made his master agree to fall off his horse. He will do it again, literally, a few pages later. The master still is not convinced, as his intellect is too weak to understand Jacques's argument. His feelings predominate over his reason: 'Cela est trop fort pour moi, mais en dépit de ton capitaine et de toi je croirai que je veux quand je veux' (*JF*, p. 868). Since the master cannot comprehend his servant's point, Jacques can only demonstrate that 'on passe les trois quarts de sa vie à vouloir sans faire' and 'à faire sans vouloir' through a concrete illustration (*JF*, p. 868). This practical demonstration is not made immediately afterwards. Jacques demonstrates his argument a few pages later with the tampering with the saddle, taking both the master and the reader by surprise. Pausing to catch their breath after the master's furious chase after his servant, Jacques asks:

> N'est-il pas évidemment démontré que nous agissons la plupart du temps sans vouloir? Là mettez la main sur la conscience, de tout ce que vous avez dit ou fait depuis une demi-heure en avez-vous rien voulu? N'avez-vous pas été ma marionnette, et n'auriez-vous pas continué d'être mon polichinelle pendant un mois, si je me l'étais proposé? (*JF*, p. 880)

Though Jacques is highly amused by the trick he has played on his master, his purpose remains the demonstration of a philosophical argument.

By explaining the mechanism of his trick and demonstration, Jacques comes very close to operating an authorial metalepsis: '[le poète] opère lui-même les effets qu'il chante'.[29] This similarity between Jacques and the narrator signals a *mise en abyme*. In the same way as the master is his servant's 'marionnette', the narrator plays with his characters as he would with 'polichinelles':

> Vous voyez, Lecteur, que je suis en beau chemin, et qu'il ne tiendrait qu'à moi de vous faire attendre un an, deux ans, trois ans, le récit des amours de Jacques, en le séparant de son maître, et en leur faisant courir à chacun tous les hasards qu'il me plairait. Qu'est-ce qui m'empêcherait de marier le Maître et de le faire cocu? d'embarquer Jacques pour les Îles? d'y conduire son maître ? de les ramener tous les deux en France sur le même vaisseau? Qu'il est facile de faire des contes! Mais ils en seront quittes l'un et l'autre pour une mauvaise nuit, et vous pour ce délai. (*JF*, 670)

Here the narrator's threat does not simply concern the intradiegetic characters, but extends to the extradiegetic, or implied reader. The historical, or actual reader remains in this case untouched, yet the ease with which the narrator navigates between the narrative levels, or in other words between the metadiegetic and intradiegetic levels of the story and the extradiegetic level of fictional reality, suggests that he is able to move with equal ease between actual fiction and reality.

This has for consequence the blurring of the limits separating the two, which Raymond Federman refers to as 'surfiction', and is confirmed by a *mise en abyme* of the enunciation.[30] The *mise en abyme* draws a correspondence between Jacques and the narrator, between the master and the reader. Henceforth, the possibility that philosophical ideas may be demonstrated as tricks played on the reader should be envisaged. It seems that both the implied and historical reader have become the narrator's playthings. Yet, as for Jacques, the tricks the narrator plays on the reader are not gratuitous; they serve as practical philosophical demonstrations accompanying discussions on associationism, and cause and effect.

Once the *mise en abyme* has been established, the narrator is able to transfer play, and more importantly its purpose, that is to say philosophical demonstrations, from the metadiegetic and intradiegetic level to the extradiegetic. The debate on determinism and free will, one of the most recurring in *Jacques le fataliste* and *Tristram Shandy*, encompasses the discussion on associationism and cause and effect.[31] The content of these debates will be studied in more detail in the second chapter on ideas and their illustrations. The present chapter merely analyses how the ludic narrative acts as a method for demonstrating philosophical ideas. The necessity of moving from effect to cause in order to understand the motivation of actions is a leitmotiv in Sterne's and Diderot's work. As Will McMorran remarks, 'Tristram's intellect is trained not to select or prioritize, but to follow blindly the paths of his countless associations'.[32] The reader is left to follow these paths as well as he can. In both *Tristram Shandy* and *Jacques le fataliste*, the effort 'to come at the first spring of the events' takes the form of a game set for the reader (*TS*, I, xxi, p. 59). The origin of certain actions remains obscure, and is presented as a riddle for the reader to solve.

The challenge of the game comes from withholding information. Jacques compares himself to a little boy who did not want to say A.

> JACQUES: Un jour un enfant, assis au pied du comptoir d'une lingère, criait de toute sa force. Une marchande importunée de ses cris, lui dit: 'Mon ami, pourquoi criez-vous? — C'est qu'ils veulent me faire dire A. — Et pourquoi ne voulez-vous pas dire A? — C'est que je n'aurai pas si tôt dit A, qu'ils voudront me faire dire B.' C'est que je ne vous aurai pas si tôt dit le nom du petit homme qu'il faudra que je vous dise le reste. (*JF*, 832)

Like the little boy, Jacques and Tristram do not want to have to follow the logical progression of their stories. Most of the time, they prefer starting at Z and help the reader work his way back to A by scattering a few clues along the way. The result is a backward and forward progression and overwhelming digressions distracting the reader from the answer. Diderot and Sterne provide an answer while withholding the logical demonstration leading to it. As it is purposefully inconsistent with its starting point, it becomes a riddle in itself. In order to solve this riddle, the reader must use the information given by the narrator to trace back the origin of certain events, even though the connection between the cause and the effect seems completely improbable. And of course, the incipit of *Jacques le fataliste* offers the first example of this:

> JACQUES: Mon capitaine ajoutait que chaque balle qui partait d'un fusil avait son billet.
> LE MAÎTRE: Et il avait raison...
> (Après une courte pause, Jacques s'écria:) 'Que le diable emporte le cabaretier et son cabaret!' (*JF*, 669)

Even though the master does not question the gap in the logical progression, which creates a *coq à l'âne* effect, the reader cannot but help wonder what the missing link is between the bullet and the landlord of the wine establishment. The answer is not long in coming:

> JACQUES: C'est que, tandis que je m'enivre de son mauvais vin, j'oublie de mener nos chevaux à l'abreuvoir. Mon père s'en aperçoit; il se fâche. Je hoche de la tête; il prend un bâton et m'en frotte un peu durement les épaules. Un régiment passait pour aller au camp devant Fontenoy; de dépit je m'enrôle. Nous arrivons; la bataille se donne...
> LE MAÎTRE: Et tu reçois la balle à ton adresse. (*JF*, 669)

The first instance of unusual associations in *Tristram Shandy* works on the same principle as this. The opening chapter of Sterne's novel contains Mrs Shandy's famous untimely question: '*Pray, my dear*, quoth my mother, *have you not forgot to wind up the clock?*' (*TS*, I, i, p. 6). This seemingly out-of-the-blue question is explained in chapter iv. The winding up of the 'large house-clock' famously precedes 'some other little family concernments'.[33] Mrs Shandy has associated her husband's visits to her bedchamber to the winding of the clock, as both actions are performed on the same date. This strange and unlikely association is set as a puzzle for the reader to solve. The more bizarre the puzzle, the more challenging it is going to be for the reader. More importantly, it also serves the function of a concrete example illustrating Locke's ideas on associationism, developed in *An Essay Concerning Human Understanding*, and to which Tristram immediately refers. Indeed, Mrs Shandy offers an illustration of the type of 'strange combination of ideas, the sagacious *Locke*, who certainly understood the nature of these things better than most men, affirms to have produced more wry actions than all other sources of prejudice whatsoever.' (*TS*, I, iv, p. 9).

In the examples previously analysed, the demonstration of causality and associationism, however improbable, takes the form of an amicable game between the text and the reader. However, other demonstrations may not be as cordial. Going back to Jacques's mock horse accident, there are certain ideas so hard to receive that their truthfulness must be forced upon us. Due to the limits of his intellect, the master must feel that something is true in order to be persuaded, since understanding is sometimes insufficient. This also holds true for the reader.

Jacques's practical joke on the master works by making use of the same mechanisms as those of the narrator's play with the reader. The narrators in *Jacques le fataliste* and *Tristram Shandy* give the impression of disorganisation. Yet, at a closer look, they both follow a particular method of writing: incompletion always seems to be intended. In the ninth volume, Tristram develops the character of Maria, a young girl encountered on his travels, deranged by some secret grief. The story of a pretty girl drawn to madness by a secret sorrow represents an attractive bait for the reader. Yet Tristram chooses not to develop her story and abruptly disregards her. Diderot displays similar devices in *Jacques le fataliste*. The narrator teases the reader by drawing the first lines of an alluring story and then deceiving him in his expectations by abandoning it. For example, the mystery surrounding the funeral convoy bearing the captain's sword will never be explained. Jacques and the reader will never know if 'ce sont des contrebandiers qui auront rempli cette bière de marchandises prohibées' or 'un enlèvement' (*JF*, p. 708). The narrator leaves the reader with the same conclusion as the master leaves his servant: 'Ce sera tout ce qu'il te plaira' (*JF*, p. 708). Remarking on the strangeness of these interruptions, McMorran talks of a 'refusal to exploit the romanesque potential of such meetings'.[34]

Most of the digressions in Sterne's and Diderot's novels are constituted by interrupted stories. Such a narrative structure represents an antithesis to the novelistic construction the reader is accustomed to. *Jacques le fataliste* and *Tristram Shandy* constantly contradict the reader's expectations. The sense of frustration arising from this contradiction is exacerbated by the fact that it concerns the intradiegetic level, and not the metadiegetic one. Secondary stories are predictable to the point of being uninteresting, since they offer an over-simplified version of stereotypical narratives. Thus the story of Amandus and Amanda, inserted in *Tristram Shandy*, is reduced to its main narrative articulations. The same effect is visible in the story of the master who is continually interrupted by Jacques's correct guesses as to its continuation. Some of these secondary stories are so predictable they would not have been worth telling, if it were not for the fact that they act as counterpoints to the main narrative. By constantly disappointing the reader's expectations concerning the progress of the main narrative, the narrator gives the impression that the story will end in a *non finito*. In *Jacques le fataliste*, the *non finito* constitutes yet another *trompe-l'oeil*, for the narrator does indeed keep his promise by completing his narrative just when the reader is least expecting it. Just as Jacques catches his master at the last moment as he falls from his horse, the narrator keeps his word with the reader, by concluding *in extremis* the long-awaited-for love story of Jacques and

Denise. However, this ending is so conventional and rushed despite its long build-up that it passes unnoticed.

The ending of *Jacques le fataliste* is an extremely complex one and has been studied in detail by Derek Connon.[35] The narrator abruptly stops his story just as Jacques is about to be taken to prison: 'Et moi, je m'arrête, parce que je vous ai dit de ces deux personnages tout ce que j'en sais.' (*JF*, p. 881) The narrator advises the reader to invent his own ending, to visit Mlle Agathe, or even to seek out Jacques in prison. He then mentions 'des mémoires, [qu'il a] de bonnes raisons de tenir pour suspects' (*JF*, p. 882), and offers to check their authenticity. This is followed by the insertion of three paragraphs taken from the alleged memoirs and which seem to be more individual episodes rather than being narratively connected. As Connon remarks, this ending with all its different parts 'gives every impression of having been cobbled together.'[36]

Connon raises our attention to the fact that the narrator's abrupt interruption would have constituted a perfectly acceptable conclusion. The separation of Jacques with his master should put an end to the story after all entitled *Jacques le fataliste et son maître*. The end of the journey and the killing of Saint-Ouin bring the metadiegetic level of the master's story to a close. Jacques receives the same answer as Aesop to his *quo vadis* question. And as the reader has been warned time and time again, he will not know the end of Jacques's love story.[37] This would have been a very neat ending indeed, but here lies the rub: 'when we do find happy and conclusive endings rounding off narratives that have purported to be true, they are accompanied by indications that we should mistrust them because of their conventionally literary nature.'[38] This first possible ending would finally reconcile the different narrative levels; but Diderot offers a tidy ending only to replace it by three paragraphs quoted from an unreliable memoir, and offers one last example of how 'the structure of imbrication works so that the framing tale and the tale inserted play against each other'.[39]

The first describes a quarrel between Jacques and Denise. The second shows Denise rubbing Jacques's knee. These two paragraphs are fairly anecdotal, and would have easily fitted in with the rest of the narrative. However, as Connon points out, their trustworthiness is constantly undermined. They mark a change within the narration: the narrator ceases to tell directly his story to the reader, and is replaced by a second person, unknown to us, editing his work. The first paragraph seems to be original, but the reader's attention is brought to inconsistencies within the text, thus making its authenticity highly questionable.[40] As for the second paragraph which seems the most *vraisemblable*, it has been dismissed by the 'éditeur' as 'évidemment interlopé' (*JF*, p. 882). Connon argues that Diderot's motivation in choosing to single these paragraphs out and continually stressing on their unreliability, was to avoid a conventional ending at all costs. The end is properly brought about by the third paragraph. Jacques is rescued from prison by Mandrin, he convinces the latter and his men not to ransack the house of Desglands, his benefactor. Jacques has a hero's triumphant return and is reunited to his master and Denise. They get married, have many children and live happily ever after. The über-conventionality of this ending brings it at a parodic level and devalues it.[41] Connon observes that '[one] of the most interesting features of this ending is the way that it contrives to give a sense of narrative closure whilst at the same time denying it.'[42]

Tristram Shandy and *Jacques le fataliste* upset the reader's expectation of a narrative similar to the ones he has become accustomed to in the literature he has previously read. The purpose of upsetting expectations could be understood as forcing a detachment from the plot, to correct a 'vile pruriency for fresh adventures in all things' (*TS*, I, xx, p. 53). To this interpretation may be objected the fact that this would actually encourage mechanical reading and a resignation to the narrator's every single whim. As McMorran indicates, pure and gratuitous arbitrariness from a narrator would result in turning the reader into a fatalist:

> Javitch argues that Ariosto's interruptive method in the *Furioso* stretches suspense or anticipation beyond its breaking point, that the self-conscious interruptions and intrusions turn an initially frustrated reader into a detached reader who no longer immerses himself in the fiction but observes and enjoys it from outside. According to this view, Ariosto thereby teaches the reader a stoic detachment from life's own trials and tribulations. This lesson in stoicism could be seen to have its counterpart in *Jacques* if we see the constant interruptions and intrusions in the latter as a lesson in fatalism. Neither Ariosto nor Diderot, however, would wish a reader to become so detached as to lose interest in the action; if the narratorial interference did not generate at least some local frustration in the reader there would be little point in it.[43]

Far from playing the role of the austere mentor guiding disciples down the road of resignation, Sterne's and Diderot's intentions are to make the reader react and reflect on how his reading experience has shaped his expectations and approach to a text. The fact that neither *Tristram Shandy* nor *Jacques le fataliste* offers a traditional ending is significant in the debate over free will and determinism. In any other novel, the ending is predictable, it is what the reader has been made to expect through his past readings. Yet here, the expectations based on past experience are overthrown. Through ludic narratives, Sterne and Diderot provide us with the practical demonstration that we are determined by what we have previously read which provides us with a set narrative model we expect to see repeated. *Tristram Shandy* and *Jacques le fataliste* thus succeed in avoiding a didactic approach to the treatment of determinism. The reader does not have solely to take the author's word on the matter; he is given the opportunity to experience determinism at first hand.

The Rules of the Game

Sterne and Diderot use the notion of a game to overthrow systematic thinking and monologism. The master is thrown off his horse because he is entrenched in the idea 'que je veux quand je veux' and refuses to accept any other possibility (*JF*, p. 868). By acknowledging only one truth, his own, he is acting as a pedant. Similarly, the reader's expectations are thwarted so that it can be proven to him that there is no single set narrative pattern. This chapter will now turn to another vital function of play: the refusal of systematic thinking. This is achieved by transforming the very basis on which the principles of game usually rest. *Jacques le fataliste* and *Tristram Shandy* hint at this by referring to play in the particular meaning of 'freedom or room for movement; the space in or through which a thing can or does move' (*OED*).[44] This definition may occur incidentally, as when applied to Dr Slop's obstetrical instruments which 'had so much room to play' in the bag (*TS*, III, vii, p. 148). This type of play or looseness of fit constitutes the basis of Sterne's and Diderot's ludic narratives: there is room for play in their play.

The fairness of a game depends on the respect of its rules and on the fact that all players have equal access to them. Ludic narratives may refuse to bend to this tacit agreement. As Hutchinson warns, 'of all games known to man, those in literature would seem to rely on rules the least'.[45] Rules are prescribed in ludic texts, but they are not strictly followed nor rigidly fixed. Burke thus completes Hutchinson's comment: 'each fiction actually contains its own rules, of which rule number one may well be, "the rules may change at any time without prior notice."'[46] The first rules to be disobeyed are those of writing. The unconventional self-referentiality at the extradiegetic level in Sterne's and Diderot's novel regularly remind the reader of this. It is reinforced by also occurring at the intradiegetic level. After having heard the story of Mme de La Pommeraye, the master reproaches the landlady for not having followed the classical rules of unity: 'Quand on introduit un personnage sur la scène il faut que ce rôle soit un. [...] Vous avez péché contre les règles d'Aristote, d'Horace, de Vida et de Le Bossu' (*JF*, p. 787).[47] The criticism the landlady receives may be addressed to Sterne and Diderot who can hardly be said to respect the rules of unity. Tristram has announced from the beginning his refusal to bend his writing to fixed rules: 'in writing what I have set about, I shall confine myself neither to [Horace's] rules, nor to any man's rules that ever lived' (*TS*, I, iv, p. 8). Sterne's novel offers a more dramatic case of disrespect for rules. As Huizinga underlines, 'Play begins, and then at a certain moment it is "over". It plays itself to an end'.[48] Yet *Tristram Shandy* disobeys one of the most fundamental rules of any game by not allowing the game to play itself out.

The changing of the rules in the middle of the game occurs in both *Tristram Shandy* and *Jacques le fataliste*. Lanham points out that the game to which

Tristram invites his reader 'is a new one. We try to figure out *what the rules are*. He remains to us cavalier. Follow me if you can'.[49] In Diderot's novel, the equilibrium of power between the master and his servant is reversed abruptly. Taking advantage of his master's complete dependency upon him, Jacques stipulates that from now on:

> Qu'attendu qu'il est écrit là-haut que je vous suis essentiel, et que je sens, que je sais que vous ne pouvez pas vous passer de moi, j'abuserai de cet avantage toutes et quantes fois que l'occasion s'en présentera. [. . .]
>
> Qu'attendu qu'il est aussi impossible à Jacques de ne pas connaître son ascendant et sa force sur son maître, qu'à son maître de méconnaître sa faiblesse et de se dépouiller de son indulgence, il faut que Jacques soit insolent et que, pour la paix, son maître ne s'en aperçoive pas. (*JF*, p. 798)

The master is now only master in name, and their relationship can be resumed by the newly invented proverb '*Jacques mène son maître*' (*JF*, p. 799). As the master protests, these new rules are deeply unfair, and they unbalance the game: 'à ce compte, ton lot vaudrait mieux que le mien' (*JF*, p. 798). However, it is necessary to submit to the new rules so that the story may be resumed.

The rules are changed, but they can also be broken. Sometimes the characters are caught red-handed not respecting the rules they have set themselves. Jacques and the extradiegetic narrator often complain that their respective audiences keep disobeying the rules by interrupting their stories with speculations as to their endings or with attempts to deviate onto other stories. Yet they themselves can be accused of making similar digressions. The extradiegetic narrator continually distracts the reader with digression. As for Jacques, he cannot help interfering with the master's own love story by guessing ahead. And what is worse, his guesses are usually correct and consequently spoil the master's *effet de surprise*:

> LE MAÎTRE: Tu vas anticipant sur le raconteur et tu lui ôtes le plaisir qu'il s'est promis de ta surprise, en sorte qu'ayant par une ostentation de sagacité très déplacée deviné ce qu'il avait à te dire, il ne lui reste plus qu'à se taire, et je me tais. (*JF*, 852)

Despite Jacques's promise to stop interrupting his master, it does not take him long before he resumes his bad habits. This is surprising in a man who had previously agreed that 'quand on a donné sa parole d'honneur il faut la tenir' (*JF*, 798).

Paradoxically, the worst case is when the rules are respected to the letter. While seeming to serve the purpose of the reader, they turn against him. The settlement that 'tout auditeur qui me permet de commencer un récit s'engage d'en entendre la fin' (*JF*, p. 718) binds the reader to listen to the narrator as long as there is a story to be told. A similar problem occurs when Tristram cunningly presents his attention to minutiae, often responsible for leading him off on tangents, as a mark of his consideration for the readers:

> I know there are readers [. . .] who find themselves ill at ease, unless they are let into the whole secret from first to last, of every thing which concerns you.
>
> It is in pure compliance with this humour of theirs, and from a backwardness in my nature to disappoint any soul living, that I have been so very particular already. [. . .] I find it necessary to consult every one a little in his turn; and therefore must beg pardon for going on a little further in the same way [. . .]. (*TS*, I, iv, p. 8)

Such assurances should guarantee the reader that he will eventually know Jacques's love story. A few pages before the end, the narrator threatens not to keep his word and to leave Jacques's love story incomplete:

> Et moi, je m'arrête, parce que je vous ai dit de ces deux personnages tout ce que j'en sais. — Et les amours de Jacques? — Jacques a dit cent fois qu'il était écrit là-haut qu'il n'en finirait pas l'histoire, et je vois que Jacques avait raison. Je vois, Lecteur, que cela vous fâche. Eh bien, reprenez son récit où il l'a laissé et continuez-le à votre fantaisie [. . .]. (*JF*, 881–82)

The narrator finally keeps his promise, but twists the rules by rushing the long-expected end which seems particularly succinct in comparison with its previous infuriatingly slow build-up. In *Tristram Shandy* and *Jacques le fataliste*, the rules are not set. They are constantly broken or modified. Though deeply unsettling for the reader, this of course allows a greater freedom of movement for the narrators. Yet because the play with the rules is so flagrant, it also marks Sterne's and Diderot's refusal to enclose their ludic narrative into a fixed and pre-defined system.

The impossibility of settling for a definite solution to a riddle serves a similar function. In both novels, the interest of a riddle is not diminished by the impossibility of resolving it by a unique correct answer, or even to answer it at all. In *Tristram Shandy*, the narrator every now and then promises to come back to and explain certain cryptic points in an appendix.[50] Not surprisingly, no such appendix was ever published and we may safely speculate that Sterne never had any intention of doing so. Unexplained passages also occur in *Jacques le fataliste* where the fate of father Hudson, of Jacques's captain, and of the captain's friend, have been left in suspension.[51] Jacques and the fictitious reader suppose that Hudson, the captain, and his friend are dead, but the narrator corrects them:

> L'HOTESSE: [. . .] Buvons à la santé de votre capitaine.
> JACQUES: S'il est encore vivant.
> L'HOTESSE: Mort ou vivant, qu'est-ce que cela fait? (*JF*, p. 759)

> Et pourquoi le vieux militaire ne serait-il pas ou le capitaine de Jacques ou le camarade de son capitaine? — Mais il est mort. — Vous le croyez . . . ? (*JF*, p. 847)

> Mais l'abbé Hudson est mort? — Vous le croyez? Avez-vous assisté à ses obsèques? — Non. — Il est donc mort ou vivant, comme il me plaira. (*JF*, p. 848)

The historical reader has probably forgotten these secondary characters at the time when those questions arrive in the novel. The role of the fictitious character and of Jacques is to bring them back to the reader's mind and point to the fact that the uncertainty of their fate is one of the insoluble riddles of the novel. It is worth mentioning that in *Jacques le fataliste*, the narrator regularly insists on the fact that this insolubility does not affect the progress of the narrative, as the reader may fear.[52]

Certain plays on words are particularly obscure. Whilst expounding on his theory of names, Walter asks his sceptical interlocutor 'how many [...] are there who might have done exceeding well in the world, had not their characters and spirits been totally depress'd and NICODEMUS'D into nothing' (*TS*, I, xix, p. 47). To explain the name 'Nicodemus' and its pejorative connotations, Melvyn New suggests a passage from Rabelais and the Gospel according to St John as possible intertextual references.[53] However, it is highly unlikely that the majority of readers would have been able to recognise such abstruse references. Some footnotes, supposed to clarify a point, actually introduce a new puzzle. Correcting Walter's reference to a Latin primary source, Sterne writes in one of these that Walter might have mistaken '*Lithopaedus* for *Trinecavellius*, — from the too great similitude of the names' (*TS*, II, xix, p. 133). This is misleading as the reader soon notices that there is hardly any resemblance between the two names, nor is there an evident play on words in Latin.

The reader's desire to fill in the blanks is natural and it is an inclination Sterne and Diderot rely on. However, Tristram explicitly underlines that some enigmas are deliberately made impenetrable:

> What these perplexities of my uncle *Toby* were, — 'tis impossible for you to guess; — if you could, — I should blush; not as a relation, — not as a man, — nor even as a woman, — but I should blush as an author; inasmuch as I set no small store by myself upon this very account, that my reader has never yet been able to guess at anything. And in this, Sir, I am of so nice and singular a humour, that if I thought you was able to form the least judgment or probable conjecture to yourself, of what was to come in the next page, — I would tear it out of my book. (*TS*, I, xxv, pp. 69–70)

Lanham underlines this peculiarity in Sterne's novel, and accounts for it by remarking that,

> [...] we function as audience by restoring to narrative and spiritual coherence Tristram's skilful chaos. He digs the hole; we fill it up. But this spoils the game! Misapprehends what Tristram is doing! He invites us to search for the center of the Silenus box but, as with Rabelais, from this center emerges, not the stern voice of coherence, but the Abbey of Thélème *Fay ce que vouldras*.[54]

Lanham draws attention to the ambiguity of play in *Tristram Shandy*, but his comments apply perfectly well to *Jacques le fataliste*. The incipit of Diderot's novel is constructed on such blanks which the reader unsuccessfully attempts to fill:

> Comment s'étaient-ils rencontrés? Par hasard comme tout le monde. Comment s'appelaient-ils? Que vous importe? D'où venaient-ils? Du lieu le plus prochain. Où allaient-ils? Est-ce que l'on sait où l'on va? Que disaient-ils? Le Maître ne disait rien, et Jacques disait que son capitaine disait que tout ce qui nous arrive de bien et de mal ici-bas était écrit là-haut. (*JF*, 669)

Like matadors skilfully making the bull respond to their taunts, Sterne and Diderot do indeed rely on the reader's curiosity and competitiveness to engage him in play by withdrawing information.[55] Yet the purpose is not to provide systematically a definite solution to the riddles. Blanks inevitably will remain, but this intended emptiness has its own function inside the play.

The game is played not against the reader, but against 'systematick reasoners [who] move both heaven and earth, and twist and torture every thing in nature to support [their] hypothesis' (*TS*, I, xix, p. 49). The pedant only recognises one possible solution: his own. The impossibility of filling in the blanks with one single correct answer defeats the systematic thinker's purpose, as he cannot force his views to fit as an answer. Such blanks offer breathing spaces open to multiple solutions. The Shandean dash literally offers such empty spaces. '— My sister, I dare say, added he, does not care to let a man come so near her ****' (*TS*, II, vi, p. 89). This blank may welcome different valid answers: 'Make this dash, — 'tis an Aposiopesis. — Take the dash away, and write Backside, — 'tis Bawdy. — Scratch Backside out and put *Cover'd-way* in, — 'tis a Metaphor' (*TS*, II, vi, pp. 89–90). The interest of this blank lies not in finding out what the right answer is. None is given. The significance of the dash is that it accepts not one single solution but a multitude of options proposed by the narrator to which the reader may add his own variations.

These empty spaces are where ludic dialogism takes place. For Barthes, texts requiring their readers to take an active part in the construction of the narrative belong to the writerly category, and are necessarily polysemic.[56] Writerly texts encourage the reader's participation, without the author imposing a unique solution. They emphasise the plurality of the answers: the reader's version is added palimpsestically to an open list of other possibilities. The reader may access those blanks 'par plusieurs entrées dont aucune ne peut être à coup sûr déclarée principale', 'les systèmes de sens peuvent s'emparer, mais leur nombre n'est jamais clos, ayant pour mesure l'infini du langage'.[57] The reader's participation in the meaning of the text may only be possible if the text in question is polysemic. The distinction between polysemy and monosemy corresponds to one of the criteria to differentiate between the writerly and readerly texts. Ludic participation may only occur in writerly texts, and these depend on the absence of an authoritative and dominant discourse:

> Le texte scriptible est un présent perpétuel, sur lequel ne peut se poser aucune parole *conséquente* (qui le transformerait en passé); le texte scriptible, c'est *nous en train d'écrire*, avant que le jeu infini du monde (le monde comme jeu) ne soit traversé, coupé, arrêté, plastifié par quelque système singulier (Idéologie, Genre, Critique) qui en rabatte sur la pluralité des entrées, l'ouverture des réseaux, l'infini des langages.[58]

The ludic narratives in *Tristram Shandy* and *Jacques le fataliste* serve to establish a method for practical philosophical demonstrations without imposing one particular authoritative philosophical system. By being based on the principle of play, Sterne's and Diderot's narratives engage in the inquisitive embrace of conflicting notions and the rejection of systematic thinking. The connotations associated with play and game often tend to belittle their role and significance in literary works, and restrict their function to entertainment. For these reasons, I have chosen deliberately to replace in my chapter title 'playful' by the term 'ludic'. As Lanham remarks, the Latin *ludus* 'preserves a fuller range of meanings'.[59] One of these forgotten meanings is 'school'. The connection between play and heuristics is particularly pertinent as I have argued that Sterne and Diderot use play as a method for philosophical demonstrations. However, if play offers a heuristic method, it also prevents it from imposing an authoritative discourse. Huizinga declares 'true play knows no propaganda'.[60] In *Tristram Shandy* and *Jacques le fataliste*, play rejects systematic thinking. In both novels, the rules of the game are never fixed; they are constantly changing.[61] Such inconsistency affects not only the object of the game, but also its ultimate purpose. There is no unique right answer to a riddle which may welcome as many solutions as there are players. Eventually, these same players are brought to realise that the interest of the game lies not, as Lanham puts it, in filling up the holes, but in transforming the text into a space for dialogism, where sometimes contradictory meanings interact and ensure the defeat of monosemy. Through their use of play, Sterne and Diderot have revealed themselves to be paradoxical authors 'qui ne [veulent] jamais prouver, et qui [vont] toujours prouvant, [. . .] ballotant du blanc au noir, et du noir au blanc'.[62] Indeed, the refusal of a dominant discourse inevitably leads to contradictions that both Sterne and Diderot embrace, and to which I will now turn.[63] In this chapter, I have analysed how play may be used as a form of practical demonstration of a complex notion. In the following chapter, I will take a much broader view in order to study abstract ideas and their concrete illustrations, pointing out the contradictions arising from this combination.

Notes to Chapter 1

1. *Jacques le fataliste* was published in 1796, though its first version started to circulate privately in September 1771, which is still more than four years after the publication of the final volume of *Tristram Shandy* (January 1767).

2. Jean Catrysse, *Diderot et la mystification* (Paris: A.-G. Nizet, 1970), p. 11. Author's italics.
3. In *Diderot et la mystification*, Catrysse mentions that *La Religieuse* was used to play a trick upon the Marquis de Croismare who was led to believe that the letters of the distressed nun were real, to the point that he actually wrote back to her.
4. Samuel Weber, 'Reading: "To the Very End of the World"', *MLN*, 111 (1996), 819–34, p. 824.
5. Denis Diderot, *Œuvres complètes*, ed. Roger Lewinter (Paris: le Club français du livre, 1970), III, pp. 245–46.
6. Mikhail Bakhtin, 'The role of games in Rabelais', in *Game, Play, Literature*, ed. by Jacques Ehrmann (New Haven: Eastern Press, 1968), p. 129.
7. Bakhtin, 'The role of game in Rabelais', p. 132. These two quotations were reprinted from Bakhtin's *Rabelais and his World*, trans. by Helene Iswolsky (Cambridge, Mass.: MIT Press, 1968). The following text is extracted from chapter three, entitled 'Popular festive forms and images in Rabelais'.
8. Play also briefly appears in the concept of outsideness (which I will apply to *Tristram Shandy* and *Jacques le fataliste* in the third chapter) in Bakhtin, 'Author and Hero in Aesthetic Activity', in *Art and Answerability, early philosophical essays by M. M. Bakhtin*, ed. by Michael Holquist and Vadim Liapunov, trans. by Vadim Liapunov (Austin: University of Texas Press, 1990), pp. 74–75.
9. This dissimilarity must account for the scarcity of examples of play at the intradiegetic and metadiegetic levels in *Tristram Shandy*. Indeed, the main and secondary characters, unlike those in *Jacques le fataliste*, are hardly ever seen playing games. In Sterne's novel, explicit play occurs mostly between the narrator and the fictional reader.
10. See note 1 to p. 756, in *Diderot, Contes et romans*, p. 1230.
11. For definition of *passe-dix* and its terms, see note 2 and 3 to p. 756, in *Diderot, Contes et romans*, p. 1230.
12. Mme d'Aisnon is 'réduite à tenir tripot' (*JF*, p. 760), and the usurer gives a few guesses as to the master's financial difficulties: 'La nécessité qui vous presse est une plaisante nécessité; une bouillotte, une partie de la belle, quelque fille' (*JF*, p. 839). *Bouillotte* is a card game, and *la belle* is the deciding round of a game, but in this case the expression may be playing with a double meaning implying more amorous games.
13. Just before Jacques's horse rushes for the gibbets (p. 700), during the landlady's story of Mme de La Pommeraye (p. 764), after the two main characters have left the Marquis des Arcis (p. 815), after the story of Suzon and the priest (p. 836), after the implied reader's contestation of the word 'engastrimeste' (p. 837), after the master's short quarrel with Agathe (p. 847), after the Chevalier's confession of treason (p. 856), during a rest next to a brook (p. 866), before the story of Jacques's second knee operation (p. 876), and up until the penultimate page before the attack of Desglands's castle by Mandrin's men (p. 884).
14. I will be relying on Genette's distinction between the extradiegetic, the diegetic or intradiegetic, and the metadiegetic. Distinguishing between the different narrative levels, Genette explains: 'Nous définirons cette différence de niveau en disant que *tout événement raconté par un récit est à un niveau diégétique immédiatement supérieur à celui où se situe l'acte narratif producteur de ce récit*. La rédaction par M. de Renoncourt de ses *Mémoires fictifs* est un acte (littéraire) accompli à un premier niveau, que l'on dira *extradiégétique*; les événements racontés dans ces Mémoires (dont l'acte narratif de des Grieux) sont dans ce premier récit, on les qualifiera donc de *diégétiques*, ou *intradiégétiques*; les événements racontés dans le récit de des Grieux, récit au second degré, seront dits *métadiégétiques*', Gérard Genette, in *Figures III* (Paris: Editions du Seuil, 1972), pp. 238–39.
15. David Gascoigne, *The Games of Fiction, Georges Perec and Modern French Ludic Literature* (Oxford, Berlin: Peter Lang, 2006), p. 18.
16. Peter Hutchinson, *Games Authors Play* (London and New York: Methuen, 1983), p. 12.

17. Lanham mentions the self-consciousness in Tristram's use and discussion of classic rhetoric: 'Invention, arrangement, style, memory, especially delivery are constantly subjects of conversation. It not only uses the tropes and schemes, it talks about using them, and wishes to use them correctly', in Richard A. Lanham, Tristram Shandy, *The Games of Pleasure* (Christchurch, New Zealand: Cybereditions, 2001), p. 31.
18. Genette, p. 244. We should keep in mind the term 'bouffonne' suggested by Genette as this will later be pertinent in the study of the carnivalesque in *Tristram Shandy* and *Jacques le fataliste*, in chapter 4.
19. Genette underlines instances of authorial metalepsis in Diderot's novel. The narrator addresses his reader to affirm his authority and power over the story: 'Qu'est-ce qui m'empêcherait de marier le Maître et de le faire cocu?' Inversely, he may also be more amenable to his reader's preferences: 'Si cela vous fait plaisir, remettons la paysanne en croupe derrière son conducteur, laissons-les aller et revenons à nos deux voyageurs' (*JF*, pp. 670 & 672). Genette then moves on to Sterne who asks the reader to intervene, to close the door, or to help Walter Shandy to go back to his bed. Genette thus points out to the various forms authorial metalepsis may take. The theatrical quality of *Tristram Shandy*, and in particular the stage effects, studied by Iser, present another facet of authorial metalepsis. Iser illustrates his point by referring to the cases when the narrator Tristram plays the stage-director by theatrically dropping the curtain over a scene so as to allow himself to make digressive comments. See chap. 3 'The play of the text' in Wolfgang Iser, *Laurence Sterne: Tristram Shandy*, trans. by David Henry Wilson (Cambridge: Cambridge University Press, 1988). In this chapter, Iser focuses on play within theatrical representations.
20. Hans-Georg Gadamer, *Truth and Method*, trans. by William Glen-Doepel (London: Sheed and Ward, 1979), pp. 94–95.
21. '[. . .] when a man is telling a story in the strange way I do mine, he is obliged continually to be going backwards and forwards to keep all tight together in the reader's fancy' (*TS*, VI, xxxiii, p. 416). The backward and forward movement is essential to both novels and will be a recurring theme in this study.
22. Roland Barthes, *S/Z* (Paris: Editions du Seuil, 1970), pp. 95–96.
23. Marian Hobson uses the term 'substitution' to talk of this interruption of one story by another: 'What is substituted for is absent: to retrieve it the substitution must be broken. Does this mean that in the moment of breaking the substitution, all narrative levels — from 'auteur'-'lecteur', through Jacques and his master, to the story told — can be held in mind? No: they represent vertical absences, towards which attention is orientated, but which are not actually in the field of attention.' In *The Object of Art: the Theory of Illusion in Eighteenth-Century France* (Cambridge: Cambridge University Press, 2009), p. 134.
24. Louis T. Milic, 'Information Theory and the Style of *Tristram Shandy*', in *The Winged Skull, papers from the Laurence Sterne Bicentary Conference*, ed. by Arthur H. Cash and John M. Stedmond (London: Methuen, 1971), pp. 238–39. I refer the reader back to this article for a more in-depth study of noise in *Tristram Shandy*. I will later focus on Barthes's treatment of *bruit*.
25. See Johan Huizinga, *Homo Ludens, a Study of the play-element in Culture* (London: Paladin, 1970), p. 29.
26. On the reader's curiosity, see Hutchinson, p. 21
27. Barthes, p. 29.
28. Jacques's explanation closely resembles a passage from Diderot's article 'Liberté' in the *Encyclopédie* where the servant's concrete examples (falling off from a horse or not, falling in love or not) are replaced by A and B: 'Il est question de choisir entre A & B; vous dites que, toutes choses mises à part, vous pouvez choisir l'un ou l'autre. Vous choisissez A, pourquoi? parce que je le veux, dites-vous; mais pourquoi voulez-vous A plûtôt que B?

vous répliquez, parce que je le veux: Dieu m'a donné cette faculté. Mais que signifie je veux vouloir, ou je veux parce que je veux? Ces paroles n'ont d'autre sens que celui, je veux A; mais vous n'avez pas encore satisfait à ma question: pourquoi ne voulez-vous point B? est-ce sans raison que vous le rejettez? Si vous dites A me plaît parce qu'il me plaît, ou cela ne signifie rien, ou doit être entendu ainsi, A me plaît à cause de quelque raison qui me le fait paroître préférable à B: sans cela le néant produiroit un effet, conséquence que sont obligés de digérer les défenseurs de la liberté d'équilibre'.

29. Genette, p. 244.
30. See Raymond Federman (editor), *Surfiction: Fiction Now . . . and Tomorrow* (Chicago: The Swallow Press, 1975), cited by Ruth E. Burke in *The Games of Poetic, Ludic Criticism and Postmodern Fiction* (New York: Peter Lang, 1994), p. 58.
31. For a discussion on associationism in *Tristram Shandy*, see chapter 3 of Jonathan Lamb's *Sterne's Fiction and the Double Principle* (Cambridge: Cambridge University Press, 1989).
32. McMorran, p. 182.
33. See *TS*, I, iv, p. 9.
34. McMorran, p. 218.
35. I am here using the argument Derek Connon makes in his chapter on *Jacques le fataliste*, pp. 275–313.
36. Connon, p. 276.
37. See Connon, pp. 276–79
38. Connon, p. 264.
39. Hobson, *The Object of Art*, p. 128.
40. The narrator signals the fact that if indeed in the first paragraph Denise is sitting on a chair, it should be impossible for Jacques, who is at her feet, to be able to reach her eyes with his handkerchief to wipe away her tears, unless she is sitting on an exceptionally low chair. See *JF*, p. 883.
41. See Connon, pp. 283–87.
42. Connon, p. 287.
43. McMorran, p. 229.
44. Jouer 'est appliqué à une chose, au sens de "se mouvoir librement avec aisance, dans un espace déterminé" [. . .]. Il signifie particulièrement "ne pas garder sa forme, se déplacer", en parlant d'une porte, d'un assemblage, et "fonctionner à l'aise" à propos d'un mécanisme', in article 'jouer', *Dictionnaire historique de la Langue française*, ed. by Alain Rey (Paris: Dictionnaires Le Robert, 1998), II, p. 1924.
45. Hutchinson, p. 5.
46. Burke, p. 63.
47. Le Bossu (1631–89), author of a *Traité du poème épique* (1675); Marco Girolamo Vida (1480–566), bishop and poet. See note 2 to page 787, in Diderot, *Contes et romans*, p. 1235.
48. Huizinga, p. 28.
49. Lanham, p. 90.
50. See *TS*, I, xiii, pp. 33–34.
51. Francis Pruner has discussed at length the confusion surrounding the unconfirmed death of the captain in chapter V 'L'ordre et la confusion des codes', in *L'Unité secrète de* Jacques le Fataliste (Paris: Minard, 1970).
52. 'Que vous importe que ce soit de par Dieu ou de par Belzébuth que votre cheval se soit retrouvé? En ira-t-il moins bien?' (*JF*, pp. 870–71)
53. See note 6 p. 612, Sterne, *Tristram Shandy*.
54. Lanham, pp. 110–11.
55. The comparison between the author and the matador originates from chapter XIII 'Citar', in Barthes, *S/Z*.

56. In the text Barthes describes as 'scriptible', the reader is a 'producteur du texte', whereas in the 'lisible' he is a 'consommateur'. Richard Miller translates Barthes's 'le scriptible' into ' the writerly', and 'le lisible' into 'the readerly'. Roland Barthes, *S/Z*, trans. by Richard Miller (Oxford: Blackwell, 1990). Quotations from *S/Z* all come from the edition published by Le Seuil.
57. Barthes, p. 12.
58. Barthes, p. 11.
59. Lanham, p. 36.
60. Huizinga, from *Homo ludens*, quoted by Lanham, p. 112.
61. 'To look for the "law" of *Tristram Shandy* is one of the least promising enterprises in criticism', Sigurd Burckhardt, 'Tristram Shandy's Law of Gravity', *ELH*, 28 (1961), 70–88, p. 70; also quoted by Lanham, p. 91.
62. Denis Diderot, *Œuvres complètes*, ed. Lewinter, III, p. 245.
63. In *L'Unité secrète*, Pruner praises 'M. Jacques Proust [qui] a heureusement réagi, dans sa grande thèse sur *Diderot et l'Encyclopédie*, contre la fâcheuse tendance à ne voir dans cette philosophie que ses contradictions: ce ne sont jamais que les apparences de cette méthode paradoxale de présentation derrière laquelle elle se cache. Diderot pense que la contradiction est inhérente à la double nature humaine — qui est non pas de corps et d'esprit, mais de nature originelle et de "seconde nature" sociale. Le philosophe qui constate la contradiction mérite-t-il d'être lui-même taxé de contradiction? S'il la constate en lui — honnêtement — n'est-ce pas au contraire parce que l'exercice de sa pensée est souverainement unitaire?', pp. 14–15.

CHAPTER 2

Ideas and Examples

Unconventional narrative and philosophical content are the two most defining features of *Jacques le fataliste* and *Tristram Shandy*. Jacques's fatalistic principles and his belief that everything is 'écrit là-haut' in 'le Grand Rouleau', suggest an essential connection between narrative and philosophy. Indeed, Jacques describes fate as a story already written and which the individual waits to see unfold. The novel itself is presented as a re-transcription of, and a reflection on, the characters' fate already written in the heavens. The way the Great Scroll unfolds triggers Jacques's and his master's conversations on fatalism and free will. It also stands as a metaphor for the progress of the narrative. The narrative challenges those debates, and alters the philosophical content of both texts. In the 'Discourse in the novel', Bakhtin claims Sterne was greatly influenced by 'Rabelais' "philosophy of the word" — a philosophy expressed not as much in direct utterances as in stylistic practice [. . .]'.[1]

My argument thus comes in direct lineage from Bakhtin's claim, which, in this chapter, is applied also to Diderot. The philosophical debates explicitly referred to in *Jacques le fataliste* and *Tristram Shandy* do not constitute the didactic message of either text. Their authoritative value is undermined by the narrative. The narrative does not negate the debates, but reshapes them so that they may acquire a new meaning. To support this argument, the present chapter will consider the interplay between ideas and examples.

In *Tristram Shandy* and *Jacques le fataliste*, there exist very peculiar connections between abstract ideas and concrete illustrations. The traditional literary dichotomy between didacticism and entertainment corresponds to a rephrasing of two different, but complementary, forms of understanding. Didacticism appeals to the intellect by using abstract ideas, whereas illustration, considered as a form of entertainment, appeals to the imagination. Understanding cannot be reached when an idea is not accompanied by an example, or when an illustration is not connected to a precise idea. In Sterne's and Diderot's novels, incomprehension regularly arises from the fact that idea and example have not been used jointly. Logically, once idea and example have been combined and both the intellect and imagination appealed to, then there should be no more grounds for misunderstanding.

Despite attempts to accompany an idea with its illustration, incomprehension remains and, in some cases, may even be aggravated. This occurs when the examples given do not coincide with the ideas they are supposed to explain; there arises an inconsistency between principles and actions. This is particularly clear in *Jacques le fataliste*: the reader expects the servant and the master to embody respectively fatalism and free will. However, Jacques and his master both undermine their own principles by acting contrary to them. Fatalism and free will are sabotaged by their own advocates. In other instances, certain ideas are held against common sense, and therefore cannot find a practical application. Many ideas formulated by the Shandys are doomed to remain an intellectual fantasy. *Tristram Shandy* presents yet another way for an idea and its illustration to mismatch. When explaining a point, Tristram regularly makes the illustration deviate from its purpose. Instead of proving the truth of an idea, Tristram's illustrations are used as counter-examples providing the exception to the general rule that he had just established. By preventing the combination of theory and illustration from fulfilling its original purpose, Sterne and Diderot invite the reader to re-evaluate the function of idea and example inside their novels.

The role of the discrepancy between an idea and its illustration in *Tristram Shandy* and *Jacques le fataliste* should be reassessed. I argue that this discrepancy, creating deliberate confusion, is employed as the means to avoid conclusion. In an effective combination of idea and example, there is very little room for disagreement since the validity and truthfulness of the argument has been proven and defended. Discussion is then closed. Sterne and Diderot consistently contrive not to let the philosophical debates in their novels reach closure. Straightforward questions are evasively answered; the characters and narrators refuse to express a definite opinion on a given matter; a discussion may unsatisfactorily tail off into silence without any final argument. In *Jacques le fataliste*, the narrator exacerbates this inconclusiveness by not expressing his own views. Very early on in Diderot's novel, the narrator refuses to side either with the fatalistic servant or the libertarian master. The narrator may also find a pretext to interrupt abruptly their discussions. The open-endedness of the stories in *Jacques le fataliste* and *Tristram Shandy* parallels the absence of conclusion in their philosophical debates.

Reluctance to conclude can be explained by a refusal to acknowledge that there exists only one right answer to a question. Contrary opinions and views are constantly being juxtaposed and presented as equally valid. Such juxtapositions may be considered as a form of heteroglossia promoting a multi-facetted truth expressed by a plurality of voices, and not by a single authoritative one. If Sterne and Diderot had drawn a hierarchy amongst their characters' diverging opinions, one particular view would have stood out as representative of the author's own position, and consequently all the other views would have been invalidated. However, Sterne and Diderot refrain from establishing the authorial, and so authoritative, discourse inside their own novels: few of the ideas expressed are adequately supported by their accompanying examples. I argue that what Sterne and Diderot are offering is not a system but a philosophical method envisaging truth as contradictory and multi-facetted instead of monosemous.

In this chapter, I will be following in Robin Howells' footsteps. Like him, I have used as a starting point Bakhtin's claim that 'Stupidity (incomprehension) in the novel is always polemical'.[2] Howells analyses the figures of the 'Fool', the 'Rogue' and the 'Clown' in French Enlightenment writings to argue that they '[practise] stupidity as a dialogic strategy and as an ideology'.[3] Whereas Howells focuses on the function of stupidity, I will concentrate on how incomprehension challenges and alters the apparent didactic discourse in *Tristram Shandy* and *Jacques le fataliste*. This leads me to the same conclusion as Howells. Like stupidity, incomprehension 'pluralise[s] and break[s] down the monologic claims of established discourses'.[4] If stupidity and incomprehension have the same effect, they reach it by taking different routes. Stupidity only affects the characters, and leads to a form of bonding between the narrator and reader who both remain outside the scene as spectators. Incomprehension (at least in Sterne's and Diderot's novels) spreads through the various narrative layers and touches characters, narrator and reader. It achieves its polemical function in a very different way to stupidity.

Abstract Ideas, Concrete Illustrations

Like other philosophical novels, *Tristram Shandy* and *Jacques le fataliste* are confronted with the concern of maintaining the balance between didacticism and entertainment. This equilibrium is especially important as the efficiency of the former depends on how well it is conveyed by the latter. In this chapter, I attribute to entertainment a very particular role. Entertainment complements the abstract and complex language of didacticism by providing an illustrative story easing comprehension. While both are supposed to convey the same idea, they each use a different mode for doing so. Didacticism appeals to the intellect and entertainment appeals to the imagination. The necessity for this complementarity is felt through obvious instances of didacticism failing because it has not been accompanied by an explanatory illustration. This occurs when certain characters express ideas by appealing only to the intellect. Consequently they are unable to make themselves understood.

Learned characters eager to display their knowledge often end up victims of their own pedantry. Walter Shandy and Dr Slop, who cannot resist the pleasure of flaunting their erudition, are the most prone to incomprehension from their audience. Both enjoy using technical terms that they alone are familiar with. They deliberately create incomprehension by not always explaining those terms to the non-specialists. Toby, an erudite man himself when it comes to military affairs, may also be accused of not adapting his discourse to his interlocutor. Terms such as 'the scarp and counterscarp, — the glacis and covered way, — the half-moon and ravelin' (*TS*, II, I, p. 74) have no concrete reality to the civilian, and only make sense to the soldier. In these cases, technical and abstract vocabulary cannot be understood, as they are not explained through concrete examples.

Examples may be just as incomprehensible when their connection to the idea they illustrate is not made explicit. In the middle of a conversation between Walter and Dr Slop on radical heat and radical moisture, Toby and Trim join in by remembering how, during the siege of Limerick, they burnt alcohol every night to stay alive. As Toby and Trim did not explain that this anecdote served as an illustration to the discussion, Dr Slop and Walter cannot make sense of it: '[all] this was as much *Arabick*' (*TS*, V, xxxvii, p. 359).

The reader is caught between two extremes. He finds himself trapped between Walter's incomprehensible abstract discourse, and Toby's just as incomprehensible concrete example. These two extremes are reassembled and summarised in the same chapter when Trim recapitulates his definition 'that the radical moisture is nothing in the world but ditch-water — and that the radical heat, of those who can go to the expence of it, is burnt brandy'. This definition, turned meaningless by its excessive specificity, is followed by Dr Slop's own version, as little enlightening as Trim's: 'It is inherent in the seeds of all animals, and may be preserved sundry ways, but principally in my opinion by *consubstantials*, *impriments*, and *occludents*' (*TS*, V, xl, p. 362). These passages provide two opposite instances of how incomprehension arises. Trim only tenuously links his concrete illustration to the abstract idea. The simple verb 'is' does not suffice to comprehend the connection. Incomprehension occurs when an idea is not clarified by a concrete illustration, or when the link between the two has not been justified. In both cases, the words are precise, the grammar simple, and yet the content remains obscure. In the case of Dr Slop, incomprehension arises from obscure language. The doctor's scientific jargon appears even more arcane in comparison with Trim's 'ditch-water' and 'brandy'. Here, we witness a clash between two opposite registers of language. Bakhtin invites us to be attentive to the 'intentional dimensions' of polylinguism. 'Generic languages' are of course perfectly comprehensible to those who speak them. But for those who are not familiar with them, 'these languages become *things*, limited in their meaning and expression'.[5] Because Dr Slop's language is as foreign to his audience as to the reader, its purpose is to obscure his discourse in order to mystify and impress his audience.

In *Jacques le fataliste*, the same problem is depicted, but this time coming from quite unexpected quarters. It is the servant who is prone to playing with complex ideas which his master finds himself unable to grasp. Jacques loses his master's and the reader's attention through the complexity of his ideas, after having defined prudence as 'une supposition, dans laquelle l'expérience nous autorise à regarder les circonstances où nous nous trouvons comme causes de certains effets à espérer ou à craindre pour l'avenir' (*JF*, 676). Incomprehension arises from the density of Jacques's ideas, and not from his expression. Jacques leaves his master in such a state of perplexity that the latter is unable to proceed further with the discussion. The master can only express his surprise that his servant is capable of understanding such a definition. Jacques avoids pedantry by employing a simple vocabulary and his sentence is grammatically correct, yet he remains incomprehensible. The source of the incomprehension lies in the fact that abstract vocabulary is too limited to express fully the intricate subtleties of Jacques's thoughts.[6] Jacques should not have relied solely on abstract language to define prudence, but should have included concrete words and illustrations.

Even though there are some occurrences of incomprehension between Jacques and his master, these are not as widespread as in the Shandean entourage, at least for those living upstairs. As for those living in the servants' hall, there seems to be a perfect understanding. When learning of the sudden death of his eldest son, Bobby, Walter finds consolation in indulging in a discourse on death. His dirge starts by an impersonation of Cicero on the loss of his daughter, followed by a reappropriation of 'an extract of *Servius Sulpicius*'s consolatory letter to *Tully*' and ends with an aphorism. The mounting on his hobby-horse seems to have most effectively consoled Walter. Tristram remarks that by the end of his father's speech 'he had absolutely forgot my brother *Bobby*'. Yet Walter fails in conveying to Toby any sense of the reality of death. Toby, who does not share his brother's classical education, can only reconcile Walter's actual situation to his references to Antiquity, by supposing 'that his misfortunes had disordered his brains' (*TS*, V, iii, p. 320). And at the end of a long reasoning on why death is not to be feared, Toby is left to ponder on an aphorism. Far from bringing home the idea of death, it only succeeds in puzzling him further:

> [. . .] 'tis terrible no way — for consider, brother *Toby*, — when we *are* — death is *not*; — and when death *is* — we are *not*. My uncle *Toby* laid down his pipe to consider the proposition; my father's eloquence was too rapid to stay for any man — away it went, — and hurried my uncle *Toby*'s ideas along with it. (*TS*, V, iii, p. 321)

Walter's speech on the occasion of his son's death is closely followed by Trim's own oration. The content is just as banal, as it muses on the suddenness of death. However, the method for its delivery is quite different. Whilst Walter only addressed himself to Toby's intellect, Trim appeals to the heart of his audience and accompanies his discourse with a concrete illustration:

> Are we not here now, continued the corporal, (striking the end of his stick perpendicularly upon the floor, so as to give an idea of health and stability) — and are we not — (dropping his hat upon the ground) gone! in a moment!
> — 'Twas infinitely striking! (*TS*, V, vii, p. 325)

Unlike Walter, who succeeded only in leaving Toby in a state of perplexity, Trim manages perfectly to express his idea.

Unlike Walter and Jacques, it appears that Trim has overcome the insufficiencies of abstract language by what Meiner calls a 'compensation imagée':

> Il est nécessaire de créer des *images* qui font entrevoir l'étendue de la pensée [. . .]. La vivacité de la pensée n'a parfois pas de nom mais au lieu de rendre le discours obscur, ce déficit sémiotique est l'occasion de mettre en marche une autre dimension de la langue, celle du langage imagé qui ne dit pas mais qui fait voir la vivacité pour que le lecteur en comprenne l'idée.[7]

Trim does not compensate for the insufficiencies of abstract language by introducing a 'langage imagé' in his speech. With the use of his hat, he creates the image and gestures his idea. The effect remains the same as it offers an example of 'clarté confuse': Trim's audience understands clearly his idea, though comprehension passes through a sentiment instead of the intellect. To understand how this 'clarté confuse' is applied through the combination of idea and illustration, it is necessary to turn back to the dichotomy between didacticism and entertainment.

The importance given to the combination of didacticism and entertainment in seventeenth- and eighteenth-century novel writing is common knowledge. Yet it is necessary to remember the literary context Diderot and Sterne come from, especially as incomprehension is at the heart of the problem. Indeed, in 1669, Pierre-Daniel Huet characterised the novelistic genre as an interplay between 'le plaisir et l'instruction des lecteurs'.[8] The occasional failures of the characters to get their message across underline the fact that the balance between didacticism and entertainment is not self-evident. Yet it is on this balance that *Tristram Shandy* rests, at least according to its narrator, who 'sat down to write my life for the amusement of the world, and my opinions for its instruction' (*TS*, III, xxviii, p. 193). It is also by the attainment of this balance that Jacques's master estimates the quality of a story. He has 'un furieux goût pour les contes' since 'ils m'instruisent et m'amusent' (*JF*, p. 787). The master's standard seems to be expressed by the narrator when telling his readers that 'Si mon ouvrage est bon, il vous fera plaisir' (*JF*, p. 835). If we read 'bon' with a moral overtone, the sentence underlines a relation of interdependence where entertainment is the natural consequence of didacticism. However, there are occasions when this balance is not reached. Both didacticism and entertainment then end up wasted.

Incomprehension arises from relying only on an abstract explanation, erroneously believing that understanding passes solely through the intellect. In this respect, the Author's Preface in *Tristram Shandy* is a key text. The narrator begins by taking his distance from Locke who, in *An Essay concerning Human*

Understanding, is wary of wit. Locke regards it as an ornament to speech useful for entertainment. But when the purpose is no longer to amuse but to instruct the audience, wit is then 'wholly to be avoided'. It is 'for nothing else but to insinuate wrong ideas, move the passions, and thereby mislead the judgment'.[9] Tristram refutes Locke's claim that wit obscures judgment. On the contrary, it is because wit functions, as Locke describes (II, xi, §2), by drawing analogies, and so by bringing illustrations to the primary idea that it makes it more comprehensible. Here we understand the correlation between the two as the narrator regards wit as a form of illustration. The narrator then responds to Didius' objection 'That an illustration is no argument':

> [. . .] — nor do I maintain the wiping of a looking-glass clean, to be a syllogism; — but you all, may it please your worships, see the better for it, — so that the main good these things do, is only to clarify the understanding [. . .].
> (*TS*, III, xx, p. 174)

Tristram pursues his refutation of Locke by inverting the philosopher's observation 'that men who have a great deal of wit [. . .] have not always the clearest judgement', which parallels the narrator's wonder at 'How it comes to pass, that your men of least *wit* are reported to be men of most *judgment*' (*TS*, III, xx, p. 179).[10] To ease the understanding between the author and his reader, Tristram claims that specific, technical vocabulary, should be replaced with concrete objects, immediately at hand, 'something standing, or hanging up, which would have cleared the point at once'.

The controversy raised in *Tristram Shandy* concerning the use of concrete examples may be better understood if placed in the wider context of the debate on clarity. Meiner underlined how distrust of 'langage imagé' had influenced discourse on clarity. Examples and tropes were suspected of introducing obscurity to a discourse. They were considered as proxies only bearing a resemblance to the signified. By always being *on the side*, as it were, they would increase the screen between *res* and *verba*. Locke's own criticism of 'figurative speeches' as a cause of obscurity and confusion is illustrative of this. Meiner analysed how men such as Leibniz and Bernard Lamy refuted the mistrust of 'langage imagé'. Lamy attributed to figurative speech a 'fonction clarifiante'. It clarifies an abstract demonstration by illustrating it with a concrete example. Understanding is then achieved when a speech appeals to both the intellect and imagination:

> Ces raisonnements ont une force merveilleuse, qui consiste en ce que, joignant une proposition claire et incontestable avec une autre qui n'est pas si claire et qui est contestée, la clarté de l'une dissipe les ténèbres de l'autre; et comme ces deux propositions sont étroitement liées, si ce raisonnement est bon, que l'on ne demeure d'accord que l'autre l'est aussi.[11]

In his study of the importance for Sterne of Addison's papers in *The Spectator*, Jonathan Lamb offers us an English counterpart to Lamy. He presents

Addison's work on the pleasures of the imagination as the realisation that 'the most complex and powerful sentiments arise from a coalition of an impression and an idea which cannot conceal the imperfection of their union but can exploit it'.[12] Addison differentiates between understanding (sometimes called 'Reason'), which is infinite, and imagination (also referred to as 'Fancy'), which is limited.

> Our Reason can pursue a Particle of Matter through an infinite variety of Divisions, but the Fancy soon loses sight of it, and feels in itself a kind of Chasm, that wants to be filled with Matter of a more sensible Bulk.[13]

An idea can only become clear to the imagination if it is accompanied by a concrete illustration, which would provide a notion with 'Colour and Shape'.[14]

Meiner traces this notion of clarifying figurative speech back to Classical authors and their use of hypotyposis, which Quintilian praised for making an idea clear by placing it, as it were, under the eyes of the audience.[15] Concrete examples have indeed a hypotypotic value as they enable us to visualise an idea by giving it the shape of an object. Tristram puts this into practice. He uses 'the two knobs on the top of the back of' 'a cane chair' he is sitting on to illustrate his point on the necessity of joining wit to judgment (*TS*, III, xx, p.180). By doing so, not only does Tristram help the reader to understand his meaning, he also proves the validity of his point. Tristram invites the reader to imagine the chair with one of the knobs missing, and after underlining how ridiculous it would look, asks 'Whether this one single knob which now stands here like a blockhead by itself, can serve any purpose upon earth, but to put one in mind of the want of the other' (*TS*, III, xx, p. 181). The answer to this rhetorical question applies to wit and judgment. The two knobs represent both and illustrate the necessity for their reunion. The Author's Preface concludes on a remark tightening the relation between the concrete and the abstract. The Preface even reverses precedence, as Tristram states that 'a philosopher should [. . .] [examine] the matter of fact before he philosophised upon it' (*TS*, III, xx, p. 182). Here, concrete reality passes from the subservient role of illustration to that of producing food for thought.

The main philosophical thread in *Jacques le fataliste* is of course the debate on fatalism and free will, and Diderot makes it understandable to the reader through the combination of idea and illustration, or, in other words, of didacticism and entertainment. The debate opposing the two sides opens the first pages of the novel. 'Jacques disait que tout ce qui nous arrive de bien et de mal ici-bas était écrit là-haut'. His master, unconvinced by such a sweeping claim, challenges him by retorting 'C'est un grand mot que cela' (*JF*, p. 669). Jacques's justification of fatalism triggers the story of his love-life which starts with the fact that 'chaque balle qui partait d'un fusil avait son billet'. Having received his bullet in the knee, the consequence is his falling in love '[par] un coup de feu' (*JF*, p. 670). In the course of the novel, Jacques constantly uses his love-story to illustrate his famous expression that 'c'était écrit là-haut'. Indeed, concrete illustration is necessary to make the abstract idea of fatalism understood by his master and the reader.

Similarly, the narrator is often faced with the reader's incomprehension. As a consequence, he must combine abstract explanations with concrete illustration so as to make his point understood. Tristram frequently resorts to this solution to explain to the reader the principle of association of ideas 'which strange combination [. . .], the sagacious *Locke* [. . .] affirms to have produced more wry actions than all other sources of prejudice whatsoever' (*TS*, I, iv, p. 9). The narrator enlightens us on this by using a series of illustrations, one of the most famous being how his mother ultimately associated the winding up of the clock with her husband's visits to her bedchamber. The necessity of accompanying the explication of an abstract notion with a concrete illustration does not only occur in the case of philosophical discussions. Toby resorts to the same method by using a map to accompany his explanations of the battle of Namur. Toby's account otherwise would have been completely obscure to his audience. The same happens at the metadiegetic level in the inserted Slawkenbergius tale. The trumpeter's wife, who is one of the happy few to have seen the incredible nose of the stranger, describes it to the Strasburgers who did not have this opportunity. She uses as a hypotyposis her husband's trumpet, 'the best apparatus the straitness of the time would allow' for 'the illustration of her theory' (*TS*, IV, Slawkenbergius's Tale, p. 231).

In these examples, comprehension is reached by appealing to both intellect and imagination through a short story. This serves to illustrate an idea fictively transposed to a practical dimension. Owing to the novel's concern with conveying didacticism via entertainment, Huet linked it to philosophical writing:

> [. . .] quand les préceptes de la philosophie sont revêtus de ses ornements, ils trouvent une entrée bien plus libre dans l'âme des jeunes personnes, que quand ils se présentent avec toute leur austérité. Aussi la plupart des philosophes ont employé le ministère des fables pour l'établissement de leurs dogmes et ont excessivement vanté l'utilité de ces impostures qui nous trompent à notre profit [. . .].[16]

Huet sternly implies that authors need to trick the reader into receiving their 'préceptes' by coating them with 'ornements' and 'fables' to overcome intellectual idleness. But novelists may also use fables as illustrations of abstract and complex notions so as to prevent incomprehension. Philosophers commonly resort to this practice. To choose one example from a thousand others, Descartes, in the *Discours de la méthode*, describes in very vivid terms a piece of bees-wax. He mentions its shape, its consistency, its colour, its smell before and after having been heated by fire. Descartes thus explains that the senses are not sufficient to inform us about the nature of objects. Tristram recuperates Descartes's wax. This time it is manipulated by '*Dolly* your chamber-maid' to demonstrate 'the cause of obscurity and confusion, in the mind of man' (*TS*, II, ii, p. 77). There is a flaw however in this demonstration, and we will come back to it later.

In the examples quoted above, illustration takes the form of a story inserted in the discourse. However, the speaker may also choose to convince his interlocutor by using experience rather than imagination as a form of illustration. Illustration through experience is a method particularly favoured by Jacques whose master often proves stubborn in his beliefs. When abstract explanation and illustrative anecdotes have had no effect, Jacques resorts to experience, usually unpleasant, to make his point. The following example is not of Jacques's doing but serves his purpose. The master impertinently refuses to believe that a wound in the knee '[est] une des plus cruelles', even after hearing Jacques's description of his own sufferings. But the master is interrupted as his horse trips, and he falls to the ground: 'son genou va s'appuyer rudement sur un caillou pointu' (*JF*, p. 680). Having experienced the pain of a wounded knee and given way to the suffering in a rather undignified way, the master is forced to acknowledge his mistake to the gleeful servant.

A similar incident happens at the end of the novel, this time concerning the key debate on fatalism and free will. Jacques tries to convince his master that none of his actions are free. Here again he clarifies his abstract explanation by accompanying it with a concrete illustration:

> Mais si vous êtes et si vous avez toujours été le maître de vouloir, que ne voulez-vous à présent aimer une guenon, et que n'avez-vous cessé d'aimer Agathe toutes les fois que vous l'avez voulu? Mon maître, on passe les trois quarts de sa vie à vouloir sans faire. (*JF*, p. 868)

Despite the illustration appealing to his imagination, the master remains unconvinced. Jacques promises to offer him a demonstration in the course of time.[17] The demonstration finally comes at the end of the master's love-story, that is to say when the master, and the reader, least expect it. Jacques intentionally provokes an argument with his master by loosely arranging his saddle, which triggers the mechanism of set responses from the master planned by the servant. Having failed to explain his idea by stimulating his master's imagination through the example of the female ape, Jacques is forced to resort to a more practical demonstration. In this case, illustration takes the form of experience. Howells has observed in other eighteenth-century French works the importance of experimentation in a character's confrontation with the world. He refers to this type of character as 'a Lockean subject' in the sense that he acts as an empiricist, receptive to the world and forming deductions based on his experience.[18]

Problems in the Application of an Idea to Reality

When an abstract explanation is accompanied by a concrete illustration, it becomes much more comprehensible. It allows a balance between didacticism and the entertainment of a lighter yet still instructive form of discourse, usually under the form of an anecdote or a short story. When the author adds an empirical demonstration to a complex idea, didacticism takes a stronger hold and becomes persuasive. We could then easily imagine that Sterne and Diderot used this method to win over the reader and persuade him to adopt their own views. Yet this is far from being the case. *Jacques le fataliste* and *Tristram Shandy* constantly blur their authors' views. Numerous instances of problematical applications of an idea to a concrete situation prevent those views from being clear-cut.

Far from clearing incomprehension, a concrete example often increases it. This occurs when there is no indication as to how that example verifies an idea, or even in what way it is illustrative. Coming back to the passage in *Tristram Shandy* of Dolly handling a piece of wax, the narrator recognises that the illustration does not apply to his argument. After Toby's explanation of the siege of Namur, the critic asks Tristram to explain how 'a military man, and whom you have represented as no fool, — be at the same time such a confused, pudding-headed, muddle-headed fellow' (*TS*, II, ii, p. 76). Tristram undertakes to expound 'the cause of obscurity and confusion, in the mind of a man': 'Dull organs, dear Sir, in the first place. Secondly, slight and transient impressions made by objects when the said organs are not dull. And, thirdly, a memory like unto a sieve, not able to retain what it has received' (*TS*, II, ii, p. 77). All three causes are progressively illustrated by Dolly handling 'an inch [...] of red seal-wax' to which 'dull organs' are likened. The hardening of the wax which makes it impossible for the seal to leave an impression, answers the second cause. And Dolly's distraction, this time responsible for the wax not receiving a print, illustrates the third. However, the narrator leaves the reader perplexed:

> Now you must understand that not one of these was the true cause of the confusion in my uncle *Toby*'s discourse; and it is for that reason I enlarge upon them so long, after the manner of great physiologists, — to shew the world what it did *not* arise from. (*TS*, II, ii, p. 78).

The narrator then puts an end to the suspense by very briefly saying that Toby's confusion arose from 'the unsteady uses of words' (*TS*, II, ii, p. 78).

Arguments may be distorted to the point that a particular notion continues to be defended against all common sense. A dinner reuniting theologians and other learned men has been organised to discuss the validity of Tristram's christening. Walter's attention is caught by a claim which not only tickles his passion for puzzling paradoxes, but also his wish to monopolise domestic matters: '*That the mother is not of kin to her child*'. The 'Duke of *Suffolk*'s case' serves as an illustration to the argument, as it reached the same conclusion. This is followed by obscure and spurious reasonings which lead the congregation more and more astray and even further than they would have liked, for their logic would then hold true for both parents. During the discussion, Toby is the only one unconvinced by such sophistry and stays faithful to plain common sense. Characters like Walter take such pleasure in toying with abstract ideas that their concurrency with reality is no longer relevant. As a result, concrete illustrations cannot possibly serve to verify such notions. They only emphasise the character's obstinacy and blindness in attempting forcefully to turn and twist a situation to suit his views. Non-coincidence between the idea and its illustration may serve as a comical resort. Nonetheless, it is completely counterproductive in solving incomprehension.

Examples may cease to coincide with the ideas they are supposed to explain when there arises an inconsistency between principles and actions. Jacques is often aware of the inconsistency of his behaviour regarding his fatalistic system. When mentioning his brother's 'malheureux voyage de Lisbonne', Jacques cannot help crying. In trying to comfort his servant by reminding him that 'cela était écrit là-haut', the master places him in front of his own contradictions. Sorrow becomes irrelevant in fatalism as such accidents, especially the Lisbon earthquake which many interpreted as a manifestation of God's will, are inevitable and follow cosmic order. Jacques is perfectly conscious of this inconsistency. Yet the heart seems to ignore the mind: 'avec tout cela je ne saurais m'empêcher de pleurer' (*JF*, p. 698). Later on in the novel, Jacques expresses his annoyance that he should react so emotionally when he believes that everything is pre-ordained. When he cries, he feels like a fool, and when he laughs, '[je] trouve encore que je suis un sot; cependant, je ne puis m'empêcher ni de pleurer ni de rire et c'est ce qui me fait enrager.' To redress this fault, Jacques '[a] cent fois essayé [. . .] [de se] moquer de tout', but to no avail (*JF*, p. 730).

The master discovers another proof of Jacques's inconsistency when he learns with surprise that his servant sometimes prays. Prayer, at least when it takes the form of an entreaty, is incompatible with fatalism. It suggests that man might be able to change what has already been pre-ordained. Here again, Jacques acknowledges his own contradictions:

> Je prie à tout hasard, et quoi qu'il m'avînt, je ne m'en réjouirais ni ne m'en plaindrais, si je me possédais, mais c'est que je suis inconséquent et violent, que j'oublie mes principes ou les leçons de mon capitaine, et que je ris et pleure comme un sot. (*JF*, p. 793)

Despite believing in fatalism, Jacques leaves the door open by continuing to pray, in case his principles might be wrong. This is reminiscent of Pascal's wager: one should believe in God as a precautionary measure. If God does exist, one gains beatitude, if He does not, one has lost nothing. But if one has not applied this measure and God exists, then one has everything to lose. By praying, Jacques takes the precautionary measure of still having a certain influence over events in case fatalism fails.

Throughout Diderot's novel, Jacques recognises that his behaviour is inconsistent with his ideas. He has even come to accept this inconsistency as the common rule: 'qu'est-ce qu'il y a de commun entre la doctrine que l'on professe et les prodiges qu'on opère?' (*JF*, p. 870). However, the servant's lucidity is not shared by the master acting as a counterpoint. The first believes in fatalism, the second in free will; and the friction between these two sparks off the debate. Yet the master does not have Jacques's lucidity. Unlike his servant, he is unaware that his behaviour often contradicts his libertarian principles. The master is described as '[un] automate': '[il] se laisse exister, c'est sa fonction habituelle' (*JF*, p. 686). The bizarre image of the machine cannot be more opposite to free will, but its appropriateness is gradually justified. The master's actions betray the fact that, despite his libertarian cant, he is the most superstitious character of the novel. The master is the first to suggest that Jacques's horse galloping towards gibbets 'est de fâcheux augure' (*JF*, p. 700). The second time the horse does this, the master is convinced that he will soon lose his servant to the hangman. While Jacques is only wondering 'Est-ce un signe du destin?', the master, far from laughing at such superstition as any libertarian would, firmly believes there is no possible doubt and talks to him as to a man condemned to death (see *JF*, p. 711).

Jacques would prove by his actions the practicality of fatalism; his master would persuade the reader that free will is well founded. However, in *Jacques le fataliste*, principles are sabotaged by their own advocates. Now and then, Jacques's behaviour betrays his fatalistic convictions; the master's actions often seem to be more in agreement with fatalism than libertarianism. In *Jacques le fataliste*, the characters are not the only ones to act in a way which is incoherent with their principles. From the beginning, the narrator warns the reader that the story of Jacques and his master is neither a novel nor a tale. A scenario is offered but then dismissed on the grounds that it would then be nothing but pure literary invention:

> Vous allez croire que cette petite armée tombera sur Jacques et son maître, qu'il y aura une action sanglante, des coups de bâton donnés, des coups de pistolets tirés, et il ne tiendrait qu'à moi que tout cela n'arrivât; mais adieu la vérité de l'histoire, adieu le récit des amours de Jacques. Nos deux voyageurs n'étaient point suivis. J'ignore ce qui se passa dans l'auberge après leur départ. [...]
>
> Il est bien évident que je ne fais point un roman, puisque je néglige ce qu'un romancier ne manquerait pas d'employer. Celui qui prendrait ce que j'écris pour la vérité serait peut-être moins dans l'erreur que celui qui le prendrait pour une fable. (*JF*, p. 678)

A few pages later, the narrator reiterates this warning by using the same method of mentioning one possible scenario and then dismissing it:

> Vous allez croire, Lecteur, que ce cheval est celui qu'on a volé au maître de Jacques, et vous vous tromperez. C'est ainsi que cela arriverait dans un roman un peu plus tôt ou un peu plus tard, de cette manière ou autrement; mais ceci n'est pas un roman, je vous l'ai déjà dit, je crois, et je vous le répète encore.
> (*JF*, p. 697)

The narrator describes the story he is telling in negative terms, refusing to place it in any literary category whatsoever. Only the vague word 'histoire' is used. The narrator's contempt of literary forms partly explains his insistence on not seeing his story associated with them. The narrator 'n'aime pas les romans, à moins que ce ne soit ceux de Richardson' (*JF*, p. 847), and he finds tales and novels remarkably easy to spin: 'Qu'il est facile de faire des contes!', 'rien de plus aisé que de filer un roman' (*JF*, p. 670, 848). The narrator's suspicion regarding literary forms stems from his insistence on the distinction between truth and fiction. This distinction is particularly important as, according to the narrator, only truth arouses interest: 'on ne peut s'intéresser qu'à ce qu'on croit vrai.' (*JF*, p. 882) As Connon points out, '[we] might expect [. . .] that the shattering of the illusion would signal the end of the drama, that, after the revelation of the artificiality of the spectacle, there would be no going back [. . .].'[19] The reader should then be careful not to confuse fact and fiction: 'soyez circonspect si vous ne voulez pas prendre dans cet entretien de Jacques et de son maître le vrai pour le faux, le faux pour le vrai.' (*JF*, p. 715)

The narrator's advice is ambiguous and acts as a warning: the story of Jacques and his master is not completely true. Truth and fiction are intermingled, despite chronological incongruities. The narrator also raises the problem of *vraisemblance* within the novel in a very paradoxical way. A writer may decide to leave out an extraordinary yet real event on the grounds that it is unlikely and might consequently shed doubt on the authenticity of the entire work. The narrator addresses this problem through the word 'engastrimeste'. It is highly unlikely that this unusual term should belong to a servant's lexicon; and it is reasonable that the reader should raise his eyebrows when hearing it on Jacques's lips.

> Et Jacques s'est servi du terme *Engastrimeste*? — Pourquoi pas, Lecteur? Le capitaine de Jacques était Bacbutien, il a pu connaître cette expression, et Jacques, qui recueillait tout ce qu'il disait, se la rappeler; mais la vérité, c'est que l'*Engastrimeste* est de moi, et qu'on lit sur le texte original *Ventriloque*.
> (*JF*, p. 837)

The narrator's justification makes sense and would be another case of a real but unlikely detail.[20] However, the narrator destroys this argument in favour of the text's authenticity by admitting that this detail is pure invention. And far from helping the reader to disentangle truth from fiction, the narrator is caught complicating the knot.

The exact literary status of the text is ultimately questioned by the fact that the narrator behaves in a way inconsistent with what he says. If the narrator is openly critical of certain scenarios for being too *romanesque*, some stories end in a very conventional way.²¹ As Hobson remarks, '[his] work appears both like other novels and better than other novels; the 'auteur' forces certain stories down the 'lecteur''s throat, yet refuses others'.²² Behind this playful construction and deconstruction of the narrative, Hobson argues that Diderot is setting an essential question: '[it] is clear that the novel is not merely using burlesque techniques but is also posing the question of *what is real* — not metaphysically but aesthetically real.'²³ The question of what is 'aesthetically real' is implicitly raised, but receives no explicit answer, leaving the reader to ponder without being given Diderot's own position on the issue.

By introducing doubt as to the authenticity of his story, the narrator invites the reader to reflect on the relationship between truth and fiction, but by doing so he invalidates one of his assertions: 'on ne peut s'intéresser qu'à ce qu'on croit vrai' (*JF*, p. 882). Yet Connon justly observes that, despite the narrator's best efforts to make us seriously doubt the text's claim to authenticity, we remain interested and read on to know the end of Jacques's love story.

> And yet, as he touches us, he also makes sure that we are aware of the mechanisms of the fiction which achieves this: if only what we know to be real could interest us we would not have read on; we have read on, and we have been involved and interested, but Diderot will not let us forget how this has been achieved.²⁴

Diderot does indeed need the reader to be aware of the narrator's inconsistencies as it is used as the means to raise the question of what is real.

In *Tristram Shandy*, didactic messages are also regularly undermined. This occurs when the illustration of an idea remains obscure. The apparent didactic message may also be impaired when the idea has departed so far from common sense that no concrete illustration can be found for it. Sterne's novel presents yet another way for an idea and its illustration to mismatch. When explaining a notion, Tristram often makes the accompanying illustration deviate from its original function, that is to say validating an idea. Instead, he uses the example as a counter-example, thus providing the exception to the rule.

Walter, who never thinks as other men do, incarnates this law of the exception to the rule. The affirmation 'that it is an irresistable and natural passion to weep for the loss of our friends and children' is justified by the examples of '*David*' who 'wept for his son *Absolom* — *Adrian* for his *Antinous* — *Niobe* for her children, and [...] *Apollodorus* and *Crito* [...] for *Socrates* before his death'. However, the appropriateness of the adjective 'irresistable' crumbles when Tristram comes to the case of Bobby and Walter, the exception to the rule who 'managed his affliction otherwise' (*TS*, V, iii, p. 317).

Yorick is another character who proves an idea wrong by being the exception to it. Every now and then, Tristram refers to the idea of national character, of which he is a staunch believer, to account for certain mindsets. But this does not work for Yorick who, though 'of *Danish* extraction' (*TS*, I, xi, p. 23), displays no signs

> [. . .] of that cold phlegm and exact regularity of sense and humours, you would have look'd for, in one so extracted; — he was, on the contrary, as mercurial and sublimated a composition, [. . .] with as much life and whim, and *gaité de Coeur* about him, as the kindliest climate could have engendered and put together. (*TS*, I, xi, p. 24)

If the parson's eccentricity 'stagger'd [Tristram's] faith in regard to *Yorick*'s extraction', the reader is more likely to conclude that the notion of national character is not wholly reliable. Tristram himself is the living refutation of his father's system on Christian names. Far from being 'extreamly mean and pitiful', his 'life and opinions are likely to make some noise in the world' (*TS*, I, xix, p. 50 & I, iv, p. 8). Tristram maximises the impact of the exception to the rule by following the same carefully constructed order. First, he enunciates the general rule, the veracity of which has no reason to be questioned. This rule is usually a commonplace originating from authoritative authors like Seneca and Aristotle. The narrator then introduces one of the Shandean characters, famous for their eccentricity rather than their wisdom, as the exception to the general rule. *Tristram Shandy* seems to invite the reader to re-evaluate the function of the concrete illustration. Far from being limited to the role of making an idea more understandable and validating it, a concrete illustration can also extend to refutation by providing the exception to the rule.

Refusal to Conclude

Sterne's and Diderot's characters and narrators expect that an illustration will instantly lift the veil of abstraction from an idea and make it comprehensible. Their expectations are thwarted each time they stumble upon cases when idea and reality do not coincide. Confusion, and not greater clarity, then results from the combination of idea and illustration. As we have seen, this occurs when the logic of an idea is pushed until it blatantly contradicts common sense. In this case, the speaker can only employ spurious examples to illustrate his idea and maintain the illusion of its validity. Confusion may be replaced by downright contradiction when the illustration provides the exception to the rule, or when experience refutes an idea. These frequent disjunctions between an idea and its practical application prevent ideas from being brought to a conclusion. I will now analyse how narrators and characters in *Jacques le fataliste* and *Tristram Shandy* manage to avoid conclusion.

In the first pages of his autobiography, Tristram presents himself as a trustworthy and truthful narrator. Mentioning the spelling of the name Yorick throughout the centuries, Tristram corrects himself by replacing a guess with the admission of his ignorance:

> I was within an ace of saying nine hundred years; — but I would not shake my credit in telling an improbable truth, however indisputable in itself; — and therefore I shall content myself with only saying, — It had been exactly so spelt, without the least variation or transposition of a single letter, for I do not know how long. (*TS*, I, xi, p. 23)

Tristram's circumspection and noncommittal answers reappear in chapter xxi. In this chapter, he muses on the discord between Walter and Toby on the subject of Dinah's disreputable relation with the coachman. The following passage is particularly telling:

> Possibly at the very time this happened, it might have something else to afflict it; and as afflictions are sent down for our own good, and that as this had never done the SHANDY FAMILY any good at all, it might lye waiting till apt times and circumstances should give it an opportunity to discharge its office. — Observe, I determine nothing upon this. (*TS*, I, xxi, pp. 58–59)

In the first sentence, Tristram alternates affirmations with evasive propositions expressing possibilities through the adverb 'possibly' and the modal verbs 'might' and 'should'. The next sentence draws the reader's attention on to the narrator's cautious reservations as he concludes with a refusal to conclude. Tristram's circumspection continues one paragraph later with Toby's 'most extream and unparallel'd modesty of nature', 'tho' I correct the word nature, for this reason, that I may not prejudge a point which must shortly come to a hearing; and that is, Whether this modesty of his was natural or acquir'd' (*TS*, I, xxi, p. 59). The text never actually establishes this last point. The narrator seems to use circumspection as a tactic to guard himself against attacks from the over-punctilious 'hyper-criticks'.

In *Jacques le fataliste*, the narrator finds himself harassed by the fictional reader, just as bothersome as Tristram's critics. The fictional reader constantly tries to jump ahead of the story. He importunes the narrator with questions in order to skip over the progression and know the outcome more quickly. These questions usually concern the characters' destination, which the narrator succeeds in keeping secret until the end of the novel. When faced with the inquisitive landlady of the Grand-Cerf, Jacques resorts to the narrator's technique of offering only evasive answers to straightforward questions

> L'HÔTESSE: Ces messieurs vont-ils loin ?
> JACQUES: Nous n'en savons rien.
> L'HÔTESSE: Ces messieurs suivent quelqu'un ?
> JACQUES: Nous ne suivons personne.
> L'HÔTESSE: Ils vont ou ils s'arrêtent, selon les affaires qu'ils ont sur la route ?
> JACQUES: Nous n'en avons aucune.
> L'HÔTESSE: Ces messieurs voyagent pour leur plaisir.

JACQUES: Ou pour leur peine.
L'HÔTESSE: Je souhaite que ce soit le premier.
JACQUES: Votre souhait n'y fera pas un zeste, ce sera selon qu'il est écrit
    là-haut.
L'HÔTESSE: Oh! c'est un mariage.
JACQUES: Peut-être qu'oui, peut-être que non. (*JF*, p. 741)

The obsequious landlady is trying to worm out from Jacques the same information the reader desires to know, but her attempts to discover the characters' destination and aim are just as unsuccessful. Yet, the narrator unexpectedly offers the reader a clue from the mouth of the landlady, and which can only be understood retrospectively: the end of the master and the servant's journey will indeed end in a wedding, that of Jacques and Denise.

Tristram does the same as Diderot's narrator when he leaves the question of 'which ever way my uncle *Toby* came by' his modesty undecided (*TS*, I, xxi, p. 59). Tristram seems to have acquired one of his uncle's traits: to retreat when confronted by rhetoricians more skilled than he. Both prefer to withdraw from a discussion as soon as they feel argued down by their interlocutor. Because he does not possess his brother's rhetorical powers, Toby's plain and good common sense can never prevail over Walter's bizarre reasonings. To avoid having to listen to spurious arguments he is unable to refute, such as in the case of the conversation on how mothers are not akin to their children, Toby applies military tactics to conversation. He retreats by using his last resort: the '*Argumentum Fistulatorium*' (*TS*, I, xxi, p. 62). By 'whistling half a dozen bars of *Lillabullero*', he is able to withdraw from the conversation, left without a conclusion (*TS*, I, xxi, p. 61).

Toby does not have recourse solely to the *argumentum fistulatorium*, baffling his interlocutor with its idiosyncrasy. He keeps up his sleeve a much more common argument: to bring a matter to a conclusion by referring to God's will. This leaves Walter deeply frustrated as it robs him of the pleasure of arguing. Divine will provides only a hackneyed conclusion 'cutting the knot [. . .] instead of untying it' (*TS*, IV, vii, p. 250):

> There is no cause but one, replied my uncle *Toby*, — why one man's nose is longer than another's, but because that God pleases to have it so. — That is *Grangousier*'s solution, said my father. — 'Tis he, continued my uncle *Toby*, looking up, and not regarding my father's interruption, who makes us all, and frames and puts us together in such forms and proportions, and for such ends, as is agreeable to his infinite wisdom. — 'Tis a pious account, cried my father, but not philosophical, — there is more religion in it than sound science. (*TS*, III, xli, p. 217)

Unable to convince Walter of the soundness of such a conclusion, Toby finally withdraws from the discussion by 'whistling *Lillabullero*'.

The discussion on the length of noses resurfaces in Slawkenbergius's Tale. This time, both sides use divine will as their main argument. The 'Popish' 'Nosarian' doctors, who believe that 'God's power is infinite', declare that 'he can make a nose, if he thinks fit, as big as the steeple of *Strasburg*'. The 'Lutheran' 'Antinosarians', for whom 'infinite power [...] extends only to all possible things', 'denied that a nose of 575 geometrical feet in length could be worn' (*TS*, IV, Slawkenbergius's Tale, pp. 237 & 238). As Tristram affirms, the debate no longer concerns noses but divine will. By slipping from the role of argument in a dispute, to that of the dispute itself, divine will ceases to be a solid, irrefutable claim. Furthermore, it opens a whole new abyss as it escapes human depth and spirals down 'into *Thomas Aquinas*, and *Thomas Aquinas* to the devil' (*TS*, IV, Slawkenbergius's Tale, p. 238). It cannot be brought to a conclusion. Inevitably, the debate goes round in circles and the doctors of theology reveal their impotence by opposing to each other ungrounded claims ("Tis above reason', ''Tis below reason', ''Tis faith', ''Tis a fiddle-stick', ''Tis possible', ''Tis impossible', *TS*, IV, Slawkenbergius's Tale, p. 237).

In Diderot's novel, Jacques and his master also reach a dead end when discussing divine will:

> LE MAITRE: Et qui est-ce qui a écrit là-haut le bonheur et le malheur?
> JACQUES: Et qui est-ce qui a fait le grand rouleau où tout est écrit? Un capitaine, ami de mon capitaine, aurait bien donné un petit écu pour le savoir [...] (*JF*, p. 677)

Necessary evil constitutes a branch of divine will on which man can give no definite answer. Jacques believes in a cosmic order escaping human understanding: 'Mon maître, on ne sait de quoi se réjouir, ni de quoi s'affliger dans la vie. Le bien amène le mal, le mal amène le bien' (*JF*, p. 730). Jacques's refusal to judge of the benefits of an action occurs in the episode of the landlady's wrath against two of her customers. By intervening, Jacques prevents the quarrel from degenerating into a fistfight. Despite having prevented 'cette femme de se faire assommer', he cannot decide on the good of his action, 'Peut-être un bien, peut-être un mal, qui le sait?' (*JF*, p. 734). A few pages before the end of the novel, the same pattern reappears as the master calls the arrival of the mother a 'fâcheuse visite' as Jacques is about to tie a garter on her daughter's leg. Surprisingly, Jacques does not wholly agree with his master's comment. By replying 'Peut-être qu'oui, peut-être que non', Jacques suggests that even a matter as trivial as this belongs to cosmic order (*JF*, p. 879).

Trim and Toby parallel Jacques and his master in their resignation to the fact that a discussion can only be concluded by silence. As Trim falls into melancholy at the sight of his 'dismally tarnish'd and fray'd' Montero-cap, Toby voices his servant's thoughts (*TS*, VIII, xix, p. 508):

> "Nothing in this world, Trim, is made to last for ever."
> — But when tokens, dear Tom, of thy love and remembrance wear out, said Trim, what shall we say?

> There is no occasion, Trim, quoth my uncle Toby, to say any thing else; and was a man to puzzle his brains till Doom's day, I believe, Trim, it would be impossible. (*TS*, VIII, xix, p. 509)

The characters here accept their questions will have to remain unanswered; yet this constitutes the exception rather than the rule. As in the case of the nosarians and antinosarians, Jacques and his master's conversation often degenerates into an argumentative quarrel. The more heated the discussion, the less the speakers are capable of arguing reasonably and responding to their interlocutor. Jacques and his master are frequently found locked in 'une querelle interminable' as they oppose to each other two antithetical views without taking the pains to justify them (*JF*, p. 684). In one instance, the narrator compares Diderot's main characters to 'deux théologiens' '[qui] disputaient sans s'entendre, comme il peut arriver en théologie' (*JF*, p. 674). The choice of the verb 'entendre' underlines the single-mindedness of the speakers as its definition mainly applies to understanding but can be extended to hearing. Jacques and his master are so engrossed in the defence of their respective ideas that they become deaf to, and consequently unable to understand what the other is saying.

The narrator usually spares his readers the tediousness of debates which go round in circles by interrupting them. Walter decides to teach Toby to recognise 'the right end of a woman from the wrong' (*TS*, II, vii, p. 90). Just as the discussion threatens to result in an accumulation of digressions on handles, hands and analogies,

> [. . .] a Devil of a rap at the door snapp'd my father's definition (like his tobacco-pipe) in two, --- and, at the same time, crushed the head of as notable and curious a dissertation as ever was engendered in the womb of speculation [. . .]. (*TS*, II, vii, p. 91)

The narrator of *Jacques le fataliste* uses the same device by resorting to convenient interruptions to end discussions. To the great relief of the reader, he breaks off their discussion on the 'grand rouleau', which threatens to be prolonged. The narrator brings to the scene 'une troupe d'hommes armés', forcing the master to end his observation that 'Il y a beaucoup de choses à dire là-dessus . . .' (*JF*, p. 677). Another interruption, under the guise of a storm, brings to a close Jacques's and his master's dispute on women 'sur laquelle ils auraient pu faire le tour du globe sans déparler un moment et sans s'accorder' (*JF*, p. 684).

Probably the most obvious trait of Sterne's and Diderot's novels is the open-endedness of many of their stories. To mention one minor example, the true social origin of Tristram's 'postillion' and the landlady of the Grand-Cerf is but one mystery amongst many others left unresolved. Inconclusiveness also affects philosophical discourse. Certain debates are doomed to remain without a conclusion. Either they degenerate into nonsense, or they go beyond human understanding, as in the case of divine will. Since that type of conversation can only go round in circles, the narrator eventually interrupts them by bringing in a timely storm or a knock at the door. The narrator thus spares the reader the tediousness of such digressions. In other cases, refusal to conclude becomes a source of frustration to the reader as simple and direct questions only receive evasive answers, playing on double-meanings.

Jacques le fataliste strikingly opens on the narrator's wilful elusiveness and roundabout refusal to provide any information on the characters' background. To answer the fictional reader's questions, the narrator alternates between extreme banality, and more questions echoing the unanswered ones. The reader starts the novel doubly frustrated. The main characters' only defining trait consists in their ordinariness, and the narrator wilfully misconstrues the meaning of the penultimate question. This is just the first occurrence of a play on the double meaning of *quo vadis*, repeated throughout *Jacques le fataliste*. The superposition of its literal (indication of a place) and symbolical (where life takes us) meaning is made explicit by the episode of Aesop going to the baths but ending up in prison. Jacques Berchtold has analysed Diderot's wilful confusion of the geographical and philosophical meaning of the verb *aller*. Such plays on semantics become 'des jeux d'esquive' in which the narrator disorientates the reader and leads him in a game of blind man's buff. Berchtold suggests that *aller* 'est le seul garant récurrent de la continuation du parcours et fournit le renseignement à la fois minimal et maximal au-delà duquel tout n'est qu'incertitude: tant que les personnages 'vont', le récit peut survivre et se poursuit'.[25] The narrative's elusive structure combined with a tension between the reader's persistent questioning and the narrator's evasive answers provides the dynamics of the text.

In the cases previously mentioned, narrators avoid conclusion by evasive, roundabout responses. They may also simply ignore the question. In Sterne's and Diderot's novels, the narrators promise to come back to such and such a story and complete it. Volumes I, II, III, IV, VI and VII share the novel's refusal to conclude. Instead of bringing an episode to a close, they leave it hanging, sometimes listing unanswered questions regarding it, but with the promise of completion postponed for the next volume. The end of volume II enumerates a series of conjectures: how Toby 'could bear up against' Walter and Dr Slop, how he 'got his modesty by the wound he received upon his groin', how Tristram was given the name his father most abhorred (*TS*, II, xix, p. 136): 'The reader will be content to wait for a full explanation of these matters till the next year, — when a series of things will be laid open which he little expects' (*TS*, II, xix, p. 137).

Sometimes, the narrators do keep their word but too late for the reader to notice. The long-desired story ends up forgotten, and when it resurfaces, it is as a digression interrupting a more interesting episode. Sometimes, the narrators do not hold their promise and leave certain stories incomplete. Despite declaring that the danger of 'a wish coming sideways' 'will be fully illustrated to the world in my chapter of wishes' (*TS*, III, I, pp. 141, 142), Tristram never actually writes the said chapter. Similarly, the link between Toby's modesty and his wound is never made explicit. And, regardless of the narrator's assurance, the chapters of '*pishes*', '*chamber-maids*' and '*button-holes*' do not explain if Walter's 'interjection was levelled at *Susannah*, or the button-hole' (*TS*, IV, xiv, p. 259).

The mystery around the death of Jacques's captain, the enigma concerning how Jacques left his father's house to sleep with Justine, and the substitution of the master's clothes with those of the Chevalier de Saint-Ouin, all remain unsolved throughout Diderot's novel. Despite what Berchtold seems to suggest, Jacques's and his master's final destination also remains unknown.[26] The purpose of their travel was not to visit the master's adopted son and pay the 'bonne nourrice' and 'le maître d'école' for his keeping. That is but a convenient stop along the way: 'Ce n'est pas loin de l'endroit où nous allons, je profite de la circonstance pour payer à ces gens ce qui leur est dû, le retirer et le mettre en métier' (*JF*, pp. 874–75). Berchtold pertinently interprets this visit to the wet nurse in conjunction with the story of Aesop. As in the case of the Greek slave ordered by his master to go to the baths, Jacques is sent to look for 'la demeure du nourricier'. But before he can reach the door, 'on lui lie les mains sur le dos et on le conduit devant le juge du lieu qui l'envoie en prison' (*JF*, p. 881). These repetitions increase the reader's impression that the text is going round in circles.

As we saw in the first chapter, the reader's participation in the writing of the text constitutes some of the ludic features in *Jacques le fataliste* and *Tristram Shandy*. Invitations to participate sometimes take the form of enigmas disseminated throughout the text for the reader to ponder upon. By leaving the last word to a third person, either absent or unqualified, the narrator expresses his refusal to conclude. The narrator simply initiates debates without joining in, instead leaving it to the readers to decide on the matter outside the novel:

> Whether it is in the choice of the clay — or that it is frequently spoiled in the baking [...] — or whether this great Artificer is not so attentive [...] — or that her Ladyship sometimes scarce knows what sort of husband will do — I know not (*TS*, IX, xxii, p. 569)

By offering a number of possibilities from which to choose, the narrator guides the reader to an open-ended conclusion. However, when he withdraws the options by saying that none of them are applicable, the narrator makes it impossible for the reader to conclude. After having listed a number of bizarre causes of love, involving most improbably water-drinking, 'a man with a pined leg', 'weavers, gardeners, and gladiators', the narrator concludes in the following chapter that none of these apply to Toby in his affair with Widow Wadman (*TS*, VIII, v, p. 492). And *vice versa*, the particular example of Toby and Wadman cannot provide 'a description of *what love is*'. On the thorny point of love, individual cases are insufficient to create a universal principle. Tristram has to come back on the 'inconsiderate' promise that 'the following memoirs of my uncle *Toby*'s courtship of widow *Wadman*' 'would turn out one of the most compleat systems, both of the elementary and practical part of love and love-making, that ever was addressed to the world' (*TS*, VI, xxxvi, p. 420). Just like divine providence and taste ('*De gustibus non est disputandum*, *TS*, I, viii, p. 14), love belongs to that class of conversation doomed never to be concluded.[27]

In *Jacques le fataliste*, the narrator chooses not to take part in his characters' discussions. This is rather problematical when conversation degenerates into an argument where each stubbornly keeps to his views and is deaf to the opinions of his interlocutor. The reader then wishes the narrator to arbitrate in the same way as the landlady of the Grand-Cerf did to settle a quarrel between Jacques and his master. The narrator manifests very early on his decision to side with neither the libertarian master nor with his fatalistic servant. He interrupts a debate on fatalism, but not to offer his own opinion on the subject, which as a narrator would be the authoritative one. He ends the conversation by remarking on the futility of trying to find a conclusion to 'un sujet dont on a tant parlé, tant écrit depuis deux mille ans, sans en être d'un pas plus avancé' (*JF*, pp. 673–74). In this excerpt, the narrator declines to side with either of his characters; ten pages later, he does the exact opposite by agreeing with them both. The result remains the same: refusal to conclude. As a transcript of their dispute on women, the narrator simply offers a list of adjectives and their antitheses: 'Et les voilà embarqués dans une querelle interminable sur les femmes; l'un prétendant qu'elles étaient bonnes, l'autre méchantes, et ils avaient tous deux raison; l'un sottes, l'autre pleines d'esprit, et ils avaient tous deux raison' (*JF*, p. 684). The account goes on for seven more lines, structured exactly on the same model, where one set of opposite adjectives immediately follows another. By settling the dispute with the paradox that 'ils avaient tous deux raison', the narrator fails in his role as an arbitrator.

There is however one instance in the text where the narrator disagrees with Jacques's views:

> Je l'ai plusieurs fois contredit, mais sans avantage et sans fruit. En effet, que répliquer à celui qui vous dit: Quelle que soit la somme des éléments dont je suis composé, je suis un; or une cause une n'a qu'un effet; j'ai toujours été une cause une, je n'ai jamais eu qu'un effet à produire, ma durée n'est donc qu'une suite d'effets nécessaires. (*JF*, p. 803)

The narrator recognises he has failed and been silenced by his character. Jacques's rhetorical victory is made visible by the fact that his reported speech has taken the place of what should have been the narrator's counter-argument.

Despite regularly making the reader feel his mastery over his narrative, the narrator seems to have relinquished his claim to omniscience. After having laughed at Jacques's claims that pain on that part of the body was the most excruciating, the master falls on a sharp stone and wounds his knee. He does not know if Jacques, notwithstanding his good nature and his affection for him, secretly rejoiced at such a convenient accident remarkably proving his servant's point. The narrator then asks for the reader's opinion on what might be the master's state of mind at that moment:

> Une autre chose, Lecteur, que je voudrais bien que vous me dissiez, c'est si son maître n'eût pas mieux aimé être blessé, même un peu plus grièvement ailleurs qu'au genou, ou s'il ne fut pas plus sensible à la honte qu'à la douleur? (*JF*, p. 681)

Like the narrator of Diderot's novel, Tristram ends up by admitting his own intellectual insufficiencies and his failure to bring an answer to a problem. When discussing how impressions, at first sight, end up dominating the mind, Tristram leaves the reader to decide whether Walter's eccentricity comes from his ideas, from his judgment, or simply from an extraordinary capacity to behold the truth (see *TS*, I, xix, p. 49).

Multi-facetted Truth

If *Tristram Shandy* and *Jacques le fataliste* initiate debates, they rarely bring them to completion. The subject of some of these debates makes it impossible to formulate definite answers. However, the reason may also be found in the narrator's unwillingness to conclude. That an author should decide to leave open a philosophical debate naturally shocks; yet it is not uncommon. Howells has noticed 'this refusal to construct or conclude' in many French works of the same period.[28] Bakhtin affirms that a novelist should refuse to side with a particular discourse:

> [...] he makes use of this verbal give-and-take, this dialogue of languages at every point in his work, in order that he himself might remain as it were neutral with regard to language, a third party in a quarrel between two people [...].[29]

Bakhtin draws a distinction between the didactic message of the various discourses brought into a novel, and the message of the novel itself. The didactic substance of the novel is the result of its combination of external discourses. I will apply Bakhtin's remark to Sterne's and Diderot's novels and argue that the reluctance to conclude can be explained by a refusal to acknowledge an answer as the only truthful one.

We have already come across one instance of antithetical opinions placed side by side in Jacques's and his master's disagreement on women. By repeating that 'ils avaient tous deux raison', the narrator rejects a single-sided, authoritative answer. In an attempt to come as quickly as possible to the heart of the matter, the master takes the conversation to 'pucelage' and declares 'qu'on aime celle à qui on le donne, comme on est aimé de celle à qui on le ravit' (*JF*, p. 817). Instead of taking the bait by offering his own story as an illustration, Jacques contests his master's affirmation by replying 'Quelquefois oui, quelquefois non' (*JF*, p. 817). The reader is already acquainted with this enunciative pattern. The only difference here is the slight variation of the adverb passing from 'peut-être' to 'quelquefois', which maintains the same indecisiveness. Like the narrator, Jacques objects to systematic truths: one version can be just as valid as its opposite.

Juxtaposition of two antithetical views also occurs in *Tristram Shandy*. Toby yet again interrupts 'the story of the King of Bohemia and his seven castles', by praising Trim on his choice of the word '*happening*'. According to Toby, '*happening*' befits the situation as ''twas a matter of contingency, which might happen, or not, just as chance ordered it'. Trim replies by mentioning King William's 'opinion' 'that everything was predestined for us in this world'. He illustrates this by applying the phrase 'every ball (has) its billet' to his belief that the purpose of his knee-wound was to bring him to serve his present master. Toby does not refute his servant's necessitarian views, as might have been expected.[30] He appears to corroborate them by replying that the direct link between Trim's wound and Toby's household 'shall never [...] be construed otherwise' (*TS*, VIII, xix, p. 515). Chance and determinism, though antithetical, do not actually contradict each other. Applying to different cases, they coincide, which allows Toby to recognise the two as equally valid. The belief that there can be only one answer to a question smacks of intolerance. The episode of Aesop's arrest while on his way to the baths, reflects this: 'Où vas-tu? — Où je vais? répond Esope, je n'en sais rien. — Tu n'en sais rien! Marche en prison' (*JF*, p. 704). The guards of 'la patrouille d'Athènes' refuse Aesop's metaphorical answer to their question, and make him pay the price by superimposing a literal meaning, the only meaning they recognise as valid.

The multiplicity of points of view in Sterne's and Diderot's novels reflects the plurality of voices uttering them. From a Bakhtinian perspective, heteroglossia constitutes one of the main defining features of the novel as a genre. Heteroglossia is a prominent trait in *Jacques le fataliste* and *Tristram Shandy* where it appears through the use of multiple registers of language. Abstract and concrete language may be considered as two different registers. And indeed Jacques regards the language of abstraction as distinct from that of concrete illustration (see *JF*, p. 676). More traditionally those registers vary according to class and profession. Different registers of tone appear in Jacques's and his master's respective love stories. Albeit the theme remains the same, the tone and choice of words vary whether applied to the servant's version, resembling the medieval *fabliaux*, or to the master's, much closer to the novelistic style of the day.[31]

Juxtaposition of conflicting ideas acts as a vehicle for heteroglossia. In volume III, Tristram informs the reader of his purpose when he first sets out on this formidable autobiography: 'to write my life for the amusement of the world, and my opinions for its instruction' (*TS*, III, xxviii, p. 193). The conventionality of Tristram's aim as an author, balancing didacticism and entertainment, belies the originality of his achievements. Sterne's novel does not do what it says on the label. Contrary to what its title suggests, the novel is not wholly centred on 'The Life and Opinions of Tristram Shandy'. The life and opinions of Walter, Trim and Toby take just as much space. This juxtaposition of opinions furthers heteroglossia as Bakhtin understood it, that is to say promoting a multi-facetted truth expressed by a plurality of voices, and not by a single authoritative one.

To present different versions of the same story or subject offers a way of underlining the plurality of opinions and interpretations. The dispute on women, already mentioned, provides an obvious example of this. The metadiegetic level brings more opportunities to underline heteroglossia by including the characters' diverging reactions to a secondary story. The interest of the anecdote concerning M. Le Pelletier lies in its controversial nature. Having solicited M. Aubertot too hard for charitable donations, M. Le Pelletier receives 'un soufflet'. Yet this does not dampen his perseverance, and he replies: 'Cela, c'est pour moi, mais mes pauvres?' At such a display of Christ-like humility, 'tous les auditeurs s'écrièrent d'admiration, excepté mon capitaine'. Far from praising Le Pelletier, Jacques's captain calls him 'un gueux, un malheureux, un lâche, un infâme' for not caring for his honour (*JF*, p. 710). The story of Mme de La Pommeraye serves the same purpose. Every now and then, Jacques and his master interrupt the landlady with their divergent opinions on the characters of her story. Whereas Jacques regards Mme de La Pommeraye as 'une méchante femme', the master shows himself more understanding and puts the blame on her unfaithful lover, the Marquis des Arcis (*JF*, p. 777). An entertaining story does not necessarily create a unique moral lesson.

When pushed to the extreme, heteroglossia becomes a source of comedy. Some characters amuse and surprise by their eccentric views. An obvious Shandean example is Walter for whom 'every object before him presented a face and section of itself to his eye, altogether different from the plan and elevation of it seen by the rest of mankind' (*TS*, V, xxiv, p. 344). In *Jacques le fataliste*, Gousse provides the most striking example of this, especially during a meeting with the narrator's wife. The conversation is structured around banal and polite questions followed by bizarre answers. Here is an extract from this peculiar dialogue:

> Comment se porte votre femme? — Comme il lui plaît; c'est son affaire. — Et vos enfants? — A merveille! — Et celui qui a de si beaux yeux, un si bel embonpoint, une si belle peau? — Beaucoup mieux que les autres; il est mort. (*JF*, p. 716)

Gousse plays the role of the fool, the jester, who revivifies the meaning of words by refusing to acknowledge authoritative discourse, in this case polite conversation where questions and answers are set by convention. Direct speech and the immediate juxtaposition of the two conflicting voices create a rapid tempo in the dialogue. The reader is not given time to imagine Gousse's answers; he stays surprised and amused by them. Sterne plays with typography to emphasise that a response may be just as valid as its opposite. While conversing on the subject of women, Walter and Toby both shake their heads as if sharing the same views. But, the narrator warns us,

> [...] never did two heads shake together in concert, from two such different springs.
> God bless ⎱ 'em all — said my uncle *Toby* and my father,
> Duce take ⎰ each to himself. (*TS*, IV, xii, p. 256)

To undermine a dominant speech, Gousse offers as an alternative his own original voice and presents it as equally valid. This absence of hierarchy amongst conflicting versions visually appears through typography interweaving multiple voices on the page.[32]

In *Tristram Shandy*, comedy also arises from heteroglossia when the number of opinions on a trivial matter grows out of proportion. The inhabitants of Strasburg, fantasising on the nose of the stranger, spend their night 'slitting and dividing it into as many noses of different cuts and fashions, as there were heads in *Strasburg* to hold them' (*TS*, IV, Slawkenbergius's Tale, p. 228). Each Strasburger forms his own idea of the stranger's nose, but they agree on the essential point, that it is extraordinary. Intertextuality similarly illustrates the convergence of differing ideas on one particular point. Worried about the effects of his son's accidental circumcision, Walter consults '*Spencer de Legibus Hebraeorum Ritualibus* — and *Maimonides*'. There he finds a long list of nations, 'the EGYPTIANS, — the SYRIANS, — the PHOENICIANS, — the ARABIANS, — the CAPPADOCIANS, — [...] the COLCHI, and TROGLODYTES', and the mention of 'SOLON and PYTHAGORAS' (*TS*, V, xxvii, p. 347). They all approve of circumcision, albeit for different reasons. In the example from *Jacques le fataliste*, Gousse's replies, however eccentric, coincide with his interlocutor's questions. Differing visions still converge to form a conversation. In the case of the Strasburgers and Spencer's work, we find the same convergence of different cultures and religions reaching the same conclusion. Walter himself is particularly fond of reaching commonly accepted conclusions by taking untrodden routes. Walter thus sends Yorick to 'the first book of the Institutes of *Justinian*, at the eleventh title and the tenth section', to find written that '*The son ought to pay her* [his mother] *respect*'. Yorick replies that he 'can read it as well [...] in the Catechism' (*TS*, V, xxxi, p. 353).

Heteroglossia does not solely refer to divergences in content. It also embraces divergences in modes of expression. Musing on sleep, Tristram humbly leaves the last word to '*Sancho Pancà*' whose metaphor of sleep covering 'a man all over like a cloak', 'speaks more to [his] heart and affections, than all the dissertations squeez'd out of the heads of the learned together upon the subject' (*TS*, IV, xv, p. 261). Sancho Panca does not however bring the discussion to a close, as Tristram at first thought a little hastily. One intertextual reference calls for another. As Montaigne comes back to his mind, Tristram feels that he must also do him justice. Before quoting 'by memory', Tristram progressively revises his hierarchy. Sancho Panca's view on sleep is not the only one worth quoting. The narrator does not 'altogether disapprove of what *Montaigne* advances upon' sleep. He even goes so far as admitting that ''tis admirable in its way' (*TS*, IX, xv, p. 261). Just as for Jacques and his master, the words of the uncouth peasant are just as valid as those of the noble man of Letters. Both praise sleep; the only difference is that one uses a concrete image, the other a more abstract language.

Heteroglossia abolishes hierarchy in ideas, but also in the way they are expressed. Sancho Panca and Montaigne act as a hypotextual parallel to the couple Trim/Walter. The two servants are simple men, 'without wit or antithesis', 'going strait forwards as nature could lead [them], to the heart'. Though they strike a different chord in their audience, their words are just as valid and effective as those of their counterparts, the two men 'of deep reading — prompt memory — with *Cato*, and *Seneca*, and *Epictetus*, at [their] fingers ends' (*TS*, V, vi, p. 324). As Bakhtin remarks, the 'novelist does not strip away the intentions of others from the heteroglot language of his work'. He does not purify a form of expression from its content to replace it by his own values. The novelist juxtaposes those various external discourses which each possess their particular lesson. It is through this combination that they may '[refract] *at different angles*' didactic messages specific to the novel which has assembled them.[33]

A conclusion to the various philosophical debates would have provided a clear-cut didactic message. If Sterne and Diderot had established a hierarchy amongst their characters' diverging points of view, one would have been singled out as representative of the author's own voice, whilst the others would have been disqualified. The reader would have then recognised this particular view as the legitimate and authoritative one, since the author would have endorsed it. However, neither *Tristram Shandy* nor *Jacques le fataliste* offers such a convenient conclusion. None of the philosophical demonstrations are supported by their concrete illustrations. Ideas may even sometimes be contradicted by their practical applications, but never are they fully negated. An idea may hold true in certain cases, but not in others. Both Sterne and Diderot are prompt to give the exception to the rule. As there is no didactic discourse pinning down absolute truth, the reader is left in limbo, uncertain even as to what the didactic message of the text might be. The preference given to heteroglossia over the establishment of an authoritative stance does not annul the didactic value of our two novels. On the contrary, heteroglossia forges it.

Tristram Shandy and *Jacques le fataliste* should not be regarded as cynical texts denying truth because they refuse to set up a dominant discourse. What they are challenging is the representation of truth as unique and absolute. For Bakhtin, the heteroglossic nature of the novel calls for the profanation of 'the authoritative word', since the latter is exclusive and cannot combine with any other language: 'its semantic structure is static and dead, for it is fully complete, it has but a single meaning, the letter is fully sufficient to the sense and calcifies it.'[34] An author must either fully endorse 'the authoritative word' or profane it so that his own voice may be heard.

To recognise that there is more than one answer to a question, that a situation is more likely to be multi-faceted than clear-cut, becomes problematical, especially when it comes to morality. The demolition of 'Dunkirk, and the mole' has left Trim with mixed feelings. He cannot decide whether military strategy or the preservation of the town weighs heavier in the balance of his conscience. Addressing his master, Trim declares in the same sentence that 'It was a thousand pities [...] to destroy these works — and a thousand pities to have let them stood'. Far from disentangling the conundrum by siding with one of the two views, Toby maintains their coexistence by telling his servant he is 'right' 'in both cases' (*TS*, VIII, xix, p. 507).

Morality stands for the authoritative discourse judging whether an action is good or wrong. Fatalism shakes the very foundations of morality. Without free will, an individual cannot choose to act according to his conscience. Jacques denies that a man may decide to fall in love even if it entailed turning a 'bienfaiteur' into a 'cocu'. This may smart his conscience, but he is not free to decide of his actions:

> Est-ce qu'on est maître de devenir ou de ne pas devenir amoureux? et quand on l'est, est-on maître d'agir comme si on ne l'était pas? Si cela eût été écrit là-haut, tout ce que vous vous disposez à me dire, je me le serais dit; je me serais souffleté; je me serais cogné la tête contre le mur; je me serais arraché les cheveux, il n'en aurait été ni plus ni moins, et mon bienfaiteur eût été cocu.
> (*JF*, p. 673)

Jacques's fatalism shocks his master who objects that 'en raisonnant à ta façon, il n'y a point de crime qu'on ne commît sans remords' (*JF*, p. 673). The master puts his finger on the paradox that Jacques believes he has no free will and yet still feels remorse for certain actions. Logically, fatalism and conscience should be mutually exclusive. However, Jacques proves that practically they may coexist.

Here again, we find another instance where an idea is contradicted by its concrete application. Jacques seems to have dissociated conscience and morality. More than once in the novel has Jacques displayed his generosity and benevolence. For example, he does not hesitate to save from destitution a wretched mother by giving her 'deux gros écus', even though he is himself in need of money (*JF*, p. 728). But Jacques acts out of sympathy, not out of a sense of morality. In fact, he does not believe in morality as '[il] ne connaissait ni le nom de vice, ni le nom de vertu' (*JF*, p. 802). Despite '[l'avoir] plusieurs fois contredit', the narrator actually shares Jacques's misgivings (*JF*, p. 803).

Far from regarding morality as a perennial and invariable standard for judging man's actions, the narrator debunks this representation by using the example of Jacques's captain and his friend. The extreme sense of honour of both men is considered by their contemporaries as 'leur coin de folie', but would have perfectly well fitted in with 'l'esprit de la chevalerie' of the Middle Ages. What men deem praiseworthy varies with time and changes as a fashion: 'Chaque vertu et chaque vice se montre et passe de mode' (*JF*, p. 719). The narrator suggests that along with truth, the representation of morality must also be questioned. Far from being absolute, morality is subject to change and cannot offer a definite clear-cut judgment on whether an action is right or wrong. Consequently, the legitimacy of morality to stand as the dominant and authoritative discourse of the novel is sapped.

Indirectly, heteroglossia challenges a particular representation of man. As we have seen, a character may act in a way inconsistent with his beliefs and hold contradictory views. His voice inside the text is not fixed and monosemous, but offers a combination of diverging views. The most telling example is that of the landlord of the Grand-Cerf. At the beginning of the episode, he refuses to lend some more money to a poor peasant, on the brink of becoming a wandering beggar, and who is already his debtor. The landlord insults him, calls him a 'gredin' who deserves his fate (*JF*, p. 741). But his heart gradually softens as the peasant paints the bleak future awaiting his children: 'ma fille servira, mon garçon s'engagera' (*JF*, p. 742). The argument has then turned round as it is the landlord who is begging the peasant to accept his money. The peasant stubbornly refuses the eleemosynary offer of 'un homme dur'. The scene ends on the landlord admitting that 'Nature m'a fait l'homme le plus dur et le plus tendre, je ne sais ni accorder, ni refuser' (*JF*, p. 743). The landlord is not the only protagonist whose character is composed of contradictory dispositions. After the bawdy stories of Jacques's iterative "first time", the fictional reader marvels at 'Comment un homme de sens, qui a des mœurs, qui se pique de philosophie, peut-il s'amuser à débiter des contes de cette obscénité?' (*JF*, p. 834).

This should be read with Jacques's and his master's criticism of the landlady's story of Mme de La Pommeraye for not having made coherent characters: 'je vous demanderai, notre charmante hôtesse, si la fille qui complote avec deux scélérates est bien la femme suppliante que nous avons vue aux pieds de son mari?' (*JF*, p. 787). Jacques and his master's reproaches to the landlady are the same as those the fictional reader addresses to the narrator. And indeed, *Jacques le fataliste* disobeys the rule of unity in classical taste. Both characters view the debate on whether or not a novel should combine diverging elements in terms of verisimilitude. However, the refusal of monosemy also has an aesthetical dimension.

Far from being lamented, man's inconstant and dual nature is praised in *Tristram Shandy*. In his elegiac speech on Bobby's death, Trim is on the edge of committing a *faux pas* with Susannah. Playing on the commonplace of man's material reality, Trim captivates her attention by implicitly referring to her as 'a flower of the field', and then as 'the finest face that ever man looked at'. But his conclusion threatens to offend Susannah as he exclaims that flower and face are 'but corruption' (*TS*, V, ix, p. 328). Trim rescues the situation by unexpectedly transforming the insult into praise: 'Now I love you for this — and 'tis this delicious mixture within you which makes you dear creatures what you are' (*TS*, V, ix, p. 329).

Later on in the novel, Tristram pursues Trim's meditation on time and women, only shifting the object of his musings from Susannah to Janatone. The beautiful 'inn-keeper's daughter' is worthier of being drawn than 'the fascade of the abbey of Saint Austreberte'. Whereas the abbey is set in stone for all eternity, Janatone '[carries] the principles of change within [her] frame'. There is an emergency to capture her beauty, all the more precious because it is volatile. The abbey may wait 'fifty years' longer (*TS*, VII, ix, p. 441). The value of Janatone's beauty can only be truly appreciated in conjunction with its transience. Tristram continues with a prospective description of the girl he so much admires and who, 'e'er twice twelve months are pass'd and gone, [...] mayest grow out like a pumpkin' (*TS*, VII, ix, pp. 441–42). Tristram here signals his aesthetics as an author. He is not interested in a fixed moment in time offering only a single facet of Janatone. His work celebrates 'this delicious mixture' which embraces Janatone as a whole, and is consequently just as volatile.

The juxtaposition of two contrary views presented as equally valid favours a representation of truth as multi-facetted. The confrontation of diverging views may also lead to the emergence of another far more subtle voice. 'Est-ce que l'on sait où l'on va?': the opening paragraph of *Jacques le fataliste* asks a fundamental question which will recur time and again throughout the novel, playing on the literal and metaphysical level. Jacques and his master each offer one of the two opposite solutions: fatalism and free will. We must add a third solution, that of Diderot himself, which is determinism. To understand how these three concepts address in different ways the question of human action, it is necessary to distinguish between them. Free will, or *libre arbitre*, is the faculty to act through the sole strength of the will, without the influence of any cause. *Libre arbitre* allows chance to occur: a man may freely choose to act in a completely random way. Fatalism is the belief that one cause can only have one specific effect and this cannot be altered as it has been pre-ordained by destiny. Determinism acknowledges a flexible chain of causes and effects: as there is no fate to fix this chain, man may choose between a closed number of different and necessary possibilities.

Diderot makes his own position on the matter clear in the *Lettre à Landois*:

> Regardez-y de près, et vous verrez que le mot *liberté* est un mot vide de sens; qu'il n'y a point, et qu'il ne peut y avoir d'êtres libres; que nous ne sommes que ce qui convient à l'ordre général, à l'organisation, à l'éducation, et à la chaîne des événements. Voilà ce qui dispose de nous invinciblement. On ne conçoit non plus qu'un être agisse sans motif, qu'un des bras d'une balance agisse sans l'action d'un poids; et le motif nous est toujours extérieur, étranger, attaché ou par une nature ou par une cause quelconque, qui n'est pas nous. Ce qui nous trompe, c'est la prodigieuse variété de nos actions, jointe à l'habitude que nous avons prise tout en naissant de confondre le volontaire avec le libre. [...]
>
> Mais quoique l'homme bien ou malfaisant ne soit pas libre, l'homme n'en est pas moins un être qu'on modifie [...].35

Diderot is clearly not on the side of the master, as for him freedom is but an empty word since our actions are always motivated. But nor is Diderot on the side of Jacques: he believes that a man may be changed and that his will, alongside external causes, participates in his choice of action.

Fatalism and free will are the most obvious philosophical views present in *Jacques le fataliste*, and the reader may well wonder which one will offer the most reliable and definite answer to the question 'Est-ce que l'on sait où l'on va?' But the reader soon understands that neither Jacques nor his master are capable of answering this. We have seen earlier that the characters behave in a way that is inconsistent with their beliefs, which seems to point out to the fact that their respective philosophical systems are not actually practical or viable to live in accordance with. The master's *libre arbitre* refuses to acknowledge that actions have any motivation whatsoever other than the individual's free will. In this sense, a man's actions can absolutely not be predicted. Though Jacques is far more intelligent, articulate and convincing than his master, he recognises that he cannot fully live in a manner conforming to his system. Fatalism is also incapable of answering the *quo vadis* question. Its major flaw is that it can only be understood retrospectively:

> L'évenement fatal tient à des causes cachées, ou est considéré dans ses rapports avec celles d'entre ses causes qui nous sont inconnues. Si dans la disposition d'une bataille je vois un homme placé vis-à-vis de la bouche d'un canon prêt à tirer, sa situation étant donnée, & l'action du canon étant prévûe, je ne regarderai plus sa mort comme *fatale* par rapport à ces deux causes que je connois; mais je retrouverai la *fatalité* dans cette multitude de causes éloignées, cachées & compliquées, qui ont fait qu'entre une infinité d'autres parties de l'espace qu'il pouvoit occuper également, il occupât précisément celle qui est dans la direction du canon.36

As Morellet, the author of the article 'fatalité' in the *Encyclopédie*, makes it clear, events may only become clear *ex post facto*. Connon points out that the fatalistic system can provide no help whatsoever to the individual wanting to take control of his existence.37

Fatalism relies on faith in the idea of a ruling destiny. If one cannot alter the course of events, one can still try to anticipate them by looking for signs: 'Nous croyons conduire le destin, mais c'est toujours lui qui nous mène; et le destin, pour Jacques, était tout ce qui le touchait ou l'approchait, son cheval, son maître, un moine, un chien, une femme, un mulet, une corneille' (*JF*, p. 691). Commenting on this passage, Hobson reflects that '[l']effort de Jacques consiste à projeter une relation de cause à effet, ou de symbole à signification, là où il y a pur accident. Selon un système de signes avertisseurs ou probables, il fait de chaque accident une destinée.'[38] Hobson has justly commented on the fact that, in the novel, these signs seem at first to confirm the existence of an overarching destiny, but finally disprove it. Despite his horse systematically rushing towards gibbets, kissing the executioner in a Socratic-like way, and ending up in prison, Jacques does not end his life on the scaffold.

The disavowal of destiny appears very blatantly in the story of the broken ring. All the signs forewarning the old wife that her husband will not survive the operation appear: at the very moment that the husband is under the surgeon's knife, the wife's ring, on which her spouse's name is engraved, falls from her finger, broken. The wife is convinced that this is a clear sign of fate and expects to hear the news of her husband's death. However, the letter she receives is from her husband telling her that the operation was a success and that he will soon be back home. As Hobson remarks, '[les] signes avertisseurs sont contredits'.[39] The master's foreboding that his servant will end on the scaffold is closely connected with this story. Indeed, the master tells the story of the old couple to explain his fears of the fated end of his servant, and his theory that 'les pressentiments dont il est impossible de se défendre, ce sont surtout ceux qui se présentent au moment où la chose se passe loin de nous, et qui ont un air symbolique' (*JF*, p. 724). In this case, the example does indeed properly illustrate the master's theory. But as Jacques points out, the story shows that the master's forebodings are completely groundless. The answer of Jacques the fatalist to this problem is that 'le destin [est] cauteleux' (*JF*, p. 725). Fate exists but cannot be predicted as its intentions are hidden. For the reader, the story actually seems to disprove the existence of an over-ruling fate. There are multiple readings possible in this passage which is further complicated by the master's own contradictions. Hobson, who has offered a very intelligent analysis of this passage, notes:

> Cette histoire qui se retourne est enchâssée dans un argument du maître qui, lui, se contredit: il a voulu prouver qu'il y a des pressentiments dont il est impossible de se défendre, et qui s'avèrent dénués de fondement — mais c'est pour revenir à son idée que Jacques est mal parti, et que les signes probables, eux, le condamnent. Nous ne savons plus où aller: la relation entre les différents moments des anecdotes nous fait problème et nous déroute.[40]

Free will and fatalism occur, as we have seen, within the philosophical debates and the various stories told along the way. They also participate in the structure of the narrative. Jacques's fatalism allows the play at the extradiegetic level where the author is presented as all-powerful over his literary creation. As characters, Jacques and the master have no control over the events in *Jacques le fataliste*; their story has been fixed by the author. As Loy remarks, '[fatalism] knows of no change; determinism is interesting as a doctrine only because of change, but change by reason of sequences or successions of elements leading to the change.'[41] At certain times, the narrator claims that he is telling a true story, and that he refuses to depart from the truth in favour of a more *romanesque* version. This truth prior to the telling of the story acts within the narrative as fate: there is only one line to follow and it admits of no change. Yet at other times, the narrator emphasises the fact that his story is not set in stone, and that it may change its course, at the whim of the narrator, and the choosing of the reader.[42]

The contradictions within Jacques and his master's debates and within the apparent narrative structure lead the reader to reflect on the inconsistencies of fatalism and free will. Yet from this reflection arises a third possibility, determinism, whose presence in the text is much more subtle. The master has been proven that his decisions are motivated, and not completely free of any influence. Jacques's inflexible fate is not only highly dubious but also pointless, and leaves no room for morality. Without being explicitly mentioned, determinism must appear to the reader as an alternative to free will and fatalism since it does not need to rely on the existence of a force that cannot be proven, and takes into account both the individual's will and external motives within the chain of cause and events.

Determinism is not imposed upon the reader by the author, nor does Diderot explain in what way it may answer the question 'Est-ce que l'on sait où l'on va?' Determinism is the intellectual process of recognising patterns and correlations between various events. In this, it is the very opposite of chance: 'Nous regardons une chose comme l'effet du hasard, lorsqu'elle n'offre à nos yeux rien de régulier ou qui annonce un dessein, et que nous ignorons d'ailleurs les causes qui l'ont produite.' Determinism is but a term used to refer to our interpretation of what links an event to another; and just like fatalism and free will, it 'n'a donc aucune réalité en lui-même'.[43] All three represent different ways for man to try to understand and give meaning to the impact the outside world has on his existence. Determinism may be the means to offer guesses as to what likely effect a cause may have, but it is just as incapable to predict man's future. Determinism as a possible middle way appears nowhere explicitly within the novel, but is suggested from the discussions on fatalism and free will and from their contradictions.

Conclusion

The (dis-)connection between an idea and its illustration radically alters the apparent lesson conveyed by the texts. The principal function of concrete illustrations is to clarify abstract reasoning. When the two are joined together, 'clarté confuse' is reached as both the intellect and the imagination are stimulated, and consequently make understanding possible. However, idea and example in *Tristram Shandy* and *Jacques le fataliste* are more often than not in a state of discord. An example supposed to support an idea actually contradicts it. Illustrations then lose their 'fonction clarifiante' (Meiner's expression) and become at first a source of confusion. The didactic message is blurred and conclusions cannot be reached, as the number of conflicting discourses multiplies. This exactly corresponds to Sterne's and Diderot's purpose. The misunderstanding arising from the unresolved juxtaposition of contradictory views furthers the dialogue whilst preventing one particular voice from imposing itself as the authoritative discourse in the novel.

It has become a commonplace in the study of *Tristram Shandy* and *Jacques le fataliste* to mention the absence of conclusion in their stories. However, it is a commonplace the reader and the critic are unavoidably drawn to. The understanding of the (dis-)connection between ideas and illustrations in these two novels renews the significance of this theme. Indeed, these stories often act as illustrations to the ideas being discussed. Diderot and Sterne do not wish to close the discussion initiated by their novels, but on the contrary, to prolong it. In order to do so, those ideas must not be brought to a conclusion by convincing illustrations, but must be left open-ended through the means of examples which question their validity without completely denying it. The open-endedness of the illustrative stories then complements that of the philosophical debates in the same way as the concrete example acts as the complementary version of the abstract idea, though appealing to a different part of the mind.

Notes to Chapter 2

1. Mikhail Bakhtin, *The Dialogic Imagination, four essays*, trans. by Caryl Emerson & Michael Holquist (Austin: University of Texas Press, 2008), pp. 311–12.
2. Bakhtin, *The Dialogic Imagination*, p. 403.
3. Robin Howells, *Playing Simplicity, Polemical Stupidity in the Writing of the French Enlightenment* (Oxford: Peter Lang, 2002), pp. 9, 10 & 307.
4. Howells, p. 10.
5. Bakhtin, *The Dialogic Imagination*, p. 289.
6. Carsten Meiner has written a history of clarity leading to the notion of 'clarté confuse', in which he has specifically focused on Marivaux's work. According to Meiner, Marivaux noticed the shortcomings of abstract language, which despite clarity of grammar, still led to incomprehension. See Carsten Meiner, *Les Mutations de la clarté, exemple, induction et schématismes dans l'oeuvre de Marivaux* (Paris: Honoré Champion, 2007), pp. 24–25.

7. Meiner, p. 25
8. Pierre-Daniel Huet, *Lettre-traité sur l'origine des romans* (Paris: A.-G. Nizet, 1971), p. 47.
9. John Locke, *An Essay concerning Human Understanding* (London: Penguin Books, 1997), Book III, chap. x, §34, p. 452.
10. Locke, Book II, chap. xi, §2, p. 153.
11. Bernard Lamy, *La Rhétorique ou l'art de parler* (Paris: PUF, 1998), pp. 225–26, quoted by Meiner, pp. 163–64.
12. Lamb, p. 4.
13. Joseph Addison, 'Imagination contrasted with understanding: imaginative importance of history, natural philosophy, etc: bounds and defects of imagination' (n°420, 2 July 1712) in Richard Steele and Joseph Addison, *Selections from* The Tatler *and* The Spectator (Harmondsworth: Penguin, 1988), p. 400.
14. Addison, 'Appeal to the imagination in writing on abstract subjects by allusion to the natural world: imagination liable to cause pain as well as pleasure' (n°421, 3 July 1712), in Steele and Addison, p. 401.
15. See Meiner, pp. 48–49.
16. Huet, p. 143.
17. The following example has already been studied in the first chapter which focused on its ludic nature. This chapter concentrates on its function as an illustration to an abstract idea.
18. Howells, p. 30.
19. Connon, p. 34.
20. 'What is *invraisemblance* in a fiction is *vrai* in reality and thus, by conversion, becomes *vraisemblance* in fiction. Where in the seventeenth-century theory there was a stable divorce between true and seeming true, with the seeming true, *vraisemblance*, being adequate to a norm, here there is a parasitic relation. If truth as the *vraisemblable* is what is left after the truth which is surprising has been excised, then even the most unlikely narrative can define its reality by reference to the more unlikely it has omitted.' Hobson, *The Object of Art*, p. 93.
21. Jacques's lucky rescue from prison by Mandrin's men, his transfer from the peasants' cottage to Desglands's castle, and his escape from a violent death thanks to a timely noise which frightens off the robbers intent on killing him, are all examples of slips into the *romanesque*. On this point, see Connon, pp. 305–07.
22. Hobson, *The Object of Art*, p. 128.
23. Hobson, *The Object of Art*, p. 129.
24. Connon, p. 298.
25. Jacques Berchtold, *Les Prisons du roman (XVII°–XVIII° siècle), lectures plurielles et intertextuelles de* Guzman d'Alfarache *à* Jacques le fataliste (Geneva: Droz, 2000), pp. 682 & 683.
26. See Berchtold, pp. 683–85.
27. See Lamb, p. 8.
28. Howells, p. 20.
29. Bakhtin, *The Dialogic Imagination*, p. 314.
30. Eighteenth-century philosophers used terms different from those we employ today: upholders of determinism were called necessitarians; supporters of free will were referred to as libertarians.
31. Juxtaposition of opposite registers will be analysed more in depth in chapter 4.
32. It is interesting to note that one of the most remarkable differences between *Tristram Shandy* and *Jacques le fataliste* is the fact that one novel boldly experiments with typography whilst the other does not. One may hazard a guess that Diderot was simply not interested in using typography; indeed, there are no particular uses of typography in the

rest of his corpus. But one may also surmise that because Sterne's daring typographical practices are so visually and immediately striking that they have in a sense become the hallmark of his novel, Diderot was careful to preserve the original voice of *Jacques le fataliste* instead of just writing a French take on *Tristram Shandy*.

33. Bakhtin, *The Dialogic Imagination*, pp. 299 and 300.
34. Bakhtin, *The Dialogic Imagination*, p. 343.
35. Denis Diderot, *Œuvres complètes*, ed. Lewinter, III, p. 13.
36. *Encyclopédie*, article 'fatalité'.
37. See Connon, p. 289.
38. Marian Hobson, '*Jacques le fataliste*: l'art du probable', in *Diderot: les Dernières Années 1770–1784*, ed. by Peter France and Anthony Strugnell (Edinburgh: Edinburgh University Press, 1985), pp. 180–96 (p. 186).
39. Hobson, '*Jacques le fataliste*: l'art du probable', p. 183.
40. Hobson, '*Jacques le fataliste*: l'art du probable', p. 183.
41. Loy, p. 131.
42. 'Destin et hasard seraient l'effet d'instances narratives [. . .]. Si l'auteur semble jouer au destin, à d'autres moments il renie toute autorité pour proclamer qu'il suit un manuscrit qui fait foi; ou, au contraire, qu'il n'est pas une instance supérieure à ses personnages, et qu'il ne peut suivre à la fois le maître et Jacques. Parfois, on l'a vu, il proclame sa parfaite liberté de dire n'importe quoi, pour ensuite refuser cette liberté et annoncer sa soumission à la vérité.' Hobson, '*Jacques le fataliste*: l'art du probable', p. 186.
43. P. S. Laplace, *Œuvres complètes* (Paris: Gauthier-Villars, 1886), VIII, p. 145; quoted in Hobson, '*Jacques le fataliste*: l'art du probable', p. 188.

CHAPTER 3

Mindscapes: Descriptions and Spatial Representations

Various philosophical discourses are progressively undermined by the very characters supposed to uphold them. In our two novels, no particular philosophical stance stands out as the authoritative one. Since all systems are equally subject to refutation, none can be representative of the author's didactic intentions. Submitted to constant contradictions, no discourse can develop into a complete system. The purpose of chapter 3 is to analyse the correlation between these fragmentary and inconclusive philosophical discourses and the description of the characters and their surroundings. Though restricted to space, my argument corroborates Bakhtin's claim that 'The architectonic of the world in artistic vision organizes not only spatial and temporal features, but also features that relate purely to meaning; there is not only spatial and temporal form, but meaning-governed form as well.'[1]

The eponymous hero of Diderot's novel offers the most obvious evidence of the existence of such a correlation. The title *Jacques le fataliste* connects the character to his philosophical views. Jacques is made to embody fatalism. The narrator encourages such a connection by opposing the fatalistic servant to his counterpart in station and convictions: the libertarian master. Naturally, the reader expects that each character will fully hypostatise the philosophical stance he represents. But as underlined in chapter 2, the characters fall short of this and, far from justifying the views they champion, they actually invalidate them.

In chapter 3, I analyse the characters' search for an outside perspective. I will focus on descriptions of characters and of outside surroundings, since both provide an external perspective. The external gaze is of particular importance as my argument is grounded in Bakhtin's concept of outsideness. In his essay 'Author and Hero in aesthetic activity', Bakhtin introduces outsideness as an aesthetical construction present in most novels. The external gaze of the author embraces the existence of the character so as to reconstruct it as a whole and complete entity. Originally, outsideness only applies to descriptions of characters. I am extending it to descriptions of surroundings on the grounds that spatial representation is itself usually reconstructed and given a unity by an external viewer. Outsideness would enable the characters to visualise and clarify the intricacies of their thoughts.

However, *Tristram Shandy* and *Jacques le fataliste* strike us by the fact that they offer no such outside reconstruction, either for characters or for landscapes. Despite the characters' efforts, their attempts to construct an outside perspective fail. The reader is placed in a similar problem to the characters. He too desires an overall view of the characters and their itineraries, of the landscapes, and of the narratives. *Jacques le fataliste* and *Tristram Shandy* offer none of these. Sterne and Diderot give very little information, and what they do yield is scattered throughout their novels. Using the little he has, the reader is tempted to perform the outside reconstruction himself. As for the characters, the aim of the reader's outside reconstruction is to simplify his approach to the texts and to disentangle their progression by a reordering. Yet we must remember that this external perspective is a rewriting of *Tristram Shandy* and *Jacques le fataliste* by the reader, and does not actually belong to the novels as written by Sterne and Diderot.

I contend that the conspicuous absence of outsideness participates in the refusal of a closed and complete authoritative perspective. To justify my reading, I will first explore how movement and the outside surroundings can unveil the characters' thoughts and influence the directions their minds take. The power of travelling to reveal the meanderings of the mind is particularly visible in *Jacques le fataliste* where the characters' journey constitutes the main pretext for their engaging in philosophical debates and more personal conversations. Both Diderot and Sterne strengthen the correlation between reflection and movement, may it be travelling or simply taking a stroll, by inserting references to the figure of the wandering philosopher. These references redefine the correlation as one between spatial and philosophical wanderings. In the same way as the interest of the philosophical debates lies not in reaching a conclusion, the importance of wandering as an aim in itself has supplanted that of the destinations which invariably turn out to be disappointing.

Travelling appears more and more as a metaphor for the characters' intellectual meanderings. For both spatial and intellectual wanderings, Sterne and Diderot have shifted the focus from the destination, or in other words the conclusion, to the actual process of travelling and thinking. The connection between travelling and intellectual meanderings is not limited to a metaphorical value. It extends to a more direct and practical application in that space may participate in the shaping of ideas and tropes. Even though the landscape surrounding the characters sometimes takes their thoughts in a certain direction, it cannot put an end to their errancy. Space then takes the form of a labyrinth or travel sickness, and becomes associated with loss of orientation, dizziness and the impossibility of finding a fixed point. This errancy is caused by the absence of an overall perspective which would have allowed the recognition of a trajectory leading to a conclusion, or destination.

The second part of this chapter concentrates on Bakhtin's concept of outsideness. Outsideness corresponds to the author's external and comprehensive perspective of his characters, both physically and biographically, necessary for providing an exhaustive description. Outsideness is opposed to the individual's internal, disjointed and fragmented perspective. Outsideness offers completion, whereas internal views are necessarily left open-ended. According to Bakhtin, outsideness is the most common model of description in novels. I am interested in how and why descriptions in *Tristram Shandy* and *Jacques le fataliste* depart from outsideness. After having offered an outline of outsideness, I confront Bakhtin's concept with descriptions in both novels in order to argue that Sterne and Diderot do not provide the author's external, all-embracing and structuring gaze. Instead, the reader is left with the characters' internal, fragmented and discontinuous perspectives.

In *Tristram Shandy*, autobiographical writing prevents outsideness from being achieved as the coincidence between author and character makes it near impossible to reach the distance necessary for an external perspective. Sterne complicates this by making Tristram merge living and writing. The completion, or, to use Bakhtinian terminology, consummation brought about by outsideness would be synonymous with death. In *Jacques le fataliste*, the master attempts to provide the outside authorial gaze supposed to make sense of Jacques's biography as a whole. However, instead of simply witnessing this biography, he anticipates it and announces his servant's end. Sharing Tristram's reasons, Jacques actively tries to avoid the biographical completion brought about by outsideness, as this would lead to his death. Indeed, Bakhtin's concept of outsideness closely ties completion of the hero, in that it is biographical and not just physical, to that of the narrative. The dependence of the narrative on the main character is particularly obvious in the case of Sterne's and Diderot's novels where Jacques and Tristram are the eponymous heroes of both texts.

If Jacques and Tristram both shun biographical completion, they yearn, as the other characters do, for the panoramic perspective which would make their thoughts understandable to themselves and others. The third part is concerned with the characters' use of spatial representations, geometry being one of the most notable methods employed, as visual illustrations for clarifying their ideas. This use of maps and geometry manifests outside intentions, since they offer external perspectives on fragmentary views so as to make them complete. Such spatial representations could indeed stand as substitutes for the outside perspective in that they would offer an overall and comprehensive external projection of the characters' meanderings and would reconstruct them as a coherent whole. In *Jacques le fataliste* and *Tristram Shandy*, the characters and narrators use geometry to give greater precision to descriptions. However, far from bringing greater clarity to language, geometry often ends up completely obscuring descriptions. Spatial representations are doomed to fail as substitutes for outsideness since outsideness can only be performed by the author's external gaze on his characters. Nevertheless, these representations do succeed as external projections of internal states of mind. Instead of helping to clarify the characters' thoughts, they are effective in representing their mental confusion.

If the characters are desperately trying to recreate authorial outsideness, so is the reader. The fourth part closely looks at descriptions of characters in *Tristram Shandy* and *Jacques le fataliste*, since descriptions contain the most obvious indicators of outsideness. Information on the characters is frustratingly scarce, fragmented, and scattered throughout the texts. The digressive nature of the narrative structure of *Tristram Shandy* and *Jacques le fataliste* affects the representation of the characters and the landscapes. This type of description signals the absence of authorial outsideness, thwarts the reader's expectations and complicates his understanding of the novels. Using the case of Smietanski's work on *Jacques le fataliste*, I argue that the reader is tempted to remedy such confusing disruptions in the descriptions by painstakingly collecting the fragments of information on the characters and reassembling them to attempt to recreate authorial outsideness. However, this constitutes a rewriting of the text and mistakes the intentions of the author. An outside view would enclose the text in a unique and monosemous perspective.

The final part takes a similar approach to part four, in that it is also concerned with the fact that readers may be tempted to supply this outside perspective themselves for exactly the same reason as for the characters: clarification. I extend Bakhtin's concept of outsideness to descriptions of the characters' surroundings and landscapes which are equally affected by the absence of an authorial perspective. Descriptions of landscapes bear the same symptoms as descriptions of characters: details are few and far between, and generally insufficient to offer the setting the reader is likely to expect. I start by contrasting spatial descriptions in *Jacques le fataliste* and *Tristram Shandy* to descriptive methods commonly found in travel writing. I come to the conclusion that, as travelling only appears in certain sections of both novels, it cannot account for the scarce and fragmented nature of Sterne's and Diderot's spatial descriptions, constant throughout their novels. Consequently, as in the case of the characters' descriptions, the absence of outsideness must explain these particular characteristics.

Here again, I use the example of the scholars Smietanski and Fredman to demonstrate the reader's temptation to reconstruct for himself the spatial descriptions as if through the authorial gaze. The description of the characters and their surroundings is just as fragmentary and incomplete as the philosophical views they hold. The description of the speaker and his discourse share the same characteristics. Both are fragmentary and left incomplete, and thus illustrate how the narrative structure shapes the philosophical debates. In turn, the narrative, and more specifically here the description, becomes a 'meaning-governed form as well' as its primary function is an organising structure.[2] Indeed, the absence of outsideness in the descriptions argues against an authoritative perspective in the same way as the incompletion of philosophical debates contests the dominancy of a unique complete system.

Backwards and Forwards: The Wandering Philosopher

Descriptions of landscapes offer the reader information both on what is being perceived and the person perceiving it. The obvious purpose of spatial representations is to provide a setting. In a more subtle way, these representations also reveal something about the person making the description. As soon as it is grasped by a human conscience, every landscape bears the stamp of subjectivity and becomes an external projection of an individual's perception of the world. Thus Weisgerber invites us to reconsider the truth of what is usually regarded as an easy cliché: that 'le paysage est un "état d'âme"'.[3] The fact that descriptions pass through the prism of those perceiving them means that spatial representations tell us as much about the landscape, the outside world, as about the individual's mind contemplating it. Landscapes can thus be turned into 'mindscapes'.

Travels are propitious to conversation, which can disclose biographical information or lead to philosophical reflections. Travelling invites Sterne's and Diderot's characters to engage in conversation, and the landscape through which they are passing has an impact on the elaboration of their thoughts. Spatial representations create an inside-out effect by exposing inner views and feelings. However, the landscapes do not simply receive the impression of the characters' minds through description. Space interacts with the characters in that it may shape the direction their thoughts take. It is necessary first to comprehend the property of disclosure in landscapes to understand why the characters try to recreate it.

In the essay "De Democritus et Heraclitus", Montaigne suggests that a man's mind may be reflected by his bodily motions and generally by the way he inhabits space. Montaigne speaks of journeys as uncovering the traveller and revealing some of his nakedness: "Tout mouvement nous découvre."[4] It seems that Montaigne's saying may be taken literally when applied to Sterne's and Diderot's novels. To while away the time during their long travel, Jacques and his master entertain each other by telling stories, which progressively get more and more intimate. Yielding to his master's insistent request, Jacques eventually agrees to recount the loss of his virginity. The master repays his indiscretion by telling his servant how he became a cuckold. If the road invites travelling companions to tell such delicately private anecdotes, it may also comically take an active role in the confirmation of Montaigne's saying. Movement may uncover the body just as well as the mind. An importunate country doctor, sharing his saddle with a young peasant girl, invites himself into an argument between Jacques and his master on the pain of knee wounds. In the heat of the conversation, 'il pousse sa compagne, lui fait perdre l'équilibre et la jette à terre, un pied pris dans la basque de son habit et les cotillons renversés sur sa tête' (*JF*, p. 671). On this occasion, movement has uncovered more than the peasant girl would have cared for.

The faculty of movement to disclose information about the traveller can be accounted for by the fact that the long time spent on the roads is propitious to conversations. As we have seen in the case of Jacques and his master, travelling companions may entertain themselves by engaging in frivolous discussions. In *Jacques le fataliste*, conversation is presented as the travellers' favoured means to while away the time. 'Ils continuèrent leur route' 'trompant l'ennui et la fatigue par le silence et le bavardage comme c'est l'usage de ceux qui marchent' (*JF*, p. 678). The novel, set on the roads of France, is mostly constituted by Jacques and his master's conversations.

In *Tristram Shandy*, however, conversation whilst travelling only occurs once. Moreover, it is in 'the chapter [Tristram] was obliged to tear out', when Toby and Walter were set 'in deep roads and dissertations' (*TS*, IV, xxv, p. 283). Yet the effect of movement and thought is not completely absent from Sterne's novel. The correlation between travelling and conversation is tightened by the fact that travelling affects the speech. This is one of the explanations Yorick forwards to justify his choice 'for riding a meek-spirited jade of a broken-winded horse' instead of 'one of mettle':

> For on such a one he could sit mechanically, and meditate as delightfully *de vanitate mundi et fugâ saeculi*, as with the advantage of a death's head before him; — that, in all other exercitations, he could spend his time, as he rode slowly along, — to as much account as in his study; — that he could draw up an argument in his sermon, — or a hole in his breeches, as steadily on the one as in the other; — that brisk trotting and slow argumentation, like wit and judgment, were two incompatible movements. — But that, upon his steed — he could unite and reconcile every thing, — he could compose his sermon [...]. (*TS*, I, x, pp. 19–20)

Yorick is here suggesting that the rhythm and motion of a specific mode of transport are propitious to the good development of its corresponding rhetorical exercise, in this case, the composition of sermons. Travelling may also allow a greater freedom of expression. Yorick answers 'with a hop, skip, and a jump' 'if the subject was started in the fields.' But he would have to remain silent 'if close pent up in the social chimney corner, [...] barricado'd in, with a table and a couple of chairs' (*TS*, I, xii, p. 27).

In *Jacques le fataliste*, the mode of transport imposes its own rhythm on the character's speech.

> Ici Jacques s'arrêta, et cela lui arriva plusieurs fois dans le cours de son récit, à chaque mouvement de tête que son cheval faisait de droite à gauche. Alors pour continuer il reprenait sa dernière phrase, comme s'il avait eu le hoquet. (*JF*, p. 712)
>
> Comme le ministre n'avait eu d'autre intention que de séparer ces deux hommes bizarres, et que les procédés généreux touchent toujours, il fut arrêté . . . Maudite bête! tiendras-tu ta tête droite? . . . il fut arrêté que mon capitaine resterait au régiment, et que son camarade irait occuper le commandement de place. (*JF*, p. 713)
>
> Il arrive . . . Va donc où tu voudras! Y a-t-il encore là quelque gibet qu'il te plaise de visiter?. . . Riez bien, monsieur, cela est en effet très plaisant . . . Il arrive [. . .]. (*JF*, p. 713)
>
> [. . .] mon capitaine qui était riche, comme je vous l'ai dit . . . J'espère, monsieur, que vous ne me condamnerez pas à finir notre voyage sur ce bizarre animal . . . Mon capitaine qui était riche avait exigé de son camarade [. . .]. (*JF*, p. 714)

These extracts are taken from Jacques's four-page long story about the love-hate relationship between his captain and another officer. Jacques has been unnerved by his horse's habit of suddenly rushing towards gibbets close by. Now made anxious by any unusual movement of his horse, Jacques is distracted from his story. The pauses and repetitions in Jacques's speech, and which the narrator likens to hiccupping, correspond to the horse's 'mouvement de tête'.

Conversations in *Jacques le fataliste* may take a more serious and profound tone. Travel literature can be easily used for didactic purposes.[5] Tristram endorses this by inviting the reader to travel from Norway to the '*Asiatick Tartary*' so that he may observe how climates affect people (*TS*, III, xx, p. 177). Here, travel is used as an illustration to justify Tristram's idea that a people's wit depends on its weather. I am not interested in didactic travelling as an illustration of ideas already formulated, with the intent to convince of their truthfulness, as in the example just quoted. This remains a minor occurrence in *Tristram Shandy* and *Jacques le fataliste*. I prefer to focus on how travelling, and movement in general, encourage reflection and generate thought, without necessarily leading to set ideas.

Returning to *Jacques le fataliste*, servant and master use their journey as a pretext for engaging in a philosophical argument on fatalism and free will. While playing on the *topos* of literature as travel, both Diderot and Sterne interweave inside the archetype of the wandering philosopher, through intertextuality. Berchtold thus points out the allusion in *Jacques le fataliste* to the story of the ancient philosopher Thales of Miletus who fell in a well whilst contemplating the stars.[6] Jacques indirectly refers to Thales's accident by warning against the dangers of deciphering the Great Scroll and constantly looking at the heavens instead of what is lying ahead. According to Jacques's fatalistic system, even if he did know what Fate was keeping in store for him, he would be unable to act upon it: 'En éviterais-je pour cela le trou où je dois m'aller casser le cou?' (*JF*, p. 677). Thales is mocked by his servant who sees him falling in a well while walking gazing at the sky to decipher its mysteries.⁷ The example of Thales of Miletus confirms the parallel between spatial and intellectual errancy, while the story of Aesop epitomises the old question *quo vadis?* concerning both a spatial destination and man's fate, a double meaning on which Diderot constantly plays to trick the reader. The interest lies not in the destination itself, but in the route that leads to it. The frequency in *Jacques le fataliste* of the verb *aller* as opposed to *arriver*, marks the narrative's concern with the long and tortuous trajectory instead of the immediacy of the arrival.

In *Tristram Shandy*, destinations are often disappointing for both Tristram and the reader. In the chapter of 'vexation upon vexation' (VII, xxx, p. 467), the sightseeing in Lyon is continuously frustrated as the lovers' tomb is nonexistent, the mechanism of the 'great clock of Lippius Basil' is 'all out of joint' and the library holding 'thirty volumes of the general history of China' is shut '*For all the* JESUITS *had got the cholic*' (*TS*, VII, xxxix, p. 479). Tristram sometimes simply offers a listing of the different cities he has passed through during his Grand Tour, but without saying anything about them (VII, x, p. 442, and VII, xv, p. 446). Tristram is not in the least intent on bringing his autobiography to a conclusion. Nor is he interested in the destinations, in the touristic spots of his Grand Tour. Tristram regards travelling as an end in itself, not as the tiring means for sightseeing. He focuses on the actual process of travelling, and says very little on the places he traverses. For example, he tells us nothing of Chantilly (only ' I [...] saw every thing at Chantilly in spite') or of St Dennis ('I pass'd through St. Dennis, without turning my head so much as on side towards the Abby —', *TS*, VII, xvi, p. 448).

As the absence of an ending in *Tristram Shandy* seems to indicate, the notion of arrival appears to have been suppressed. The same may also be said of *Jacques le fataliste*, though with one reservation. The narrator does offer a conclusion to both Jacques's love story which ends in a marriage, and to the master's story with his rival in love whom he kills in a duel. However, the narrator rushes through these at such a great pace, allowing them but a ridiculously small space in the book, and complicates the conclusion in such a way that the reader is left with the false impression there has been no ending at all. Both Sterne and Diderot echo, each in their own way, Montaigne's saying: 'J'entreprends seulement de me branler, pendant que le branle me plaît, et me promène pour me promener'.⁸ Wandering has no other aim but itself. Here again, spatial movement agrees with the motions of the mind. The interest of the characters' philosophical debates lies not in the conclusions they reach, for there are none. We are encouraged to refocus our attention on the progressions of the mind instead of on the truths attained.

Truth is traditionally viewed as something set and permanent, and to reach this fixed point would be the end of the journey. Such a vision would concentrate on the importance of the destination instead of the trajectory. By not following this rule, Sterne and Diderot may give the impression of having failed in the sempiternal quest, apparently confirmed on a miniaturised scale by the fact that they have been unable to bring their narrative to an end. Turning back to Bakhtin, this interpretation would be valid if we were dealing with *monological* novels. However, *Tristram Shandy* and *Jacques le fataliste* belong to the second category, that is to say *dialogical* works, where dialogue between different views has replaced the imposition of a single authoritative truth. This focus on the process of mental reflection instead of on the conclusions, externally projected and enabled by wandering, brings us very close to the principles of peripateticism.[9] I limit the similarity between peripateticism (from the Greek *peripatetikos* 'walking up and down') and Sterne's and Diderot's novels to the method of generating thought through movement. I am not concerned with the philosophical views of the Peripatetic School.

The directions we take when travelling through a particular landscape may influence the direction of our thoughts and shape our choice of images. Whilst taking a stroll in 'le Jardin du roi' with the Marquis des Arcis, Mme de La Pommeraye mentions Mlle d'Aisnon whom they have just encountered:

> Comme cela me vieillit! Quand cela vint à Paris, cela n'était pas plus haut qu'un chou. — Vous parlez de la fille de cette dame que nous avons trouvée à la promenade? — Oui. C'est comme dans un jardin où les roses fanées font place aux roses nouvelles [. . .]. (*JF*, p. 769)

We can guess that Mme de La Pommeraye's choice of images ('chou' and 'roses'), has been influenced by the Jardin, which was dedicated to the study of botany.[10] The capacity of the environment to nourish our thoughts explains why wandering has been used as a philosophical method. The peripatetic method is used in *La Promenade du sceptique*, by the philosopher Cléobule whose topics of conversation 'étaient presque toujours analogues aux objets qu'il avait sous les yeux':

> Je compris que Cléobule s'était fait une sorte de philosophie locale; que toute sa campagne était animée et parlante pour lui; que chaque objet lui fournissait des pensées d'un genre particulier, et que les ouvrages de la nature étaient à ses yeux un livre allégorique où il lisait mille vérités qui échappaient au reste des hommes.[11]

We see the influence of the landscape on the train of ideas in *Jacques le fataliste*.

Jacques and his master decide to shelter from the heat and rest 'au bord de ce ruisseau', in an 'endroit [. . .] charmant' (*JF*, p. 866). However, the 'mouches' and 'cousins' coming from the stream prevent Jacques from sleeping. Unable to rest, Jacques and his master transform this into an opportunity to engage in a philosophical debate on hidden order and necessary evil, using the stinging midges to illustrate their discussion:

> LE MAÎTRE: Quand tu as ou trop de sang ou du mauvais sang que fais-tu? tu appelles un chirurgien qui t'en ôte deux ou trois palettes. Eh bien, ces cousins dont tu te plains sont une nuée de petits chirurgiens ailés qui viennent avec leurs petites lancettes te piquer et te tirer du sang goutte à goutte.
>
> JACQUES: Oui, mais à tort et à travers, sans savoir si j'en ai trop ou peu. Faites venir ici un étique, et vous verrez si les petits chirurgiens ailés ne le piqueront pas. Ils songent à eux, et tout dans la nature songe à soi et ne songe qu'à soi. (*JF*, pp. 866–67)

The description also mentions that master and servant 's'étendent sur l'herbe', and are resting 'à l'ombre de ces arbres' (*JF*, p. 866). Their conversation moves from the midges to 'la fable de Garo'. This new topic has most certainly been brought along by the similarity of Jacques and his master's situation to that of Garo who fell asleep under a tree:

> Si au lieu de glands le chêne avait porté des citrouilles, est-ce que cette bête de Garo se serait endormi sous un chêne? Et s'il ne s'était pas endormi sous un chêne, qu'importait au salut de son nez qu'il en tombât des citrouilles ou des glands? (*JF*, p. 867)

In *Tristram Shandy*, the effect of movement upon ideas takes a more physiological turn as Tristram talks of it in terms of communication. The 'most rapid motion' of the coach driving him 'from Stilton to Stamford', ''twas communicated to my brain — my heart partook of it' (*TS*, V, I, p. 309). The influence of wandering on the shaping of the mind becomes even more internalised, and is pushed to an extreme in *Tristram Shandy*. Talking of animal spirits, Tristram affirms

> [. . .] that nine parts in ten of a man's sense or his nonsense, his successes and miscarriages in this world depend upon their motions and activity, and the different tracks and trains you put them into; so that when they are once set a-going, whether right or wrong, 'tis not a halfpenny matter, — away they go cluttering like hey-go-mad; and by treading the same steps over and over again, they presently make a road of it, as plain and as smooth as a garden-walk, which, when they are once used to, the Devil himself sometimes shall not be able to drive them off it. (*TS*, I, i, pp. 5–6)

This excerpt repeats the inside-out pattern: man has turned into a garden where his animal spirits wander. A man's reason and good sense depend on whether his animal spirits follow the right track at a steady pace or whether they go astray 'cluttering like hey-go-mad'. The motion of the animal spirits constitutes the motor of the autobiography. Not only did they bring about Tristram's conception, but they also shaped his particular mindset. Walter's animal spirits set in motion those of his son, but Elizabeth's 'unseasonable question' 'scattered and dispersed' them. Walter's animal spirits were unable to safely escort the homunculus (Tristram at the state of seed) 'to the place destined for his reception' (*TS*, I, ii, p. 6). Tristram portrays his homunculus self as a young traveller, embarking on a journey in his mother's womb, and whose 'own animal spirits' are 'ruffled beyond description' (*TS*, I, ii, p. 7). The son thus blames the scattered trajectory of his father's animal spirits at his conception for the fact that he is himself scatterbrained.

In peripateticism and our two novels, intellectual peregrinations never follow a straight, pre-determined line. Conversation carries in its etymology the notion of movement. The Latin *conversari* translates as 'to turn with'. It thus seems that the meanderings of discourse follow the meanderings of the road. As Montandon remarks, their progress is a digressive one. For Montaigne and Diderot (and I will add Sterne), the importance lies in the trajectory, in the meanderings of the mind, and not in the destination:

> L'aspect décousu du texte, la liberté avec laquelle l'écrivain dispose sans ordre visible sa pensée apparentent sa démarche à celle d'un flâneur. 'Montaigne sait bien ce qu'il dit, mais il ne sait pas toujours ce qu'il va dire. S'il a dessein d'aller en un lieu, le moindre objet qui lui passe devant les yeux le fait sortir de son chemin' (Guez de Balzac). C'est l'inspiration du moment, l'idée qui apparaît au détour du chemin, l'humeur qui l'engage dans telle voie qui déterminent le cours hasardeux de la pensée, guidée par la fortune. 'Il suit sans art l'enchaînement de ses idées; il lui importe fort peu d'où il parle, comment il aille ni où il aboutisse. La chose qu'il dit, c'est celle qui l'affecte dans le moment. Il n'est ni plus lié ni plus décousu en écrivant, qu'en pensant ou en rêvant' (Diderot).[12]

The characters' wanderings quickly become errancies, even in familiar surroundings. The errancies of Toby's mind in his own bedroom, carried away by his obsession for calculations, illustrate this. The theme of the labyrinth, studied in an article on *Tristram Shandy* by Soud, is commonly used by both Sterne and Diderot as an external projection of the internal errancy of the mind.[13]

The impression of dizziness, of loss of orientation the characters undergo is described as a sort of *mal de transport*, a travel sickness. In *Tristram Shandy*, it finds an illustration in the crossing of the Channel from Dover to Calais:

> Sick! sick! sick! sick! —
> — When shall we get to land? captain — they have hearts like stones — O I am deadly sick! — reach me that thing, boy — 'tis the most discomfiting sickness — I wish I was at the bottom — Madam! How is it with you? Undone! undone! un — O! undone! sir — What the first time? — No, 'tis the second, third, sixth, tenth time, sir, — hey-day — (*TS*, VII, ii, p. 433)

The impossibility of finding a fixed point, some solid ground on which one could safely walk, produces not only nausea but can also be responsible for falls. In the first pages of *Jacques le fataliste*, the interfering country doctor inadvertently pushes off the peasant girl riding behind him. Jacques is knocked unconscious due to his horse rushing in the hangman's house, and thus making the rider's head violently collide with the lintel. When trying to dismount, the master falls to the ground because of his servant's tampering with the stirrups. In these three cases, oversight and the absence of a general view of the situation are responsible for the falls. The most telling example, however, is to be found in *Tristram Shandy*. Dr Slop is 'coming slowly along, foot by foot, waddling thro'' the dirt upon the vertebrae of a little diminutive pony'. Obadiah is 'mounted upon a strong monster of a coach-horse, prick'd into full gallop, and making all practicable speed the adverse way' (*TS*, II, ix, p. 93). The mischief is caused by 'a sudden turn, made by an acute angle of the garden wall' (*TS*, II, ix, p. 94), which prevents the characters from avoiding crashing into each other.

Travel invites the characters to reflection in both meanings of the word, as the journey is propitious to philosophical musing and private confidences. Whilst travelling, the characters willingly make some personal revelations. However, locomotion and landscapes may shape and influence the direction their thoughts take. In such cases, spatial representations externally project a mental process, which consequently becomes more easily understandable. Yet space can impose its own constraints and prevent an overview of the situation, as in the example of the collusion between Dr Slop and Obadiah.[14] In other instances, it is an overall view of their own confused ideas that the characters are lacking. Their mental errancies are then externally projected as spatial wanderings. It is this very absence of a panoramic view which is preventing the characters from disentangling their thoughts from contradiction, in the same way as it is checking them from seeing what lies ahead on the road. An overall perspective would allow a totalising view revealing the bigger picture. Diderot illustrates this in the 1767 salon where the narrator tries to console the 'abbé' with the sand irritating his eye by explaining to him the notion of cosmic order:

> Mon très-cher abbé, lui dis-je, oubliez pour un moment le petit gravier qui picote votre cornée, et écoutez-moi. Pourquoi l'univers vous paraît-il si bien ordonné? c'est que tout y est enchaîné, à sa place, et qu'il n'y a pas un seul être qui n'ait dans sa position, sa production, son effet, une raison suffisante, ignorée ou connue.[15]

The 'abbé' is missing an overall perspective to understand that what he feels at first as a source of annoyance has a place and a purpose in the general order of things.

It is this same panoramic view our wandering characters are lacking to make sense of their situation and their ideas. In the essay 'Author and hero in aesthetic activity', Bakhtin studies the function of this all-embracing outlook, which he calls outsideness, in literary works, and more precisely regarding the way the author constructs his characters. I will now turn to Bakhtin's concept of outsideness so as to explain how it can be used to define with a greater precision what I have been periphrastically referring to as an overall and panoramic perspective.

Outsideness

In 'Author and Hero in Aesthetic Activity', Bakhtin coins the term *outsideness* to explain how an exhaustive description is attained. One of the peculiarities of *Tristram Shandy* and *Jacques le fataliste* is that outsideness, a feature common to most novels according to Bakhtin, is not achieved. Sterne's and Diderot's descriptions depart from conventional rules, as they do not provide an overall and comprehensive view of the characters and their surroundings. Before analysing how the descriptions in *Jacques le fataliste* and *Tristram Shandy* depart from Bakhtin's notion of outsideness, it is necessary first to understand what outsideness actually refers to.

To clarify the concept of outsideness, Bakhtin sets momentarily aside literature and refers to social relations. Man can never directly perceive himself entirely. He only has access to a fragmentary vision of his body and the physiognomic messages it is sending. Man feels his outside presence from the inside, and this in a disjointed, discontinuous way. He needs the external gaze of another person for his exterior presence to be reconstructed as a coherent whole, or, to use Bakhtin's terminology, to be consummated.

> For self-consciousness, this integral image is dispersed in life and enters the field of seeing the external world only in the form of fortuitous fragments. And what is lacking, moreover, is precisely *external* unity and continuity; a human being experiencing life in the category of his own *I* is incapable of gathering himself by himself into an outward whole that would be even relatively finished. The point here is not the deficiency of material provided by outer vision (although the deficiency is in fact considerable); the point, rather, is the absence in principle of any unitary axiological approach from within a human being himself to his own outward expressedness in being. No mirror, photograph, special self-observation will help here. At best, we might get an aesthetically spurious product, created for one's own selfish purposes from the position of a possible other who lacks any standing of his own.
>
> In this sense, one can speak of a human being's absolute need for the other, for the other's seeing, remembering, gathering, and unifying self-activity — the only self-activity capable of producing his outwardly finished personality. This outward personality could not exist, if the other did not create it: aesthetic memory is *productive* — it gives birth, for the first time, to the *outward* human being on a new plane of being.[16]

This reconstructive gaze of a spectator, reassembling and reorganising as a whole the fragments of what we perceive of ourselves, corresponds to Bakhtin's outsideness. Outsideness is not restricted to the appearance of the body. Through outsideness, Bakhtin embraces both the spatiality of the body and the temporality of the biography. Man cannot have a sense of his own biography since the opening and conclusion of its narrative (that is to say birth and death) escape his consciousness.[17] The narrative of our personal biography can only be constructed by the memory of others.

For example, Tristram says he stands 'indebted' to his uncle Toby for the anecdote of how Walter was interrupted by a question about the clock, the night of his conception (see *TS*, I, iii, p. 7). If it had not been for Toby's recollection, Tristram would have been ignorant of the circumstances of his conception. Yorick is the only character benefiting from a complete description.[18] This may be explained by the fact that he is also the only character to whom the rules of outsideness have been applied. In the first volume, Tristram laments Yorick's death by the famous black page, and his last moments have been recorded by Eugenius. Having witnessed Yorick's existence, Eugenius is able to deduce from the parson's past the cause of his death: a broken heart (see *TS*, I, xii). The same applies to Le Fever, whose life and death, witnessed by Toby and Trim, is told in volume VI, with a description of his general aspect, of his character and his biography. Death is the condition for Yorick's and Le Fever's biographical consummation.

Just as for the perception of our body, our life appears to us as a fragmented and overwhelming accumulation of events without any completion. The completion of my existence does not belong to me but can only be achieved through the memory of others.

> I come to know a considerable portion of my own biography from what is said by others, by people close to me, as well as in the emotional tonality of these others: my birth and my descent, the events of family life and national life in my early childhood (that is, everything that could not have been understood or simply could not even have been perceived by a child). All these moments are indispensable for reconstructing an even minimally intelligible and coherent picture of my life and its world; I — as narrator of my own life — come to know all of them from the lips of others who are its heroes.
>
> Without these stories told by others, my life would not only lack fullness and clarity in its content, but would also remain internally dispersed, divested of any value-related *biographical unity*.[19]

In the same way as man needs the external gaze of another person for his physical appearance and his biography to be reconstructed and complete, a character can only become a complete unit through the author's outside view. Bakhtin calls *transgredience* the information escaping the character's consciousness but to which the author alone has access. The 'plastic-pictorial, spatial values which are *transgredient* to the hero's consciousness and his world' 'consummate him from outside, from another's consciousness of him — the consciousness of the author/contemplator'.[20] It is worth noticing Tristram's efforts to offer an outside reconstruction of his biography by gathering and criss-crossing various family reminiscences. This is particularly visible in Tristram's speculations on the exact date of his conception:

> Now it appears, by a memorandum in my father's pocket-book, which now lies upon the table, "That on *Lady-Day*, which was on the 25th of the same month in which I date my geniture, — my father set out upon his journey to *London* with my eldest brother *Bobby*, to fix him at *Westminster* school;" and, as it appears from the same authority, "That he did not get down to his wife and family till the *second week* in *May* following", — it brings the thing almost to a certainty. (*TS*, I, iv, pp. 9–10)

Despite Tristram's hopes, the time of his conception cannot be fixed with any great certainty to a particular date. The information Tristram provides to justify his speculative date is insufficient and even contradictory.

Outsideness corresponds to this principle of consummation (or in other words completion) made possible by transgredient information. Thus, Bakhtin defines outsideness as an 'aesthetically productive'

> [...] relationship in which the author occupies an intently maintained position *outside* the hero with respect to every constituent feature of the hero — a position *outside* the hero with respect to space, time, value, and meaning. And this being-outside in relation to the hero enables the author (1) to collect and concentrate *all* of the hero, who, from within himself, is diffused and dispersed in the projected world of cognition and in the open event of ethical action; (2) to collect the hero and his life and to complete him to the point where he forms a *whole* by supplying all those moments which are inaccessible to the hero himself from within himself (such as full outward image, an exterior, a background behind his back, his relation to the event of death and the absolute future, etc.); and (3) to justify and to consummate the hero independently of the meaning, the achievements, the outcome and success of the hero's own forward-directed life.[21]

Supposing that *Tristram Shandy* and *Jacques le fataliste* complied with outsideness here broadly outlined, the characters' physical aspects and biographies would have been consummated by the narrator's external gaze. However, when actually confronting description in the two novels to Bakhtin's concept of outsideness, we are struck by the absence of an outside consummating reconstruction. Description remains fragmentary, elliptic and diffused throughout the texts to the point that the reader struggles to picture the characters as a whole.[22] There is no outsideness to consummate the characters 'to the point where [they form] a *whole*'.

As Todorov underlines, Bakhtin is aware that outsideness constitutes a norm from which some novels escape.[23] Bakhtin mentions the case of autobiographical writing where the hero coincides with the narrator. This is particularly relevant to the study of *Tristram Shandy*. For outsideness to be attained in autobiographies, 'the author must take up a position outside himself, must experience himself on a plane that is different from the one on which we actually experience our own life'.[24] But Tristram seems to reject such a distancing from the self as he merges living and writing in one. He admits that to 'live' and to 'write' '[mean] the same thing' (*TS*, III, iv, p. 145).

To understand what is at stake in the connection between living and writing, we should include travelling in the equation. Tristram embarks on the Grand Tour so as to flee from Death, pursuing him hot on his heels. Travelling is consequently associated with living and writing. On his Grand Tour, Tristram continues his autobiography 'writing-galloping' (*TS*, VII, iv, p. 434). Tristram must continue to write and move in order to stay alive. To bring his autobiography to a conclusion is synonymous with death.

> If I am consummated and my life is consummated, I am no longer capable of living and acting. For in order to live and act, I need to be unconsummated, I need to be open for myself — at least in all the essential moments constituting my life; I have to be, for myself, someone who is axiologically yet-to-be, someone who does not coincide with his already existing makeup.[25]

Here, Bakhtin puts his finger on the narrator's refusal to conclude his autobiography. This resistance to completion makes outsideness impossible, both at the biographical and descriptive level.

Jacques experiences a similar situation to Tristram. The master interprets as sinister omens his servant's being regularly rushed to gibbets by his horse, and most of all his affectionately embracing an executioner. Like the reader, the master seems desirous to know the conclusion of Jacques's story. As is his custom, he is too impatient to wait for the end and prefers to guess. Taking *The Life of Socrates* for model, the master predicts that Jacques will end up in the same way as the Athenian philosopher, and keeps warning his servant of this, so that he may prepare himself for his fate.

> Jacques, mon ami, vous êtes un philosophe, j'en suis fâché pour vous, et s'il est permis de lire dans les choses présentes celles qui doivent arriver un jour, et si ce qui est écrit là-haut se manifeste quelquefois aux hommes longtemps avant l'événement, je présume que votre mort sera philosophique, et que vous recevrez le lacet d'aussi bonne grâce que Socrate reçut la coupe de la ciguë. (*JF*, p. 723)

But as always, the master's guesses are way off the mark. Unlike Socrates, Jacques is not condemned to death, as his horse's strange attraction for the gibbet would suggest. Instead, Jacques is released from gaol by the fellows of the famous bandit Mandrin, thus enabling him to return back to Denise and marry her. Following Bakhtin's model, the master corresponds to the outside gaze supposed to complete and unify Jacques's biography. But instead of silently witnessing the end of this biography, the master tries to anticipate it and lets his servant know. Jacques is understandably uncomfortable about these predictions and fights against their completion. As for Tristram, conclusion becomes a matter of life and death, and it is in Jacques's interest not to reach it.

The master's prediction constitutes a maladroit attempt to provide an outside standpoint on Jacques's biography, so as to make sense of the horse's uncanny behaviour. In a way, the master is following Diderot's advice to the abbot with a grain of sand in his eye: to comprehend an event in the greater scheme of things. In this way, the master is representative of the other characters of Sterne's and Diderot's novels. Indeed, the master is not alone in his search for an outside perspective. Now that I have broadly outlined Bakhtin's concept of outsideness, I can explore the different ways in which the characters attempt to put it into practice and the reasons why they fail.

The Failings of Geometry

In the first volume of Sterne's novel, we find Tristram musing on the possibility of directly visualising what happens inside a man's brain. He fantasises on 'the fixure of *Momus*'s glass, in the human breast'. An author could have 'look'd in, — view'd the soul stark naked; — observ'd all her motions, — her machinations'. For the purpose of drawing his characters from a model, he could have 'then taken [his] pen and ink and set down nothing but what [he] had seen, and could have sworn to' (*TS*, I, xxiii, p. 65). In *Jacques le fataliste*, we find a similar fantasy: to read one's fate written in the skies. Both novels apply the inside-out pattern already mentioned, though one uses the heart as a window into a man's soul, the other the heavens.

More importantly for this study, these two instances constitute fantasies of access to an outside gaze. Jacques confesses he will never know 'ce qui est écrit là-haut'. As for Tristram, he dismisses Momus' glass as unfeasible since 'our minds shine not through the body, but are wrapt up here in a dark covering of uncrystalised flesh and blood' (*TS*, I, xxiii, pp. 65–66). Nevertheless, this does not deter the characters from their pursuit of outsideness. Geometry is used as a possible realisation of Momus' glass, as it is supposed to achieve what Tristram 'love[s] the Pythagoreans' for, that is to say '"*getting out of the body, in order to think well.*" No man thinks right whilst he is in it; blinded as he must be, with his congenial humours' (*TS*, VII, xiii, p. 444).

In *Tristram Shandy*, geometrical figures are a surprising yet regular feature. Tristram uses geometrical terms to describe 'a little, squat, uncourtly figure of a Doctor *Slop*, of about four feet and a half perpendicular height, with a breadth of back, and a sesquipedality of belly, which might have done honour to a Serjeant in the Horse-Guards' (*TS*, II, ix, p. 93). Geometry does not actually help to singularise Dr Slop. On the contrary, he is reduced to the geometrical shape of a circle. The learned Latin word 'sesquipedality' (from *sesquipedalis*, 'a foot and a half long') and his ball-like appearance turn him into the caricature of the little portly pedant. In this case, Dr Slop has been reduced to a geometrical figure: he is easy to visualise but he has lost his personal traits.

In other cases, the opposite happens. Geometry is pushed to such a degree of rigour and exactness that the reader can no longer visualise the description. The character has been obscured by geometry. Before Trim starts reading the sermon to Walter, Toby, and Dr Slop, Tristram insists he 'must first give' 'a description of his attitude' (*TS*, II, xvii, p. 106):

> He stood before them with his body swayed, and bent forwards just so far, as to make an angle of 85 degrees and a half upon the plain horizon; — which sound orators, to whom I address this, know very well, to be the true persuasive angle of incidence; [. . .]
>
> He stood, — for I repeat it, to take the picture of him in at one view, with his body sway'd, and somewhat bent forwards, — his right leg firm under him, sustaining seven-eighths of his whole weight, — the foot of his left leg, the defect of which was no disadvantage to his attitude, advanced a little, — not laterally, nor forwards, but in a line betwixt them; — his knee bent, but that not violently, — but so as to fall within the limits of the line of beauty [. . .]. (*TS*, II, xvii, p. 107)

This description of Trim's posture strikes by its fastidious precision. Trim's natural talent as an orator has been covered up by the measurements and geometry has failed to provide an outside perspective. It does not enable us 'to take the picture of [Trim] in at one view'. Instead of helping the reader to visualise Trim in a particular posture, the description has fragmented the character into a leg, a foot, and a knee, which, when assembled, resembles more a schematised curve than a human body.

Tristram also uses geometry to give a greater precision to his descriptions of the surroundings of Shandy Hall:

> [. . .] by which word *world*, need I in this place inform your worship, that I would be understood to mean no more than of it, than a small circle described upon the circle of the great world, of four *English* miles diameter, or thereabouts, of which the cottage where the good old woman lived, is supposed to be the centre. (*TS*, I, vii, p. 12)

Tristram delimits a circle, the Shandean '*world*' of which the midwife is the centre. This circle comprehends 'the whole hamlet' but also 'two or three of the adjacent hamlets in the skirts of the next parish'. There is 'one large grange-house and some other odd houses and farms within two or three miles' 'from the smoke of' the midwife's 'chimney' (*TS*, I, xiii, p. 33). The precision of geometrical terms such as 'circle', 'diameter' and 'centre' is undermined by the vagueness introduced by the phrase 'or thereabouts'. Tristram is conscious of the failure of his descriptions to make the geography of Shandy Hall and its surroundings apparent to the reader. The actual locality cannot fit as neatly as Tristram would wish into the exactness of a geometrical circle. Having been unsuccessful with the written language, he promises to provide a map:

> But I must here, once for all, inform you that all this will be more exactly delineated and explain'd in a map, now in the hands of the engraver, which, with many other pieces and developments to this work, will be added to the end of the twentieth volume, — not to swell the work, — I detest the thought of such a thing; — but by way of commentary, scholium, illustration, and key to such passages, incidents, or inuendos as shall be thought to be either of private interpretation, or of dark or doubtful meaning [...]. (*TS*, I, xiii, pp. 33–34)

However, the twentieth volume has never been written nor the promised map provided whose function seems to be to point at the inadequacies of Tristram's descriptions.[26]

To this normal use of geometry, Sterne adds a more unexpected one. In *Tristram Shandy*, geometrical figures are used to illustrate the various directions the characters' thoughts take. Geometry thus represents a means for mapping the mind. Even if it cannot provide an explanation for the Shandean characters' outlandish notions, geometry may make Tristram's, Toby's and Walter's thoughts more comprehensible by visually representing the meanderings of their minds. To describe the way his nephew thinks, Toby makes an interesting choice of words: 'unaccountable obliquity' (*TS*, I, iii, p. 7). If geometry fails to explain why Tristram 'should neither think nor act like any other man's child' (*TS*, I, iii, p. 7), it succeeds in showing the particularities of his intellect. Obliquity is a euphemistic and polite way of saying that Tristram does not think straight. In this instance, geometry serves description. In others, it may be responsible for shaping trains of thought and producing associations of ideas.

Losing patience with Toby's obsession with military matters, Walter is about to remonstrate with his brother, 'taking his wig from off his head with his right hand, and with his *left* pulling out a striped *India* handkerchief from his right coat pocket' (*TS*, III, ii, p. 142). This movement would have been harmless if it had not been for the fact that 'In the latter end of Queen *Anne*'s reign, and in the beginning of the reign of King *George* the first — "*Coat pockets were cut very low down in the skirt*"' (*TS*, III, ii, p. 143). Walter is caught in an uneasy diagonal bodily posture. And not only does this 'zig-zaggery' lead to an association of ideas in Toby's mind, but it also reproduces its shape, as Walter's difficulties with his jacket lead him to a similar problem he encountered 'before the gate of St Nicholas', then leading him to the 'traverses of the attack of Namur'(*TS*, III, iii, p. 144).

Both geometry and language constitute tools with particular rules to enable men to understand the world, and most of all to find a common ground in that understanding. Geometry employs measurements and theorems, whilst language uses grammar and definitions. Geometry has also its own language. To perform demonstrations, one must not only use the appropriate vocabulary but also keep to a particular linguistic procedure (the grammar of geometry as it were). In *Les Mutations de la clarté*, Carsten Meiner mentions the use of geometry in rhetoric. Geometrical language was transferred from mathematics to other forms of discourses, which would then gain in clarity. Indeed, geometry was regarded as following a logical order enabling the mind to understand the transition from one argument to another. By obeying the rules of logic, geometry was supposed to be a clear and persuasive form of language free from the risks of misunderstanding. Meiner quotes Philippe Du Bois who advocated the use of 'l'ordre géométrique' for these very reasons and defined it as

> [. . .] l'ordre de la raison qui veut que l'on commence par des choses, ou connues, d'elles-mêmes, comme les premiers principes, ou déjà prouvées, ou reçues et supposées par ceux à qui l'on parle; et que de-là on passe aux conséquences qui en naissent, et qui étant une fois admises, deviennent à leur tour des principes, d'où l'on tire de nouvelles conséquences, qui tiennent aux premiers comme les autres, mais par des liaisons plus éloignées, et qu'on ne saurait faire sentir, qu'en passant par tout ce qui est entre deux. Cet ordre est appelé géométrique parce que les géomètres l'observent inviolablement, mais il ne leur est pas particulier. Tous ceux qui veulent parler raisonnablement le suivent comme eux, parce qu'il n'y a que celui-là qui puisse donner des idées justes et précises, ni produire une pleine et entière conviction. Aussi a-t-il été observé par tous ceux que l'on regarde comme les maîtres de l'éloquence.[27]

Diderot seems to have kept in mind the advice to introduce the precision and logical rigour of geometry in rhetoric. In *Jacques le fataliste*, the narrator uses geometry as a language supposedly more precise than normal discourse:

> Ce qui reste de tabac le soir dans ma tabatière est en raison directe de l'amusement, ou inverse de l'ennui de ma journée. Je vous supplie, Lecteur, de vous familiariser avec cette manière de dire empruntée de la géométrie, parce que je la trouve précise et que je m'en servirai souvent. (*JF*, p. 687)

Contrary to his warnings, the narrator uses geometry as language only one more time:

> Ici Jacques fit halte à son récit et donna une nouvelle atteinte à sa gourde. Les atteintes étaient d'autant plus fréquentes que les distances étaient courtes, ou comme disent les géomètres, en raison inverse des distances. Il était si précis dans ses mesures, que pleine en partant, elle était toujours exactement vide en arrivant. Messieurs des ponts et chaussées en auraient fait un excellent odomètre, et chaque atteinte avait communément sa raison suffisante. (*JF*, p. 877)

The precision geometry brings to language is not, however, followed by a greater clarity for the reader. On the contrary, it obscures the narrator's discourse. Meiner alludes to the attractions geometry had for certain rhetoricians, only to study the reasons why others departed from it. By solely relying on reason and logic and only appealing to the auditor's intellect, this form of rhetoric integrating geometry was regarded as having fallen into the very flaws it wanted to avoid. The two excerpts quoted above illustrate how the desire for exact precision makes geometrical language more abstruse.

In *Tristram Shandy*, geometry is integrated in discourse in a different way to *Jacques le fataliste*. The characters and the narrator do not apply its logical exactness to clarify their language. They prefer to use geometrical figures as a substitute for rhetorical tropes. In one instance, geometry serves to describe the construction of a sentence and argument 'jumping closely in one point, so like the two lines which form the salient angle of a raveline' (*TS*, III, xv, p. 168). The connection between geometry and language is even more tightened by the fact that some geometrical figures share the same appellation as rhetorical ones. Toby 'proceeded next to *Gallileo* and *Torricellius*, wherein, by certain geometrical rules, infallibly laid down, he found the precise path [of the canon ball] to be a PARABOLA, — or else an HYPERBOLA' (*TS*, II, iii, p. 80).[28] If we compare the geometrical definitions of the two words, it is difficult to visualise the difference between a parabola and a hyperbola, as both are curves. This is an instance where geometry actually obscures meaning rather than making it more visible.

If we return to *Les Mutations de la clarté*, Meiner opposes the 'clair-distinct cartésien' which relies on logical rigour and appeals to the audience's intellect, to 'le clair-confus des idées sensibles, qui échappe à la systématicité déductive géométrique'.[29] In rhetoric, this 'clair-confus' prefers to engage with the audience's imagination and sensibility by employing tropes. These tropes can never reach the precision of the precise and abstract words used by 'clair-distinct' rhetoric. Yet, they are more striking and make the discourse easier to understand:

> La vivacité de la pensée n'a parfois pas de nom mais au lieu de rendre le discours obscur, ce déficit sémiotique est l'occasion de mettre en marche une autre dimension de la langue, celle du langage imagé qui ne dit pas mais qui fait voir la vivacité pour que le lecteur en comprenne l'idée.[30]

Tristram points to the 'clair-confus' of the figurative use of the word 'square'. He marvels at 'the great *Square*' of Calais, but adds

> [...] not that it is properly a square, — because 'tis forty feet longer from east to west, than from north to south; so that the French in general have more reason on their side in calling them *Places* than *Squares*, which strictly speaking, to be sure they are not. (*TS*, VII, v, p. 436)

Geometrically, the Calais *place* is not strictly speaking a square. Yet Tristram has chosen to translate *place* by 'square'. The geometric and rhetorical figure 'square' conveys to the reader's mind the function of the *place* in the city. The precise measurement of the *place* adds very little to the description. Its purpose lies not in spatial representation, but in a reflection on language. It draws the reader's attention to the 'déficit sémiotique' of figurative speech mentioned by Meiner.

If we compare Tristram's use of geometrical figures to Toby's, we notice that the nephew's 'square' is perfectly comprehensible, whereas the uncle fails to be understood by both himself and his interlocutors. This may be explained by the fact that Tristram uses the geometrical figure of the square as a rhetorical figure. On the other hand, Toby is solely interested in the geometrical figure exactly describing the trajectory of the cannon ball. Unlike Tristram, he does not allow for the 'déficit sémiotique' which a rhetorical figure would inevitably introduce. If we made a rough classification, Tristram's square would belong to the 'clair-confus', and Toby's hyperbola and parabola to the 'clair-distinct'.

Following Meiner's argument, the 'clair-confus' rhetoric employs figurative speech so that the audience may visualise ideas through their imagination. Tristram pushes this a step further as he uses geometry so that the narrative progression may be visualised. The narrative line is taken literally and for the first five volumes is represented through conceptual geometry, in the sense that this representation is intuitive and not constructed on precise measurements as in Euclidian geometry. We still find a certain rigour as this line shows the progression of volume V from A, 'the trip to *Navarre*', to 'the intended curve B, which is the short airing when I was there with the Lady *Baussiere* and her page', to c c c c c 'nothing but parentheses', to D. Yet these conceptual lines are striving for the 'excellency' of the straight line 'drawn as straight as I could draw it, by a writing-master's ruler, (borrowed for that purpose) turning neither to the right hand or to the left' (*TS*, VI, xl, p. 425–26). However, Tristram's choice of the straight line as the model for his narrative contradicts his satire on critics who judge of the aesthetic quality of a literary work by geometry.

> [. . .] their heads, Sir, are stuck so full of rules and compasses, and have that eternal propensity to apply them upon all occasions, that a work of genius had better go to the devil at once, than stand to be prick'd and tortur'd to death by 'em.
> [. . .] And what of this new book the whole world makes such a rout about? — oh! 'tis out of all plumb, my Lord, — quite an irregular thing! — not one of the angles at the four corners was a right angle. — I had my rule and compasses, &c. my Lord, in my pocket. — Excellent critic! (*TS*, III, xii, p. 163, 164)

The narrator is not the only one desirous to provide an outside reconstruction in order to make his descriptions more comprehensible. The characters themselves feel the need to reassemble topographies in their entirety. In the chapter of *L'Espace romanesque* consecrated to *Tristram Shandy*, Weisgerber remarks on the uncanny obsession with precise measurements. This obsession noticeably has a hold on Tristram and his father Walter, but culminates with Toby and his mathematical calculations concerning the impact of the projectile responsible for the wound on his groin.

> No sooner was my uncle *Toby* satisfied which road the cannon-ball did not go, but he was insensibly led on, and resolved in his mind to enquire and find out which road the ball did go: For which purpose he was obliged to set off afresh with old *Maltus*, and studied him devoutly. — He proceeded next to *Gallileo* and *Torricellius*, wherein, by certain geometrical rules, infallibly laid down, he found the precise path to be a PARABOLA, — or else an HYPERBOLA, — and that the parameter, or *latus rectum*, of the conic section of the said path, was to the quantity and amplitude in a direct *ratio*, as the whole line to the sine of double the angle of incidence, form'd by the breech upon an horizontal plane; — and that the semi-parameter, — stop! my dear uncle *Toby*, — stop! — go not one foot further into this thorny and bewilder'd track, — intricate are the steps! intricate are the mases of this labyrinth! (*TS*, II, iii, p. 80)

Toby's obsession with measurements is emphasised through the quickening of rhythm and the use of very technical vocabulary. This desire to circumscribe the outside world into measurements ill conceals Toby's anxiety to make sense of what happened to him on the battlefield in Flanders. Trapped in the confusion of the engagement, Toby was unable to form an outside perspective of the event since he was involved in it. The man-made labyrinths, such as mazes and fortifications, first stand as a manifestation of man's desire to control his surroundings but in the end produce the opposite effect. They reverse into the recognition of the failure to master the outside world. Returning to Bakhtin, internal errancy could correspond to the characters' fragmentary and incomplete perception of their existence. Toby's maps, calculations and miniature model of the conflict on his bowling green may be seen as a retrospective attempt to form an outside reconstruction. Shifting his position from an insider to that of a spectator, outsideness would transform Toby's perspective from fragmentary and incomplete to a comprehensive overall view of the battle.

Jacques's fatalism may sometimes take a similar turn to Toby's maps. To explain fate, Jacques refers to the commonplace spatial representation of the path:

> Il croyait qu'un homme s'acheminait aussi nécessairement à la gloire ou à l'ignominie qu'une boule qui aurait la conscience d'elle-même suit la pente d'une montagne, et que si l'acheminement des causes et des effets qui forment la vie d'un homme depuis le premier instant de sa naissance jusqu'à son dernier soupir nous était connu, nous resterions convaincus qu'il n'a fait que ce qu'il était nécessaire de faire. (*JF*, pp. 802–03)

This sentence is built on the parallel between a ball and an individual. A man's destiny may only be understood by looking at the path drawn by all the events from his birth to his death. From the individual's own perspective, this path is invisible. Jacques implies that, similarly, the route taken by the ball may at first seem completely random. But as soon as the attention moves from the ball in question to an overall view of the mountain, one observes the inclination and accidents of the terrain determining the itinerary of the object. As he considers the individual's biography, it seems as though Jacques is applying the principle of outsideness with a fatalistic twist.

In 'Author and Hero in Aesthetic Activity', Bakhtin mentions that a biography may be given a specific meaning. He thus distinguishes between classical and romantic character construction.[31] The difference between these two constructions roughly lies in superimposition of fatalism in the first case, free will in the second. I will concentrate on the classical construction, which is the most relevant to our quotation. It implies that a biography is given a fatalistic signification and is read as the accomplishment of an individual's destiny. Because he cannot perform an outside reconstruction upon himself, the individual is unaware of the workings of fate. Jacques uses the heavens where everything is written as a sort of outside substitute. He regularly confesses his ignorance as to the whys and wherefores of various events. As one of the main characters, Jacques is obviously unable to provide an outside perspective on what is happening in the novel. This does not prevent him from wishing for such a perspective, even though he cannot himself have access to it. To a certain extent, Jacques's belief in fate corresponds to his trust that there does exist an outside view completing his existence and giving sense to it as a whole. However, the reader cannot share Jacques's trustfulness, as such an outside reconstruction is nowhere to be found in the novel.

Toby's maps, Tristram's travel guides and Jacques's fatalism attempt to provide, each in their own way, an outside format. This desire to contain the outside world in a panoramic perspective corresponds to the characters' struggle to comprehend events befalling them. As Weisgerber underlines, the various maps, models and charts in *Tristram Shandy* 'renferment l'univers dans une chambre, réduisent la nature selon des méthodes scientifiques et, par un tracé précis, montrent plus directement et objectivement que les mots'.[32] Maps do provide the characters with an outside perspective enabling them to make sense of certain situations, but not all. Moreover, the reader does not have access to those maps, despite Tristram's assurances that they will be inserted at the end of the book. Unlike the reader, Toby and Tristram enjoy the outside perspective offered by maps. Even though this vantage point is restricted to the battle of Namur and the surroundings of Shandy Hall, it remains an advantage. Indeed the reader finds himself in the uncomfortable position of knowing even less than the characters. Tristram attempts to transcribe those maps by using geometrical language. But as Meiner remarks, the precision brought by geometrical rigour in language may obscure the idea being expressed.

In both *Tristram Shandy* and *Jacques le fataliste*, geometry is turned into ridicule as its pretence to bring clarity and attain truth by precision (often exaggerated by Diderot, and most of all by Sterne) fails and only leads to greater obscurity. In *Jacques le fataliste* (p. 732), the only character depicted with geometrical instruments is the twisted-minded, nonsensical Gousse. Diderot also uses geometrical instruments in the 'allée des marronniers' where he satirises the philosophers: 'On y voit tracés sur le sable des cercles, des triangles et d'autres figures de mathématiques'.[33] The failings of geometry are particularly visible in the discrepancies between geometrical representations of reality and reality itself. The 'six or seven miles riding' to reach the midwife are in practice 'almost equal to fourteen', 'the country thereabouts being nothing but deep clay' (*TS*, I, vii, p. 12). The 'precise angle of 85 degrees and a half to a mathematical exactness' maintained by Trim when reading the sermon, would in practice make people 'fall upon their noses' (*TS*, II, xvii, pp. 107–08).

And yet, the very failings of geometry are significant. This is what the article 'géométrie' of the *Encyclopédie* suggests:

> [. . .] la Géométrie envisage donc les corps dans un état d'abstraction où ils ne sont pas réellement; les vérités qu'elle découvre & qu'elle démontre sur les corps, sont donc des vérités de pure abstraction, des vérités hypothétiques; mais ces vérités n'en sont pas moins utiles.

Geometry fails as soon as a character attempts to use it to represent his thoughts as through a Bakhtinian outside perspective. A systematic instrument is inadequate to encase the meanderings of the mind. However, the shortfalls of geometry for the characters are noteworthy to the reader. Geometry as a tool for description in Sterne's and Diderot's novels functions in the same way as the description of Obadiah's knots, which is made so complicated by the profusion of detail that it is impossible for the reader to follow. But this is exactly why the description is successful. The complexity and inextricability of Obadiah's knots is emphasised by the intricacy of the description. As in the second chapter, the reader witnesses once again the failures of illustration, here taking the form of spatial representation, to make ideas comprehensible. However, these illustrations do succeed in rendering the characters' intellectual meanderings and perplexities. In this sense, the illustrations do perfectly correspond to the ideas they are representing, whether through geometry or through more conventional methods. In other words, the external projection of the characters' minds does not actually help to clarify their thoughts. Instead, it describes their mental confusion.

Description of Characters

The question of description in *Tristram Shandy* and *Jacques le fataliste* has often been studied in terms of realism. Comparing Sterne's and Diderot's depiction of characters, Alice Fredman concludes that '[despite] the differences in their ultimate points of view, both writers frequently use similar means for portraying character. Their method, as indicated by their treatment of realism, is generally one of indirection'.[34] Fredman develops her opposition between Sterne's eccentric Shandeism and Diderot's interest in human nature and society (what Fredman refers to as 'their ultimate points of view').[35] She does not, however, give any precision about realism and how it applies to Sterne's and Diderot's works, other than a brief comment on the French philosopher's admiration for 'Richardson's realistic details' expressed in the *Eloge de Richardson*.[36] The reader is expecting from the author an 'aesthetic consummation' of the characters (to use Bakhtin's terminology). Description constitutes the most obvious starting point to this process. However, the nature of the characters' descriptions in *Jacques le fataliste* and *Tristram Shandy* does not allow a completing perspective.

In normal circumstances, the reader would probably not be really concerned with the physical appearance of the characters or the depiction of their environment. Due to the fact that the narrative structure in our two novels offers no firm ground and is extremely disorientating, the reader feels more acutely the need to find reference points to help him navigate through the texts. Diderot and Sterne intentionally do not provide such benchmarks; and by creating descriptions as fragmentary and incomplete as the philosophical debates, they succeed in making the aesthetic form of their works coincide with the content.

It is easy to understand why critics were tempted to view Diderot's descriptions in terms of realism. *Les Deux Amis de Bourbonne* ends on aesthetical considerations concerning what Diderot calls *le conte historique*. If an author of such *contes* wishes to create the illusion of reality, Diderot advises him to pay attention to minutiae:

> [. . .] il parsèmera son récit de petites circonstances si liées à la chose, de traits si simples, si naturels, et toutefois si difficiles à imaginer, que vous serez forcé de vous dire en vous-même: Ma foi, cela est vrai; on n'invente pas ces choses-là.[37]

Illustrating his advice by a concrete example, Diderot looks back into his experience as an art critic to differentiate between an ideal portrait and a realistic one:

> Mais que l'artiste me fasse apercevoir au front de cette tête une cicatrice légère, une verrue à l'une de ses tempes, une coupure imperceptible à la lèvre inférieure, et d'idéale qu'elle était, à l'instant la tête devient un portrait; une marque de petite vérole au coin de l'œil ou à côté du nez, et ce visage de femme n'est plus celui de Vénus; c'est le portrait de quelqu'une de mes voisines.[38]

Diderot does not talk of realism, in this context anachronistic, but of verisimilitude. A writer must *faire vrai*. This principle is put into practice in *Jacques le fataliste* through the brief description the landlady gives of Jacques's captain: 'un grand homme, bien fait, un peu sec, l'air noble et sévère, le jarret bien tendu, deux petits points rouges à la tempe droite' (*JF*, p. 759). The similarity of this passage with *Les Deux Amis de Bourbonne* is striking. Diderot applies the same scrupulous attention to detail and has replaced the wart on the temple by two small red blemishes.

Smietanski has devoted one of his works to the study of realism in *Jacques le fataliste*. Aware of the anachronism of the term, Smietanski customizes realism, as it were, to adapt it to his object of study.[39] By attempting to adapt a nineteenth-century term to an eighteenth-century novel, Smietanski has redefined realism in such an indiscriminate way that it could include the vast majority of works of art. I am not interested in pursuing the discussion on whether or not *Tristram Shandy* and *Jacques le fataliste* can be called realist novels. But it is worth noticing that Smietanski regards Diderot's descriptions of characters and surroundings as not realist. Smietanski has already cleared the ground by producing a thorough factual account of descriptions in *Jacques le fataliste*.[40] We reach however very different conclusions.

The obvious starting point of a study of description is to try to picture the physical appearance of the characters. This proves uncommonly difficult in the case of Diderot's and Sterne's novels. As Smietanski complains of *Jacques le fataliste*, information concerning the characters' looks is scarce and scattered:

> [...] il faut scruter les quelque trois cent quatre-vingts pages du livre pour parvenir à rassembler ces miettes éparses. Jamais un portrait en règle, jamais une description du personnage. A nous encore de l'imaginer à notre guise, à partir de faibles éléments.[41]

The same may be said of *Tristram Shandy*. We learn that Tristram 'never could bear cold weather', that he caught 'an asthma' by 'scating against the wind in *Flanders*' (*TS*, I, v, p. 10). His nose has been 'squeez'd' 'flat to [his] face' (*TS*, I, xv, p. 38), and he has 'two spider legs' (*TS*, VII, i, p. 432). Tristram tells us that Walter 'was a little phthisical' (*TS*, III, xxiv, p. 190). As for Toby's physical aspect, it is never actually described. We know only about his wound in the groin. Tristram offers a more detailed description of minor characters such as the midwife (*TS*, I, vii, p. 12) and Dr Slop who is said to have 'lost his teeth' and 'the nails of his fingers and thumbs' are 'cut close' (*TS*, III, x, p. 151). But those details are only mentioned to explain why a knife had to be used to open the bag containing his obstetrical instruments. And we may add that short nails and the absence of teeth are very little to work on for the reader to picture Dr Slop.

Tristram's attention seems to be centred more on the familiar objects surrounding the characters than on the characters themselves. His father and uncle are usually represented smoking their pipes. We are also provided with some information about their clothing. Tristram tells us of his uncle's 'new pair of black-plush-breeches' (*TS*, I, xxi, p. 56), his 'laced cloaths' with 'blue and gold' 'at the sleeves', his 'white ramallie-wig', his 'thin scarlet breeches' and his 'red plush ones' (*TS*, VIII, xxviii, pp. 528, 529). Toby's old-fashioned and tattered clothing as he is about to propose to Widow Wadman is amply described in volume IX, chapter ii. Thanks to Susannah, the reader is given a sample of the contents of Tristram's mother's wardrobe: 'the green satin night-gown', 'her red damask, — her orange-tawny, — her white and yellow lutestrings, — her brown taffata, — her bone-laced caps, her bed-gowns, and comfortable under-petticoats' (*TS*, V, vii, p. 325). But this is a description of a wardrobe. At no point is Elizabeth actually described wearing any of these. The lack of description concerning the majority of the intradiegetic characters becomes even more noticeable when compared to what we find in secondary stories. Slawkenbergius's tale opens on a very conventional description:

> It was one cool refreshing evening, at the close of a very sultry day, in the latter end of the month of *August*, when a stranger, mounted upon a dark mule, with a small cloak-bag behind him, containing a few shirts, a pair of shoes, and a crimson-sattin pair of breeches, entered the town of *Strasburg*. (*TS*, IV, Slawkenbergius's tale, p. 221).

In one short paragraph, Tristram has condensed more information about Diego and his surroundings than the first four volumes provide about his father Walter and Shandy Hall.

We encounter the same refusal to provide any sufficient descriptions in Diderot's novel. From the little information he has, Smietanski reconstructs Jacques's outside appearance: 'Jacques est grand, sec, vigoureux et il boite'.[42] Not only is this an extremely meagre and frustrating description, it is also a rewriting of the text: originally, this rare information is disseminated across the novel. We may also notice that the adjective 'sec' used to describe the captain serves to qualify Jacques as well. By sharing a trait with another character, Jacques becomes even less distinguishable from the others.

The narrator gives us a few indications concerning Jacques's clothing. But these are so banal that instead of helping him stand out they actually make him even more common: he sleeps in his shirt and wears a handkerchief around his neck when he has a sore throat. Jacques's only distinctive garment is 'son énorme chapeau': 'les ailes de ce chapeau relevées lui plaçaient le visage à peu près au milieu du corps, rabattues, à peine voyait-il à dix pas devant lui, ce qui lui avait donné l'habitude de porter le nez au vent' (*JF*, p. 868).[43] This hat would have provided the reader with a reason why the narrator has not given a proper description of his hero. But the mention of the hat comes too late in the novel for the absence of a description not to be conspicuous. As for Jacques's master, the narrator gives us no information at all concerning his physical appearance. Objects, rather than bodily features, seem best to characterise the characters. Throughout the novel, the master is seen opening his snuffbox and looking at his pocket watch, whilst Jacques regularly consults his flask.

The lack of description for the two main characters of Diderot's novel makes Jacques and his master conspicuous. But most secondary characters fare hardly better. The doctor Jacques and his master first encounter is presented as '[une] espèce de paysan' and the peasant girl riding behind is only said to be 'belle sous le linge' (*JF*, pp. 671 & 672). The adjective 'sinistre' serves to qualify the entire inn Jacques and his master first rest at: 'L'hôte, l'hôtesse, les enfants, les valets, tout avait l'air sinistre' (p. 674). Mme de La Pommeraye is simply described as 'une veuve qui avait des moeurs, de la naissance, de la fortune et de la hauteur' (p. 748), but we know nothing about the appearance of the Marquis des Arcis, of Desglands, of the landlord of the Grand-Cerf, of the Chevalier de Saint-Ouin, of M. de Guerchy or of the captain's friend. No description whatsoever is given of the peasant family who offered their hospitality to the wounded Jacques, nor of the surgeon and his wife who healed him. Nothing is said either about Jacques's family: his brother Jean, his father, his grandparents, his godfather, Bigre fils or Justine. Jacques does not mention Marguerite's and Suzanne's physical attractions.

Concerning the three main love stories of the novel, we are provided with a bit more information. Denise is '[une] grande brune de dix-huit ans, faite au tour, grands yeux noirs, petite bouche vermeille, beaux bras, jolies mains' (p. 727). Mlle Duquênoi is 'jeune, belle et bien élevée' (p. 760), and 'Agathe est jeune, vive, blanche, grasse, potelée, ce sont les chairs les plus fermes [. . .] et la peau la plus douce' (p. 857). None of these descriptions are very individualising. The details focused on (hands, lips, eyes, skin) are the classical traits to represent a pretty woman and can be used interchangeably. The same applies to the description of Janatone and Nannette (*TS*, VII, ix & xliii), two young French women who caught Tristram's eye in the course of his travels.

The use of such blank adjectives is pushed to an extreme in *Tristram Shandy* with the description of widow Wadman. Tristram affirms that never did the reader 'behold [. . .] any thing in this world, more concupiscible than widow *Wadman*'.

> To conceive this right, — call for pen and ink — here's paper ready to your hand. — Sit down, Sir, paint her to your own mind — as like your mistress as you can — as unlike your wife as your conscience will let you — 'tis all one to me — please put your own fancy in it. (*TS*, VI, xxxviii, p. 422)

And indeed the narrator leaves us with the famous blank page to fill with our own idea of widow Wadman. 'Was ever any thing in Nature so sweet! — so exquisite!' (*TS*, VI, xxxviii, p. 424). The blank page sends the reader back to the blankness of the subjective adjectives 'concupiscible', 'sweet', and 'exquisite'. Neither refers to anything precise which would enable us to recognise Wadman by a specific physical trait, like the captain's blemishes. Those adjectives are blanks for the reader to fill with his 'own fancy'.

I concur with Smietanski's comment that

> Diderot pousse la généralisation du portrait jusqu'au type, c'est-à-dire jusqu'à la disparition totale des traits individuels au profit de lignes et de formes stéréotypées, traditionnellement prêtées à une catégorie d'individus dont l'allure, la mise évoquent le métier ou la fonction [. . .].[44]

Adjectives such as 'beau' and 'joli' only convey subjective impressions and do not give us any precise indication as to what the person looks like. The same problem occurs with Père Ange, described as having 'de beaux yeux, un beau visage, un bras et des mains à modeler' (*JF*, p. 699). As Smietanski remarks, 'il s'agit, en réalité, de croquis assez rapides, de simples esquisses'.[45] The narrator does not provide complete descriptions, but only light sketches, which typify the characters instead of singularising them.

Smietanski does not include in these the portrayal of the landlady and Hudson, which he considers as 'nets, développés', rendering in the novel 'un relief assez singulier':[46]

> L'hôtesse n'était pas de la première jeunesse; c'était une femme grande et replète, ingambe, de bonne mine, pleine d'embonpoint, la bouche un peu grande, mais de belles dents, des joues larges, des yeux à fleur de tête, le front carré, la plus belle peau, la physionomie ouverte, vive et gaie, une poitrine à s'y rouler pendant deux jours, des bras un peu forts, mais les mains superbes, des mains à peindre ou à modeler. (*JF*, p. 758)

The description of the landlady is, with that of Richard (see *JF*, p. 800) and Hudson (*JF*, p. 802), one of the most detailed of the novel. However, some of the adjectives are too impressionistic to be precise. 'Belle' and 'superbe' act as convenient blanks in which the reader can place whatever he sees fit. As for the description of the captain, we start by a very brief and generalised remark on the character's whole appearance. The narrator's gaze then focuses on very specific parts of the body, examined individually and detached as it were from the rest of the figure. The captain stands out from the other characters by the two red blemishes on his right temple.

The landlady should have been noticeable by the plastic beauty of her hands, if it had not been a feature she shared with Denise and the Père Ange. The comment 'des mains à peindre ou à modeler' functions in the same way (though less strikingly) as Sterne's blank page. Sterne's and Diderot's narrators invite the reader to paint or sculpt a character so as to correct the deficiencies of the description. Richard and Hudson are two exceptions. They are fully individualised and given a complete description. But this is motivated by the fact that the innocence and ingenuousness of Richard, made manifest by his demeanour, complement Hudson's deceptive charming looks.

The description of an individual's character may be perceived as more telling than that of his physical aspect. Tristram offers careful psychological portraits of the main characters. But, just as for the physical descriptions, most of these are scattered throughout the novel. In the first few pages of the book, Tristram presents his father, 'who was originally a *Turky* merchant, but had left off business for some years, in order to retire to, and die upon, his paternal estate in the county of —' as 'one of the most regular men in every thing he did, whether 'twas matter of business, or matter of amusement, that ever lived' (*TS*, I, iv, p. 9). He is later described as 'a gentleman of many virtues' but with 'a strong spice' 'in his temper' which can be called either 'perseverance' or 'obstinacy' depending on the circumstance (*TS*, I, xvii, p. 41). The portrait of Walter continues in chapter xix, where his qualities as an orator are described. The narrator does not condense Walter's moral portrait into a particular chapter. He disseminates it throughout the novel.

The same may be said, though to a lesser degree, of Toby's portrait. The narrator brings Toby on stage, waiting with Walter, for the safe delivery of baby Tristram. 'But to enter rightly into my uncle *Toby*'s sentiments upon this matter, you must be made to enter first a little into his character, the out-lines of which I shall just give you' (*TS*, I, xxi, p. 56). Despite Tristram's assurance that the portrait of his uncle will immediately follow, he falls into digressions on the effect of the climate upon the temperament, and on the cycle of war and peace, before coming back to his subject: 'But I forget my uncle *Toby*, whom all this while we have left knocking the ashes out of his tobacco pipe'.

> His humour was of that particular species, which does honour to our atmosphere; and I should have made no scruple of ranking him amongst one of the first-rate productions of it, had not there appear'd too many strong lines in it of a family-likeness, which shewed that he derived the singularity of his temper more from blood, than either wind or water [. . .]. (*TS*, I, xxi, p. 58)

We notice that Tristram does not actually say what Toby's humour consists of; he only speculates on its origin. This is followed by still more digressions until Tristram returns to Toby,

> [. . .] a gentleman, who, with the virtues which usually constitute the character of a man of honour and rectitude, — possessed one in a very eminent degree, which is seldom or never put into the catalogue; and that was a most extream and unparallel'd modesty of nature [. . .]. (*TS*, I, xxi, p. 59)

As we are told a few paragraphs later, Toby's modesty originates from a battle wound. This particular trait has nothing to do with Toby's share of the family humour mentioned previously. Tristram deviates in his moral portrait: he starts mentioning a feature, then digresses, then mentions another one. And as in the case of Toby's humour, Tristram sometimes forgets about a characteristic he has touched upon, and consequently leaves the description incomplete. The above quotation also provides a good example of how the narrator delays the key information the reader is waiting for. Here, Tristram focuses on the exceptionality of the trait and so delays having to say what that trait actually is.

What truly interests Tristram is Walter's systematic thinking, Toby's obsession with anything military, Yorick's outspokenness, Trim's love of talking. In Tristram's view, to describe a man's hobby-horse is the best way to describe the man himself. Tristram explicitly says that he has drawn his 'uncle *Toby*'s character from his HOBBY-HORSE' (*TS*, I, xxiii, p. 67). He justifies this mode of description by arguing that 'if you are able to give but a clear description of the nature of the one [the hobby-horse], you may form a pretty exact notion of the genius and character of the other' (*TS*, I, xxiv, p. 67).[47] Walter and Toby are two of the most important characters in Sterne's novel. Their moral portraits are the most extensive, albeit disseminated, fragmented and incomplete. Tristram's own portrait constitutes an extreme version of this. Nowhere does he provide a self-portrait *per se*; there are no chapters dedicated to the moral portrait of the autobiographer. The whole novel fulfils that function as it disseminates Tristram's particularities throughout the nine volumes, left for the reader to gather. Nothing is said of Elizabeth, Tristram's mother. The particularity of her character is to be completely bland, and so representative of the female members of the Shandy family who 'had no character at all' (*TS*, I, xxi, p. 58). Tristram does not mention either the moral characters of Susannah, Obadiah, and many others. Of his brother Bobby, we only know that he was the '*first* child, — coming into the world with his head *foremost*' and turned 'out afterwards a lad of wonderful slow parts' (*TS*, II, xix, p. 136).

In comparison to *Tristram Shandy*, the scarcity of moral portraits in *Jacques le fataliste* is striking.[48] While Jacques has gone in search of the watch and purse, the narrator takes the opportunity to acquaint the reader with the master:

> Il a peu d'idées dans la tête; s'il lui arrive de dire quelque chose de sensé, c'est de réminiscence ou d'inspiration. Il a des yeux comme vous et moi, mais on ne sait la plupart du temps s'il regarde. Il ne dort pas, il ne veille pas non plus; il se laisse exister, c'est sa fonction habituelle. (*JF*, p. 686)

Though amusing, this description of the master is rather unsatisfying as it reduces the master to the basic human functions. There are no details provided to singularise him as he is only characterised by his commonness. There is but one true portrait, and it appears in a secondary story told by the master. The character, who is not even named but identified as 'une veuve charmante' (*JF*, p. 861), has no role in the novel. Her only connection to it is by her relationship with Desglands, a minor character. Moreover, the portrait contains an incongruous detail that Jacques does not identify, and which should arouse the reader's suspicions: the charming widow is mourned by her husband.[49] This portrait has very little success with Jacques, and his master admits that it is 'long et ennuyeux'.

> JACQUES: [. . .] plus de portraits, mon maître; je hais les portraits à la mort.
> LE MAÎTRE: Et pourquoi haïssez-vous les portraits ?

JACQUES: C'est qu'ils ressemblent si peu, que si par hasard on vient à rencontrer les originaux, on ne les reconnaît pas. Racontez-moi les faits, rendez-moi fidèlement les propos, et je saurai bientôt à quel homme j'ai affaire. Un mot, un geste m'en ont quelquefois plus appris que le bavardage de toute une ville. (*JF*, p. 863)

It seems that Jacques's criticism concerns the fact that portraits fix the characters in a type instead of focusing on the more subtle details and inner contradictions, which would singularise them as individuals. By preferring 'un mot, un geste', Jacques favours the fleeting over the static for both moral and physical portraits.[50]

Tristram shares Jacques's preference for gestures to describe his characters: 'Attitudes are nothing, madam, — 'tis the transition from one attitude to another' (*TS*, IV, vi, p. 249). Like Jacques, Tristram believes that a momentary position is more telling than a general description. From the beginning of the novel, he has carefully noted the body language of his characters when strongly reacting to a specific event, either minor or important. This may be illustrated by the description of Walter when he learns that his newborn son's nose has been crushed 'as flat as a pancake to his face' (*TS*, III, xxvii, p. 193):

> The palm of his right hand, as he fell upon the bed, receiving his forehead, and covering the greatest part of both his eyes, gently sunk down with his head (his elbow giving way backwards) till his nose touch'd the quilt; — his left arm hung insensible over the side of the bed, his knuckles reclining upon the handle of the chamber pot, which peep'd out beyond the valance, — his right leg (his left being drawn up towards his body) hung half over the side of the bed, the edge of it pressing upon his shin-bone. (*TS*, III, xxix, p. 194)

Tristram justifies the meticulousness of the details by affirming that they are necessary to understand the extent of Walter's sorrow. But this description does not enable the reader 'to take the picture of [Walter] in at one view' (*TS*, II, xvii, p. 107). The focus of the description shifts from one specific part of the body, to another. Tristram's fastidiousness becomes counterproductive as the details obscure the characters instead of making them visible. The result is an impression of fragmentation and indistinctness. As in the description already mentioned of Trim about to read the sermon, the reader cannot perceive Walter as a whole, only as a 'right leg' or a 'left arm'. This excerpt is one of the most striking and complete examples of Tristram's mode of description of a character's posture.

This pattern is repeated throughout the novel, but usually reduced to one or two lines. Thus Toby is described 'taking his pipe from his mouth, and striking the head of it two or three times upon the nail of his left thumb' (*TS*, I, xxi, p. 56). If Tristram provides painstaking precision to the description of his protagonists' postures and moral characters, he is however conspicuously silent when it comes to their — or even his own — general physical aspect. The little information supplied has been dropped incidentally and left for the reader to garner along the way.

Smietanski concludes by saying that 'si Diderot n'ignore pas complètement la mise, il ne procède pas à des descriptions. Il ne donne que de rapides indications qui ont une valeur affective ou explicative plutôt que plastique ou pittoresque'.[51] Smietanski interprets this as Diderot not having been able to 's'être complètement affranchi de l'esthétique classique'.[52] Indeed, the presence of classical aesthetics may be found for instance in Diderot's practice of hyperbolic understatement, especially when it comes to the description of the feminine characters of *Jacques le fataliste*. Denise, Mlle Duquênoi and Agathe's function in the story is due to their beauty. Other than knowing that they are all three physically attractive, there is no need for any further characterisation. However, hyperbolic understatement cannot alone explain the dearth of description of the two heroes of the novel. To know that Jacques is tall, spare, vigorous and limps, does not add much to our understanding of him. As for his master, nothing at all is said about him. Classical aesthetics seem an unsatisfactory explanation for the paucity of description, at least in these two cases.

Smietanski is of particular interest to me in that he provides an example justifying my argument. Like any reader, Smietanski is frustrated by the scarcity of descriptions and deplores that the little we have is fragmentary and disseminated throughout the novel. The nature of description in *Jacques le fataliste* disrupts and perturbs the reader's representation of the characters. He consequently tries to remedy this by meticulously collecting the scattered descriptions and reuniting them for each character in the first part of his study. This constitutes a rewriting of the text, for Diderot according to all evidence has deliberately chosen not to provide a complete portrait of his protagonists. In *Le Réalisme dans* Jacques le Fataliste, Smietanski supplies the outside perspective, absent from the novel. By rewriting the descriptions, he tries to act as the author's proxy so as to provide himself the aesthetic completion he feels is missing.

Smietanski's frustration and desire to provide an outside perspective is shared by many readers of *Tristram Shandy* where the descriptions are just as fragmentary, scarce and scattered as in Diderot's novel. An outside perspective would consummate '[all of the cognitive-ethical determinations and values of the hero] in the form of a unitary and unique whole that is a concrete, intuitable whole, but also a whole of meaning'.[53] The characters desire to gain access to this 'whole of meaning' and so attempt to gain an outside view, though without much success. The reader is also made to feel the difficulty to grasp this 'whole of meaning' through the absence of outsideness in the descriptions.

Descriptions of Landscapes

Though Bakhtin seems to take only into account the author's relationship to the hero, I do not restrict the matter of outsideness to the description of the characters. The absence of outsideness equally affects spatial representations as descriptions of landscapes and surroundings are just as fragmentary and rare as those of the characters. Bakhtin's concept of outsideness may not be the only key to account for the particularities of the descriptions in Sterne's and Diderot's novels. Indeed, Smietanski offers an alternative by studying description in *Jacques le fataliste* in terms of realism. He considers spatial representations, which pose the same problem as the portrayal of the characters, also as a failing in realism and as bearing the mark of classical aesthetics.

Travel literature may offer another reason for the singularity of the description. The travel-book style is present in both novels. The intradiegetic (or principal) narrative of *Jacques le fataliste* is set on the road, whilst volume VII of *Tristram Shandy* focuses on the hero's Grand Tour. Details of the journey and descriptions of the landscapes and surroundings obviously form an essential part of travel literature, and follow conventions specific to the genre. Travel literature may be seen to bear an influence on spatial representations. However, travelling is fairly localised in the two novels and consequently is insufficient to account for the fragmentation and paucity of spatial descriptions, which are constant throughout the novels. Another inconsistency is that, in the passages that are set on the road or abroad, Sterne and Diderot will insert certain travel literature traits but also blatantly ignore others. So I return to Bakhtin's outsideness and explore how it may be applied to spatial descriptions in Sterne's and Diderot's novels.

Factual description is a common trait in travel literature, and more specifically in periegeses in which the author would act as guide and offer a survey of the various foreign places he has journeyed through.[54] This characteristic appears in the descriptions of *Tristram Shandy* and *Jacques le fataliste*, which seem to be very little encumbered with emotional input. Both narrators restrict themselves to factual information about the different places they travel through. Evaluating the cleanliness of the inns, the quality of the food, the warmth of the landlords' welcome, and the road taxes, are common features of travel literature, fond of such factual surveys:

> Ils s'arrêtèrent dans la plus misérable des auberges. On leur dressa deux lits de sangle dans une chambre formée de cloisons entrouvertes de tous les côtés. Ils demandèrent à souper. On leur apporta de l'eau de mare, du pain noir et du vin tourné. (*JF*, p. 674)

In *Jacques le fataliste*, the narrator is provided with many opportunities to indulge in that type of description, but he seems systematically to shun them. Waiting to be served at the inn of the Grand-Cerf, the landlady promises a feast:

'J'ai des poulets, des pigeons, un râble de lièvre excellent, des lapins, c'est le canton des bons lapins. Aimeriez-vous mieux un oiseau de rivière' (*JF*, p. 734). And for dessert, she asks her maid to bring 'des fruits, des biscuits, de la confiture' (*JF*, p. 735). The reader is anticipating a lavish description of Jacques and his master's dinner. But he is disappointed in this as the only details he is given are that the wine was good but the 'épinards étaient un peu salés' (*JF*, p. 736).

Anne F. Woodhouse recognises the attention to factual information as a general trait of eighteenth-century travel diaries.[55] To make the most of the didactic purpose of travelling, one was supposed to keep a detailed record of what was considered as typical of the country. Such a compilation led to what Woodhouse refers to as "uncontrolled eclecticism". Sterne reproduces the eclectic style of those travel diaries by having his narrator insert a whole series of random elements collected along the way. The most vivid sample of Tristram's method of 'writing-galloping' is to be found in the description of Paris seen from a coach. The description is as meandering as the streets of the city, jumping from one sight to the other: 'And prithee when do they light the lamps? What? — never in the summer months! — Ho! 'tis the time of sallads. — O rare! sallad and soup — soup and sallad — sallad and soup, *encore* —' (*TS*, VII, xvii, pp. 448–49). Arriving by coach in Paris, Tristram asks the driver various questions on the French capital, and lets his mind be taken over by the novelty of it all.

Jean-Michel Racault notices that, in travel literature, *mimesis* takes over from *diegesis*, description supplants action, which is unusual in the traditional novel configuration.[56] The type of description involved more often than not records what the senses, and especially the eye, perceive. Awareness of the weather, smells, and so forth, become more frequent. The narrator often wishes to convey as well as possible his experience as a traveller. Naturally, he will impart the sensuousness and immediacy of his first impressions by recording them as digressive fragments with no apparent structure, apart from that of his own itinerary.

At the beginning of this chapter, I have talked of the characters' mental errancies translated into spatial wandering. This feeling of wandering is communicated to the reader through the digressive style of both novels. The narrator in *Tristram Shandy* refers to his digressive mode as a 'backward and forward' movement. Even though this movement does not become a subject of conversation as in Sterne's novel, it may also be found in *Jacques le fataliste*. The most obvious example is that of Jacques who has to go back to the inn where he has forgotten his master's watch and money. This contretemps is particularly frustrating for the reader who has to follow Jacques retracing his steps when the story is only just underway. Stephen Soud more interestingly links the 'backward and forward' progression to the way one wanders in a labyrinth, thus corroborating the construction of the narrative as a maze.[57] The metadiegetic narratives are embedded and disseminated in the main story. This has as an effect the entangling of the different narrative levels and of the various chronotopes, which the reader can find hard to differentiate.[58] The reader tries to remedy this impression of wandering in exactly the same way as the characters do, that is to say by seeking the vantage point Bakhtin's outsideness would provide.

On his travels, Tristram seems to be engrossed in the collection of very precise, but also very random and useless information. However, the influence of travel literature can only explain the incomplete and fragmentary nature of a restricted part of the descriptions. Travelling is limited to volume VII, as most of *Tristram Shandy* takes place in Shandy Hall. The intradiegetic narrative of Diderot's novel is indeed set on the roads of France, but these are never described as particularly exotic to the characters. More importantly, the metadiegetic level in *Jacques le fataliste*, with its multitude of inserted stories, composes roughly half of the novel and is hardly concerned with travelling. Fragmentation and incompleteness pervade the entirety of spatial representations in Sterne's and Diderot's novels, and are not simply restricted to scenes of travelling. If Diderot did indeed include travel literature in *Jacques le fataliste*, he also focused on the representation of the less foreign, more familiar, trivial surroundings. The same may be said of Sterne. The interest of spatial representation is not limited to the seventh volume of *Tristram Shandy*, describing the protagonist's Grand Tour. It is also relevant to the eight remaining volumes set in Shandy Hall.

As travel literature reveals itself insufficient to account for the particularities of spatial representation, we must then turn back to Bakhtin and see if the concept of outsideness can shed any light on the descriptions of landscapes and surroundings, as it did for characters. Bakhtin has limited the use of outsideness to the characters' physical and biographical description. Yet it seems that the fragmentary and incomplete nature of the protagonists' description in *Jacques le fataliste* and *Tristram Shandy* also applies to the representation of the surroundings. I am extending outsideness to the description of the topography in Sterne's and Diderot's novels, as it is part of the same process. In this respect, I follow Smietanski who included the descriptions of the landscape to 'les limites du réalisme' in *Jacques le fataliste*.[59]

Just as for the characters, Smietanski complains of the vagueness of the descriptions and that 'Diderot s'est efforcé d'une façon très consciente d'exclure toute description trop précise'.[60] Any information Diderot does give out is mainly incidental, unexceptional and kept extremely brief. Neither the narrator nor the characters seem willing to take the opportunity of describing at any length their surroundings, as would normally be the case in travel literature. Those descriptions which allow slightly more details function as stage indications. This is the case for the description of Bigre's house which

> [...] consistait en une boutique et une soupente. Son lit était au fond de la boutique. Bigre le fils, mon ami, couchait sur la soupente à laquelle on grimpait par une petite échelle, placée à peu près à égale distance du lit de son père et de la porte de la boutique. (JF, p. 819)

The reader needs to visualise the layout of the space to understand the comings and goings of Justine, Jacques and Bigre fils.[61] But still the descriptions remain sketchy and insubstantial.

The only exceptions are Jacques's *tableau* and the master's description of the apartment of the disreputable moneylender Le Brun (see *JF*, p. 839). The precision of the master's description is at odds with the fact that he is talking of something which happened several years ago and which he has only seen once. It is also at odds with the rest of the descriptions in the novel, and emphasises their paucity. It seems that the master is indulging in an *exercice de style* by using this particular scene as an opportunity to create a *tableau* the better to entertain his audience. Smietanski draws a similar conclusion as for the characters. The descriptions of landscapes and surroundings are solely used as signals for the reader to recognise stereotypes. By the description of the apartment, Jacques immediately identifies Le Brun's infamous profession: 'Cela sent le faiseur d'affaires d'une lieue à la ronde' (p. 839). Landscapes and surroundings are never singularised. They are only described 'lorsqu'ils jouent un rôle particulier dans l'action dramatique ou lorsqu'ils contribuent à illustrer un caractère'. Otherwise, 'les descriptions se réduisent à de très fugitives touches et sont donc à peu près inexistantes'.[62]

The withholding of information is particularly frustrating for the reader of *Jacques le fataliste*. The narrator teasingly refuses to give any indication whatsoever concerning the heroes' destination. He turns a deaf ear to the reader's repeated question 'Où allaient-ils?', and prefers to suffer such interruptions rather than to give in. When the fictive reader asks where the main characters are going, the narrator constantly evades the question, taking delight in maintaining the uncertainty.

> Les voilà remontés sur leurs bêtes et poursuivant leur chemin. — Et où allaient-ils? — Voilà la seconde fois que vous me faites cette question, et la seconde fois que je vous réponds: Qu'est-ce que cela vous fait? Si j'entame le sujet de leur voyage, adieu les amours de Jacques ... Ils allèrent quelque temps en silence. (*JF*, p. 670)

The narrator's cruel teasing appears in the fact the verb *aller* in the last sentence is followed by indications on the manner of their going, and not on the location. The frustration concerning destinations during the narrators' travels may be extended to the entire narrative of both *Tristram Shandy* and *Jacques le fataliste* and their problem of completion. The reader feels he has not reached his destination, that the narrator has not led him from A to B but has left him somewhere along the way. In both novels, the blame for such narrative wanderings is put upon travel. In *Tristram Shandy* (VIII, 1, p. 490), the narrator justifies his inability to reach the straight line by explaining that his digressions are unavoidable as they are those of the road where any noteworthy sight or event is but another deviation.

In *Jacques le fataliste*, the deviating effect of travelling upon narrative progress is even more visible. Jacques's horse indeed governs the progress of the narrative as he interrupts Jacques's story by rushing towards gibbets and changing the conversation to digressions. Jacques and his master, who both dislike interruptions, must then evaluate what story would be most fit for a given leg of their journey, keeping digressions for short stages, the main stories for longer ones. 'LE MAITRE: Cette aventure-là sera pour la route. L'autre est courte' (*JF*, p. 794).

The reader is left to glean for himself clues concerning the route Jacques and his master are taking. From the beginning of *Jacques le fataliste*, the fictional reader questions the narrator as to Jacques and his master's destination. Yet this remains secret till the end, and even the master's visit to his alleged son is only made because it is on their way. Smietanski himself tries to reconstruct the two heroes' itinerary by speculating on the few indications collected in the novel. Caught up by a storm, Jacques and his master are forced 'de s'acheminer . . .

> — Où? — Où? Lecteur, vous êtes d'une curiosité bien incommode! Et que diable cela vous fait-il? Quand je vous aurai dit que c'est à Pontoise, ou à Saint-Germain, à Notre-Dame de Lorette ou à Saint-Jacques de Compostelle, en serez-vous plus avancé? (*JF*, p. 684)

As the reader insists on knowing the location, the narrator continues the torment by adding to the list of possible places an enigmatic castle, a brothel, a friend's house, the hospitality of 'des moines mendiants', 'la maison d'un grand', 'une grande auberge', the home of 'un curé de village à portion congrue', and 'une riche abbaye de bernardins' (*JF*, pp. 685 & 686). A few pages later, the narrator finally remembers that 'Jacques et son maître avaient passé par Conches, et qu'ils avaient logé chez M. le lieutenant général' (*JF*, p. 689). This first clue is not however as helpful as it first seems. As Smietanski underlines, more than one town was called Conches.[63] Smietanski then turns his attention to the mention of Jacques's horse who 'redescendit la montagne, remonta la fondrière' (*JF*, p. 700). Grounding his guess on such thin geological indications, Smietanski suggests that the scene takes place in the Argonne region.[64] I agree with Diderot's narrator and do not believe that it is helpful for our understanding of *Jacques le fataliste* that the characters were at one point in the Argonne. Not only is this not confirmed by the text, but it also seems risky to superimpose actual geography on a work of fiction. However, Smietanski's speculation is interesting in that the lack of detailed description leads to the need to fill the blanks and reconstruct the itinerary.

The same problem occurs in the case of *Tristram Shandy*. Fredman thus describes Shandy Hall:

> It has a small back parlor where the Shandy brothers like to sit by the fire, despite Walter's distress at the squeaking hinge on the door. There is a dark passage leading to the parlor, a front stairway with landings, a backstairs near

the nursery, a kitchen where a scullion scours fish kettles. There even are windows, albeit they are not very dependable because Trim has removed weights and pulleys for the model siege. Outside there are walks, a large uncultivated commons near the river, a fish pond, a stable yard which leads into a narrow and sometimes muddy lane running along the garden wall. Toby's cottage is very near by, its windows also in need of repair, and its kitchen garden and bowling green, protected by a hedge, are dug up and cluttered by an intricate arrangement of small fortifications and besieged towns. Through the hedge and an adjoining arbor is the widow Wadman's house.[65]

Fredman has reconstructed Shandy Hall by collecting pieces of information scattered throughout the nine volumes of the novel. Such a description does not actually appear in the text. The first detail concerning Shandy Hall is the mention of a large house-clock 'standing upon the back-stairs head' (*TS*, I, iv, p. 9). Twenty pages later, we are told about Walter's 'wall-fruit, and green gages' (*TS*, I, xvi, p. 39). One volume later, Tristram talks of 'a small crevice, form'd by a bad joint in the chimney-piece' (*TS*, II, vii, p. 91). In volume III, he then mentions the 'cornish of the room' (*TS*, III, vi, p. 147), the 'cane chair' with 'the two knobs on the top of the back of it' 'fasten'd on' 'with two pegs stuck slightly into two gimlet-holes' (*TS*, III, xx, p. 180). The creaky 'door-hinge' is discussed in a chapter of its own (*TS*, III, xxi, pp. 182–83). In volume IV, the reader is told about 'the fish-pond' (*TS*, IV, xvii, p. 264). By quoting the details we are given about Shandy Hall, we are able to see how the narrator has disseminated them in the text and how very little meat they provide. Like Smietanski, Fredman feels the need to supply herself the outside reconstruction the novel does not provide.

Smietanski's gathering of information and speculations concerning the characters' itinerary may be understood as an attempt to supply an outside perspective. The same may be said of Fredman's reconstruction of Shandy Hall. Outsideness is absent from *Jacques le fataliste* and *Tristram Shandy* as the descriptions of the landscapes, routes, and familiar surroundings, appear under the form of disseminated fragments. This leaves the reader in an awkward position since instead of benefiting from a vantage point given by the narrator, he realises he knows even less of the situation than the characters do. The fictive reader's 'fureur de deviner' (*JF*, p. 819) and the emphasis on the missing information are an incentive for the actual reader to fill in the gaps. The fragmentary and incomplete description encourages the reader to supply himself an outside perspective, just like Smietanski and Fredman, in order to form 'a unitary and unique whole [. . .] of meaning'.[66]

Conclusion

The principal function of description in Sterne's and Diderot's novels cannot be mimetic. Indeed, the fragmentary nature of the descriptions, their paucity and incompleteness are improper for imitation. We then must assume that description serves a different aim. The various philosophical debates of the two novels are fragmented and incomplete; their descriptions are exactly in the same state, and for the same reason: the refusal of 'a unitary and unique whole [...] of meaning'.[67] Outsideness corresponds to the author's standpoint enabling him to consummate the hero into such a whole.[68] Bakhtin also talks of the author's relationship to the hero as an authoritative one.[69] The contradictions between ideas and examples make it impossible for a particular philosophical stance to become the authoritative view of the texts. The absence of outsideness in the descriptions of *Tristram Shandy* and *Jacques le fataliste* confirms this.

In his preface to *Esthétique de la création verbale*, Todorov places the concept of outsideness developed early, in the rest of Bakhtin's work:

> Une telle exigence de l'exotopie supérieure est parfaitement 'classique': Dieu existe bien et reste à sa place, on ne confond pas le créateur avec ses créatures, la hiérarchie des consciences est inébranlable, la transcendance de l'auteur nous permet d'évaluer avec assurance ses personnages. Mais elle ne sera pas maintenue. En cours de route, Bakhtine se laisse influencer par son contre-exemple, Dostoïevski (ou par l'image qu'il s'en fait); son premier livre publié, en 1929, lui est consacré, et c'est un éloge de la voie précédemment condamnée. La conception précédente, au lieu d'être maintenue au rang d'une loi esthétique générale, devient la caractéristique d'un état d'esprit que Bakhtine stigmatise sous le nom de 'monologisme'; la perversion dostoïevskienne, au contraire, s'élève en incarnation du 'dialogisme', à la fois conception du monde et style d'écriture, pour lesquels Bakhtine ne cache pas sa préférence.[70]

Todorov underlines how outsideness, by acting as a counterpoint, is in the continuity of Bakhtin's work on dialogism and the rejection of systematic thinking. In order to understand the function of outsideness, it is necessary to recall what distinguishes monologism from dialogism. Following Bakhtin, monologism imposes a single dominant discourse whereas dialogism allows the coexistence of a plurality of discourses, sometimes contradictory. There is no closure in dialogism as its multiple discourses never cease to converse and dispute with each other. Closure would imply that one particular discourse has imposed itself as the authoritative one and so has put an end to all dialogue. Outsideness serves monologism in that it provides a complete and finite perspective supporting the authoritative discourse. Logically, it is antithetical to dialogism. In the next chapter, I will apply to the two novels another Bakhtinian key concept, the carnivalesque, to see how the superposition of opposite registers participates in the refusal of systematic thinking.

Notes to Chapter 3

1. Bakhtin, *Art and Answerability*, p. 138.
2. Bakhtin, *Art and Answerability*, p. 138.

3. Jean Weisgerber, *L'Espace Romanesque* (Lausanne: Editions de l'Age d'Homme, 1978), p. 18.
4. Michel de Montaigne, *Les Essais* (Paris: Le Livre de Poche, 2001), I, L, p. 490.
5. Tzvetan Todorov, who prefaced Bakhtin's essay 'Author and Hero in aesthetic activity' (a preface which I will later come back to), mentions the didactic purposes of travel literature in the context of the representation of the 'good savage'. Todorov argues that travelling is motivated by a dissatisfaction with one's own homeland which is criticised when compared to foreign countries, idealised by the traveller. See Tzvetan Todorov, *Nous et les autres. La réflexion française sur la diversité humaine* (Paris: Editions du Seuil, 1989), pp. 303–04.
6. See Berchtold, p. 686.
7. In the *Theaetetus*, Socrates briefly describes the episode of Thales ridiculed by the Thracian servant, so as to guard his interlocutor Theodorus against being absent to the world, lost in abstract thought, but unable to apprehend reality directly.
8. Montaigne, p. 1525.
9. According to Anne D. Wallace, peripatetic walking constitutes an end in itself, the interest lies not in a destination to reach but in the movement. See *Walking, Literature, and English Culture, The Origins and Uses of Peripatetic in the Nineteenth Century* (Oxford: Clarendon Press, 1994).
10. See note 1 to page 767, in Diderot, *Contes et romans*, p. 1232.
11. Denis Diderot, *La Promenade du sceptique ou les allées*, in *Oeuvres complètes*, ed. Roger Lewinter (Paris: Le Club français du livre, 1969) I, p. 315.
12. Alain Montandon, *Sociopoétique de la promenade* (Clermont-Ferrand: Presses Universitaires Blaise Pascal, 2000), p. 27.
13. Stephen Soud explores the function of the maze with regard to Toby, Walter and Tristram's 'quest for a totalizing knowledge' (p. 405). He presents the maze in Sterne's novel as being a concrete, an abstract and an aesthetical pattern. See '"Weavers, gardeners, and gladiators": Labyrinths in *Tristram Shandy*', *ECS*, 28 (1995), 397–411.
14. I am alluding to a quote by Arthur L. Loeb: 'Space is not a passive vacuum, but has properties that impose powerful constraints on any structure that inhabits it', in *Space Structures: Their Harmony and Counterpoint* (Reading, Mass.: Addison-Wesley, 1976), p. xvii.
15. Denis Diderot, *Œuvres complètes*, ed. Roger Lewinter (Paris: le Club français du livre, 1970), VII, p. 142.
16. Bakhtin, *Art and Answerability*, pp. 35–36.
17. See Bakhtin, *Art and Answerability*, pp. 99–137.
18. Unlike the other characters, Yorick is given a full description of his biography, his character and physical appearance. Instead of being scattered and fragmented, Yorick's description is concentrated in chapters x, xi and xii of volume I.
19. Bakhtin, *Art and Answerability*, p. 154.
20. Bakhtin, *Art and Answerability*, p. 27 (original italics). See also p. 12, & pp. 23–24.
21. Bakhtin, *Art and Answerability*, p. 14. In note 28 p. 235, the editors explain Bakhtin's choice of words: 'Bakhtin contracts the Russian phrase *nakhodit'sja vne* (to be situated or located outside the bounds of someone or something) into a noun — *vnenakhodimost'* (the state of being situated outside the bounds of). It should be stressed that this situatedness outside (the bounds of) the hero is a *position* assumed *in relation* to the hero or *toward* the hero. Other translators have preferred to render *vnenakhodimost* as "extopy" or "extra-location"'.
22. I will provide a detailed analysis of descriptions in Sterne's and Diderot's novels later on in the chapter
23. See Tzvetan Todorov's preface to Bakhtin, *Esthétique de la création verbale*, trans. by Alfreda Aucouturier (Paris: Gallimard, 1984).p. 12.

24. Bakhtin, *Art and Answerability*, p. 15.
25. Bakhtin, *Art and Answerability*, p. 13.
26. I am taking the liberty of including maps in my application of geometry. I justify this by referring to the word's etymology, as geometry literally stands for 'measuring the earth', which is also the purpose of maps.
27. Philippe Du Bois, *Avertissement en tête de sa traduction des sermons de Saint Augustin*, ed. by Thomas Carr (Geneva: Droz, 1992) p. 110-12, quoted by Meiner, p. 86.
28. The *Oxford English Dictionary* offers a series of definitions of the word parabola. In mathematics, it corresponds to 'a symmetrical open plane curve formed by the intersection of a cone with a plane parallel to its side'. In rhetoric, it is 'a figure of speech expressing a comparison drawn between two things or facts'. Hyperbola also carries a mathematical and a rhetorical meaning. In terms of geometry, it is defined as 'One of the conic sections; a plane curve consisting of two separate, equal and similar, infinite branches, formed by the intersection of a plane with both branches of a double cone'. Rhetorically, it appears under hyperbole and corresponds to 'A figure of speech consisting in exaggerated or extravagant statement, used to express strong feeling or produce a strong impression, and not intended to be understood literally'.
29. Meiner, p. 172.
30. Meiner, p. 25.
31. See Bakhtin, *Art and Answerability*, pp. 172-82.
32. Weisgerber, p. 186.
33. Diderot, *La Promenade du sceptique*, in *Oeuvres complètes*, ed. Roger Lewinter, I, p. 354.
34. Fredman, p. 114. Fredman's considerations are not restricted to *Jacques le fataliste* and *Tristram Shandy*; she examines Sterne's and Diderot's literary works in general.
35. See Fredman, pp. 113-21.
36. Fredman, p. 132.
37. Denis Diderot, *Les Deux Amis de Bourbonne*, in *Contes et romans*, p. 449.
38. Diderot, *Les Deux Amis de Bourbonne*, in *Contes et romans*, p. 449.
39. See Jacques Smietanski, *Le Réalisme dans* Jacques le Fataliste (Paris: A. G. Nizet, 1965), p. 19.
40. I will be regularly referring to Smietanski's first part 'Les limites du réalisme' for my study of description of characters and surroundings in *Jacques le fataliste*.
41. Smietanski, p. 38.
42. Smietanski, p. 38.
43. Smietanski also mentions Jacques's clothing, p. 38.
44. Smietanski, p. 41.
45. Smietanski, p. 39.
46. Smietanski, p. 39.
47. Fredman mentions the use of the hobby-horse in the characters' descriptions which she regards as an illustration of Shandeism, pp. 113-21.
48. It is worth remembering the importance of the portrait amongst the French seventeenth-century literati. La Bruyère's *Les Caractères* are generally considered as representative of, and having helped to establish, the portrait as a literary genre. For further reference on the subject, see Jaqueline Plantié, *La Mode du portrait littéraire en France (1641-1681)* (Paris: Champion, 1994).
49. 'Son mari, indulgent pour le seul défaut qu'il eût à lui reprocher, la plaignit pendant qu'elle vécut, et la regretta longtemps après sa mort.' *JF*, p. 861.
50. This view is supported by the editors in note 2 to p. 863, p. 1251. J. Robert Loy relates Diderot's descriptions in *Jacques le fataliste* to his work as an art critic, pp. 112-13.
51. Smietanski, p. 43.
52. Ibid., p. 44.

53. Bakhtin, *Art and Answerability*, p. 5.
54. On periegeses, see Krzysztof Jarosz who offers the following definition: 'Le terme de "périégèse" désignait dans l'Antiquité une relation de voyage, possédant un caractère plus ou moins scientifique, avec sa part nécessaire de généralisation qui concernait surtout les mœurs et le caractère des nations; mais une périégèse servait aussi de guide touristique pour les voyageurs désireux de suivre les traces de l'auteur de ce baedecker antique, ou simplement pour les lecteurs qui voulaient se renseigner sur des pays lointains. Les périégèses ou *itineraria* se prêtaient donc avant tout à une lecture référentielle qui impliquait la foi du lecteur en ce que racontaient ces pionniers de la géographie et du tourisme qu'étaient les auteurs de périégèses, tels Palémon ou Pausanias, sans oublier Hérodote qui semble avoir inauguré le genre.' in 'Périégèse hypertextuelle d'une contrée réelle: *Voyage en Italie* de Jean Giono', in *Roman et récit de voyage*, ed. by Marie-Christine Gomez-Géraud and Philippe Antoine (Paris: Presses de l'Université de Paris-Sorbonne, 2001), p. 91.
55. See Anne F. Woodhouse, 'Eighteenth-Century English Visitors to France in Fiction and Fact', *MLS*, 6 (1976), 37–41.
56. See Jean-Michel Racault, *Nulle part et ses environs, Voyage aux confins de l'utopie littéraire classique (1657–1802)* (Paris: Presses de l'Université de Paris-Sorbonne, 2003) p. 366.
57. See Soud, p. 405.
58. 'We will give the name *chronotope* (literally, "time space") to the intrinsic connectedness of temporal and spatial relationships that are artistically expressed in literature', Bakhtin, *The Dialogic Imagination*, p. 84.
59. 'Les limites du réalisme' corresponds to the first part of Smietanski's work. On the descriptions of landscapes and surroundings in *Jacques le fataliste*, see pp. 25–37.
60. Smietanski, p. 31.
61. On the description of Bigre fils' room, see Smietanski, p. 36.
62. Smietanski, p. 37.
63. Smietanski, p. 26.
64. Ibid., p. 28.
65. Fredman, p. 105.
66. Bakhtin, *Art and Answerability*, p. 5.
67. Bakhtin, *Art and Answerability*, p. 5.
68. In note 6 p. 233, the editors explain this choice of word: '"To consummate" (to bring to the utmost degree of completion or fulfillment, to accomplish) is intended to convey the definitiveness implied by the Russian *zavershit*', in Bakhtin, *Art and Answerability*.
69. See Bakhtin, *Art and Answerability*, p. 153.
70. Todorov, preface to Bakhtin, *Esthétique de la création verbale*, p. 12.

CHAPTER 4

Sentimentalism and the Grotesque

In the course of their travels, the main characters in *Tristram Shandy* and *Jacques le fataliste* prefer places of sociability to places of isolation. Both novels offer much fuller descriptions of the roads, the inns and the travellers passing through than of solitary landscapes, which go hardly noticed.[1] Though the beauty of solitary landscapes is acknowledged, it is shunned in favour of more populous locations. In the course of his Grand Tour, Tristram traverses 'the rich plains of Languedoc'. Despite admitting that '[t]here is nothing more pleasing to a traveller', he begins to regret the emptiness of the landscape, and so hurries to transform the '*plain* into a *city*' crowded with 'beggars, pilgrims, fiddlers, fryars' and women (*TS*, VII, xlii, p. 482 & xliii, p. 484). Sterne's and Diderot's characters seek social interaction and human contact, not solitude. This is understandable considering that Tristram, Jacques and his master share the eighteenth-century philosophers' interest in society and the mechanisms bonding large numbers of individuals into a coherent and functional whole. One of those mechanisms is sensibility, which takes the exacerbated shape of sentimentalism in *Tristram Shandy* and *Jacques le fataliste*.

Certain works by Sterne and Diderot have been considered as belonging to sentimental literature for their exaggerated excitement of pathos displayed in emotional scenes, used to touch the reader and make him feel for the suffering characters. *Tristram Shandy* and *A Sentimental Journey* were thus considered by their contemporaries as two of the great models of the genre. Though to a lesser degree, *Jacques le fataliste* also offered sentimental passages, which found favour with the public. But most of all, it is in the *Eloge de Richardson* (1762) that Diderot eulogises sentimentalism, using as a pretext his literary mausoleum to the author of *Clarissa*. Yet, as sentimentalism fell into disrepute, the appropriateness of the term 'sentimental' applied to *Tristram Shandy* and *Jacques le fataliste* has been disputed, and critics preferred to focus on their farcical nature, which is at the opposite end of the spectrum.

Gardner Stout very pertinently compares the controversy on sentimentalism and comedy regarding *A Sentimental Journey* to Dr Eustace's walking stick. This stick was sent to Sterne in homage to Shandeism because of its particularity of having multiple handles:

Confronted with this paradoxical spectacle, many readers have shown the tendency Sterne noted in meditating upon Dr Eustace's walking stick: to take either the 'sentimental' or the comic handle of the book, according to their sensibility. Several recent critics of Yorick's Journey have attempted to resolve its paradoxes by arguing that the 'sentimental' aspects of the book are essentially insincere — a pose Sterne adopted to regain the favor of the public, which had been pleased with the benevolence and the pathos of Tristram's 'life and opinions' and offended by their wit.[2]

Stout's comparison may be perfectly well applied to *Tristram Shandy* and *Jacques le fataliste* as both novels present to the reader the 'sentimental' and 'the comic handle'. Sharing Gardner Stout's dissatisfaction with the solution of having to choose one handle or the other, my aim in this chapter is to reconcile sentimentalism and the grotesque, through Bakhtin's notion of the carnivalesque defined in *Rabelais and his World*.[3]

Since sentimentalism can be defined as the artificial creation of sensibility, to understand it one necessarily needs to go back to sensibility, referring first to physical, and then to emotional responsiveness, and to how it influenced philosophers belonging to the moral-sense school. Sterne and Diderot partook of the interest in sensibility sometimes seen as being at the origin of society, and consequently of morality. On those grounds, it became of interest to authors concerned with giving to their works a didactic purpose. Sentimentalism does not allow emotions to manifest themselves unbridled, but makes them acceptable by channelling them through politeness. Politeness constitutes a branch of sensibility in that it also plays an essential role in social interaction and in the instruction of moral behaviour.

In *Tristram Shandy* and *Jacques le fataliste*, sensibility affects the reader at different levels of the narrative. The reader is sentimentally involved with the characters, but his relations with the narrator are based on politeness. Sentimentalism, itself polite in nature, represents a complete system encompassing sociability, morality and aesthetics all tightly linked to each other. However, the sentimental system only appears in Sterne's and Diderot's novels at the metadiegetic level, or in other words, in secondary stories, and is absent from the main narrative. Indeed, both the extradiegetic and intradiegetic levels dissent from it by being deeply impolite and juxtaposing sentimentalism with its opposite, the grotesque. Such a problematical coincidence of contraries takes meaning through the Bakhtinian carnivalesque, which prevents a dominant system from imposing itself. By combining it with the grotesque, Sterne and Diderot are not invalidating sentimentalism, but nor are they allowing it to become the only representation of reality in their novels. I will analyse how both novels differ from the aesthetics of sentimental literature, but tally with those of the carnivalesque as defined by Bakhtin.

Sterne and Diderot echo in their novels the philosophical ideas of their time on the question of sensibility. These ideas may be put into the mouths of the characters who thus hold a theoretical debate of their own on sensibility. They may also be integrated into the narrative as part of a small episode and so take the form of an illustrative occurrence of sensibility, without necessarily being explicitly connected to the theoretical debates between the characters. In this treatment of sensibility, *Jacques le fataliste* and *Tristram Shandy* share certain traits of the sentimental novel. I will explore the sociable nature of sensibility and its representation and discussion in *Jacques le fataliste* and *Tristram Shandy*. The expression of sensibility through body language is presented as a form of communication, and as such requires the presence of others who will respond to it.

Sensibility was also seen as the foundation for morality as, through sympathy, it regulates the way human beings interconnect. This idea was particularly attractive to sentimentalist authors who wished to strengthen their readers' sense of morality by artificially creating sympathy for the characters. In principle, this allowed for the didactic message to be felt rather than intellectually understood. In this sense, sentimentalism offers a complete system binding sociability, morality and aesthetics together. If both novels do engage with the question of sensibility and borrow certain aspects of sentimentalist literature in its treatment, they also depart from it in others. To understand in what ways *Jacques le fataliste* and *Tristram Shandy* diverge from the sentimentalist tradition, it is necessary to analyse the points they agree on, but also the points on which they are at variance.

As part of their treatment of sensibility, both novels expose the inconsistencies of sentimentalism. One of its failings is the fact that it does not allow for any distance between the sufferer and the spectator. This means that sensibility is reduced to a purely mechanical response to the stimulus of another's body language. The absence of distance may also imply that the spectator is only aware of his own mechanical emotional response, but oblivious of the person actually suffering. In sentimentalism, emotions may end up having a blinding effect rather than clarifying the connection between men. The two novels also contradict the notion that the expression of emotions is more reliable and trustworthy than verbal language. Diderot in particular demonstrates that gestures can be equally misunderstood and just as deceptive as words. Moreover, *Jacques le fataliste* and *Tristram Shandy* question the moral claim of sentimentalism on the grounds that it may be misplaced, and that it introduces a confusion between feelings and sexuality. By exposing its incoherencies either through philosophical discussions or scenes in the novels, Sterne and Diderot challenge sentimentalism as a complete system.

The two novels constantly transgress the aesthetics of sentimentalism, and consequently introduce a farcical register. This is first visible through representations of the human body, which by becoming exuberantly impolite, arouses laughter instead of sympathy. Diderot and Sterne have carnivalised the body of some of their characters. This carnivalisation is not restricted to the body, but pervades the entire novel. Respectable figures are humbled and laughed at, and the sentimental register combines with the farcical. Contemporaries of Sterne and Diderot, and even later critics, have found this combination of the grotesque and sentimentalism problematical. The temptation has been to take into account only one of the two registers and to ignore the other.

It is necessary to study jointly sentimentalism and the grotesque in the two novels. Indeed, this coincidence of opposites corresponds to a true carnivalesque transgression. This enables Sterne and Diderot to prevent a dominant discourse from establishing itself in their novels. The presence of the grotesque does not invalidate or annul the sentimental dimension of *Jacques le fataliste* and *Tristram Shandy*. By combining the grotesque with sentimentalism, Sterne and Diderot recreate the distance necessary for sensibility to become once again a dialogue, instead of just a mechanical reaction to a stimulus. As a result, both authors paradoxically reintroduce sensibility as a polite dialogue.

Sociable Sensibility

The connection between sensibility and sociability has been the object of Mullan's study on Hume, Richardson and Sterne, 'writers committed to the resources of a language of feeling for the purpose of representing necessary social bonds'.[4] Relying on biographical material, Mullan examines the correspondence between these three writers' reflections on sensibility and sociability as expressed in their works, and how it found a resonance in their public lives and social relations. While often running parallel to Mullan's study, my own work focuses on how *Tristram Shandy* and *Jacques le fataliste* echo discussions on the sociable nature of sensibility and further these by adapting them to a form of sociability with the reader inside the novel. The debates on the failures of language led by philosophers such as Locke and Beattie helped to trigger the interest of eighteenth-century intellectuals in emotions as a more reliable form of communication.[5]

Physiognomy offered an alternative as the body is able to express through gestures, postures and looks what is internally felt. The body can thus be read as a text. Sentimental literature relied on the belief that the body has its own universal language, and that it is much more trustworthy as there is supposed to be a perfect correspondence between an expression and an emotion, unlike verbal language where there often exists a discrepancy between signifier and signified.[6] As Anne C. Vila summarises, 'sensibility was the true inner language of the human being'.[7]

Tears are the traditional sign of sensibility, but Sterne and Diderot delighted in finding subtle physical variations such as changes of complexion, of voice, sighs, trembles and so on. In *Jacques le fataliste*, the landlady of the Grand-Cerf describes the various signs revealing the Marquis des Arcis's progressively decreasing affection for Mme de La Pommeraye.

> Peu à peu il passa un jour, deux jours sans la voir; peu à peu il manqua au dîner-souper qu'il avait arrangé; peu à peu il abrégea ses visites, il eut des affaires qui l'appelaient; lorsqu'il arrivait il disait un mot, s'étalait dans un fauteuil, prenait une brochure, la jetait, parlait à son chien ou s'endormait. Le soir, sa santé qui devenait misérable voulait qu'il se retirât de bonne heure, c'était l'avis de Tronchin. 'C'est un grand homme que Tronchin! Ma foi! je ne doute pas qu'il ne tire d'affaire notre amie dont les autres se désespéraient', et tout en parlant ainsi il prenait sa canne et son chapeau et s'en allait, oubliant quelquefois de l'embrasser. [...] Mme de La Pommeraye pressentit qu'elle n'était plus aimée [...]. (*JF*, p. 749)

Des Arcis is betrayed by his own body language expressing weariness instead of love. Mme de La Pommeraye, who is carefully recording and reading all the signs, is able to decipher the state of his feelings for her. Not only does sensibility reveal the permeability of the body to the world, but it also exposes the porous nature of the surface of the body, incapable of concealing the internal movements of the soul.

As its etymology reveals, sympathy is inherently sociable: the Greek *sumpathéia* literally translates as *feeling with*. The truth of this is verified by the fact that emotions are not purely internalised. The body lets these emotions transpire externally so that they may be visible to others. Emotions are not to be repressed; they are to be communicated and they demand the notice of spectators. Thus they take their full meaning in a social context. Lamenting the nose of his son crushed under the pressure of Dr Slop's forceps, Walter cannot hide his excessive fatherly concerns.[8] The narrator minutely describes 'the most lamentable attitude of a man borne down with sorrows, that ever the eye of pity dropp'd a tear for' (*TS*, III, xxix, p. 194).

Walter's physical expression of grief is answered by the reaction of his brother Toby who, 'having a tear at every one's service, — [...] pull'd out a cambrick handkerchief, — gave a low sigh, — but held his peace' (ibid., p. 195). Toby's sympathy needs no words to be expressed; it is the very absence of words that strengthens his body language. After a lengthy interruption on the subject of noses, the scene is picked up again, this time portraying Walter's recovery. The physical signs of this are to be found in such trivial and inane indications such as '[playing] upon the floor with the toe of that foot which hung over the bedside', '[thrusting the handle of the chamber-pot] a little more within the valance', and '[giving] a hem!' These signs indicating Walter's uplifted spirits are answered by Toby's 'gleam of sun-shine' radiating on his face (*TS*, IV, ii, pp. 246 and 247). These two passages reveal how external manifestation of grief finds a response in a sympathetic spectator.

In the same way as a person experiencing emotions demands the recognition of these by others, consciously or not, the sentimental novel demands a reaction from the readers to its sentimental scenes. Todd's view that such 'arousal of pathos' constitutes the stamp of the sentimental novel, finds an echo in *L'Eloge de Richardson*.[9] Diderot puts the emphasis on the capacity of the novel to make its readers react through sensibility. He thus gives the rather extreme example of a friend's reaction at the reading of a passage of Richardson's *Clarissa*:

> Le voilà qui s'empare des cahiers, qui se retire dans un coin et qui lit. Je l'examinais: d'abord je vois couler des pleurs, bientôt il s'interrompt, il sanglote; tout à coup il se lève, il marche sans savoir où il va, il pousse des cris comme un homme désolé et il adresse les reproches les plus amers à toute la famille des Harlove.[10]

In the preface to *La Religieuse*, it is this time Diderot who is caught by his friend shedding tears:

> Un jour qu'il était tout entier à ce travail, M. d'Alainville, un de nos amis communs, lui rendit visite, et le trouva plongé dans la douleur et le visage inondé de larmes. "Qu'avez-vous donc? lui dit M. d'Alainville. Comme vous voilà! — Ce que j'ai? lui répondit M. Diderot; je me désole d'un conte que je me fais."[11]

Both Diderot and his friend seem to be oblivious to the fact that they are sympathising with fictional characters; their feelings take the same intensity as if it were a real situation.

In a similar way, the master lets his sympathy get carried away while listening to Jacques telling the story of how he was left penniless with his wounded knee worsened after having been attacked by robbers:

> En cet endroit, le Maître jeta ses bras autour du cou de son valet en s'écriant: 'Mon pauvre Jacques, que vas-tu faire? Que vas-tu devenir? Ta position m'effraye.'
> JACQUES: Mon maître, rassurez-vous, me voilà.
> LE MAITRE: Je n'y pensais pas; j'étais à demain, à côté de toi, chez le docteur, au moment où tu t'éveilles et où l'on vient te demander de l'argent. (*JF*, p. 730)

The master has mixed up time and space, and his sympathy for Jacques has obviously left him disoriented. We may believe that the whole scene is an exaggeration of an audience's sympathetic reaction to a character's tribulations in a narrative. However, Diderot contradicts our doubts by giving us his own example and that of his own friend affected by the story of Clarissa. Both excerpts bewilder the modern reader by their dramatic intensity, which seems foreign to our own approach to texts. Paul Goring offers an answer by talking of a 'process of spectacularisation'.[12] There is a need to be seen emotionally moved by a sentimental scene, in that it artificially creates a bonding with a spectator. We see here formed a *mise en abyme* where a suffering character appeals to the sympathy of the reader who in turn appeals to the sympathy of an external spectator, witnessing, as Diderot with his friend, his emotional anguish.[13]

The sentimental novel does not content itself with the description of bodily expressions. As these do not come first-hand to the reader, they lose some of their strength through transcription. The author himself engages in some form of socialisation with the reader by translating, as it were, those expressions and naming their coinciding emotions.[14] Translation bears in its etymology the same notion as sympathy of exchange, since it comes from the Latin *translatus*, 'carried across'. Translation conveys from the start a sociability confirmed and developed by Yorick. In *A Sentimental Journey*, Yorick mentions how in normal circumstances the spectator automatically operates this translation:

> There is not a secret so aiding to the progress of sociality, as to get master of this *short hand*, and be quick in rendering the several turns of looks and limbs, with all their inflections and delineations, into plain words. For my own part, by long habitude, I do it so mechanically, that when I walk the streets of London I go translating all the way; and have more than once stood behind in the circle, where not three words have been said, and have brought off twenty different dialogues with me, which I could have fairly wrote down and sworn to.[15]

Yet, by using the very word 'translation', he also points to the literariness of the creation of sympathy inside the novel. The reader's emotional involvement in a sentimental scene necessitates a type of translation different from that of naming the emotions corresponding to bodily expressions.

Sentimentalism is a visual art; as previously underlined, it heavily relies, in literature, on description and demands spectatorship. On this account, it is not surprising that sentimentalism flourished in theatre, in particular in the *drame bourgeois* to which Diderot contributed with *Le fils naturel* and *Le père de famille*, but also in painting, with Greuze as one of its most illustrious representatives. The novel borrows from theatre and painting the technique of mediating a sentimental scene through the eyes of a witness. This witness will configure the reader's own reception of the scene. One of the most vivid sentimental scenes in *Jacques le fataliste* relies on the presence first of the Marquis des Arcis as witness so as better to strike the reader's sympathetic chord. He arrives back home in a state of wrath against his new wife who has tricked him into marrying her: 'Elle se jeta à ses pieds, la face collée contre le parquet sans mot dire. [. . .] Elle voulut se relever mais elle retomba sur son visage, les bras étendus à terre entre les pieds du marquis' (*JF*, p. 783). Then after realising that she has fallen into a swoon, the Marquis 'attacha un moment sur elle des regards où se peignaient alternativement la commisération et le courroux'.

As the wife is brought to her room, the reader believes there will no longer be a witness to her sufferings. However, he is mistaken since the Marquis secretly asks for reports on her health, which come back to him with very distressing descriptions of her state. She regularly falls into swoons, she suffocates and at one point her sufferings no longer need to be reported since 'il lui était survenu une espèce de hoquet qui se faisait entendre jusque dans les cours' (*JF*, p. 784). It is then the mother's turn to act as witness and it is through her eyes that the reader perceives the despair of the daughter, made more acute by her mother's loss as to how to react to such extreme grief:

> [...] ces deux femmes restèrent en présence l'une de l'autre sans presque se parler, la fille sanglotant, poussant quelques fois des cris, s'arrachant les cheveux, se tordant les bras, sans que sa mère osât s'approcher d'elle et la consoler. (*JF*, p. 784)

It is interesting to remark that the body language of grief with the cries, the tearing of hair, the wringing of arms, corresponds exactly to the description Jacques gives concerning women in labour. These gestures may then be said to be stock manifestations of pain.

It is then back to the Marquis to take over the role of witness, and this is the scene he is confronted with after having called his wife to him:

> Au lieu de se lever, elle s'avança vers lui sur ses genoux, elle tremblait de tous ses membres; elle était échevelée, elle avait le corps un peu penché, les bras portés de son côté, la tête relevée, le regard attaché sur ses yeux et le visage inondé de pleurs. (*JF*, p. 785)

We see that the description of Mlle Duquênoi's grief is always mediated by the presence of a witness, but also that by varying the identity of the spectator, the body language adjusts itself to its audience, as it were, and thus becomes more expressive and pathetic. Mlle Duquênoi does not express her despair in front of her mother in the same way as she does in front of her husband. Goring describes this technique as a triangulation:

> An incorporated viewing figure 'triangulates' a scene for the actual viewer or reader, directing the gaze, emphasising that the viewed object is engaging or of interest *by virtue* of its visual appearance or movements, and often modelling an appropriate response to the acting figure [...]. [...] it is a means of interpellation — a means of hailing readers and inviting them to occupy positions created within the fiction where spectatorial and ideological perspectives are integrated. It is a means of directing a mode of reading.[16]

The arousal of sympathy for the characters from the reader contains a didactic purpose without carrying the inconveniences of didacticism. Indeed, sympathy conveys emotions, considered as preceding thought, and it relies on experience instead of on intellectual understanding. Jacques thus tries to explain the empirical nature of sympathy to his master:

> Il cherchait à faire concevoir à son maître que le mot douleur était sans idée, et qu'il ne commençait à signifier quelque chose qu'au moment où il rappelait à notre mémoire une sensation que nous avions éprouvée. (*JF*, p. 681)

Sentimentalism and the Grotesque 131

The master tests the validity of this conception of sympathy by asking Jacques, rather unexpectedly, 's'il avait déjà accouché' and if he thought it was painful. The point the master is trying to make is to deny the empirical nature of sympathy for it contradicts the fact that Jacques sympathises with women in labour despite the fact that he has never given birth himself. The master's case study shares striking similarities with that offered by Adam Smith when arguing that sympathy cannot be a selfish passion:

> How can that be regarded as a selfish passion, which does not arise even from the imagination of anything that has befallen, or that relates to myself, in my own proper person and character, but which is entirely occupied about what relates to you? A man may sympathize with a woman in child-bed, though it is impossible that he should conceive himself as suffering her pains in his own proper person and character.[17]

Jacques remains unabashed and answers thus:

> Je plains ceux ou celles qui se tordent les bras, qui s'arrachent les cheveux, qui poussent des cris, parce que je sais par expérience qu'on ne fait pas cela sans souffrir; mais pour le mal propre à la femme qui accouche, je ne le plains pas, je ne sais ce que c'est, Dieu merci. (*JF*, pp. 681–82)

Jacques's answer may be understood by the fact that he knows by experience how the body expresses suffering. His sympathy is awakened by external signs of pain, even though he has not experienced that particular suffering. It is because he knows by experience the body language of suffering that he is able to imagine what this suffering is.

The theoretical debate on the subject of sympathy is illustrated by Jacques's empathy for an unfortunate woman. Jacques responds to her signs of distress: crying on the ground and tearing her hair out. She accompanies those visible signs by a plea explaining her dire situation. She accidentally broke the jar containing oil the hard-hearted steward asked her to fetch. Because of this, she will not have enough money to feed her children. However, as Jacques remarks, this is not enough to transform the pity felt by the bystanders into active charity: 'Tout le monde la plaignait, je n'entendais autour d'elle que, "la pauvre femme!" mais personne ne mettait la main dans sa poche' (*JF*, p. 728). At this point, Jacques himself is asking her for more details on her accident before deciding whether or nor to help her. The decisive trigger is the sight of her children:

> Dans ce moment survinrent les petits enfants de cette femme, ils étaient presque nus et les mauvais vêtements de leur mère montraient toute la misère de la famille, et la mère et les enfants se mirent à crier. Tel que vous me voyez il en fallait dix fois moins pour me toucher; mes entrailles s'émurent de compassion, les larmes me vinrent aux yeux. (*JF*, p. 728)

Moved by this pitiful scene, Jacques, who is a poor man himself, offers her the money from his own purse to pay back the oil. In this scene, Jacques stands out from the crowd: he is a truly sensitive man as his empathy has stirred him to act in a virtuous way.

The origin of the link between morality and sensibility comes from the principle of '*la morale sensitive*', defined by Anne Vila as 'a system of morals based largely if not exclusively on regulating sensibility's effect on moral behavior'.[18] As she reminds us, sensibility was first a physiological concern. When Rousseau declares in *Les Confessions* that 'Je sentis avant de penser: c'est le sort commun de l'humanité', he is making sensation and sentiment merge in the verb *sentir*.[19] With the evolution of its definition extending to emotions, moral philosophers in turn made use of it to explain the presence of morality in man. Hume argued that morality originates from feeling: virtue is first felt, and only later is it intellectually understood. This is the logical deduction from the fact that feeling precedes thought, as we find expressed by Rousseau.

Hume went further by affirming that man has access to morality not through reason but through sensibility: 'Morality, therefore, is more properly felt than judg'd of'.[20] Morality appears as instinctive as man's sociability. Furthermore, one could not go without the other since morality, more concerned with how the individual may harmoniously live with others than with the knowledge of good and evil which serves as its façade, is indispensable for the organisation of society. Sympathy was of particular interest to Hume, in that it is experienced, but it is also what gives us a 'feeling' of morality.

Men of letters took interest in the effect of sensibility on morality, with the idea in mind that the regulation of the *morale sensitive* could be performed artificially through novels. As Anne Vincent-Buffault phrases it, 'The pleasure of crying provided the opportunity to receive a moral education in an agreeable fashion, without the intervention of reason'.[21] Diderot himself believed in the power of art to make men more virtuous by awakening emotions such as empathy:

> Le parterre de la comédie est le seul endroit où les larmes de l'homme vertueux et du méchant soient confondues. Là, le méchant s'irrite contre des injustices qu'il aurait commises, compatit à des maux qu'il aurait occasionnés, et s'indigne contre un homme de son propre caractère. Mais l'impression est reçue, elle demeure en nous, malgré nous; et le méchant sort de sa loge moins disposé à faire le mal que s'il eût été gourmandé par un orateur sévère et dur.
>
> Le poète, le romancier, le comédien vont au cœur d'une manière détournée, et en frappent d'autant plus sûrement et plus fortement l'âme qu'elle s'étend et s'offre d'elle-même au coup.[22]

In this regard, Diderot viewed Richardson as an exemplary novelist. According to Diderot, Richardson was able to make his readers experience moral lessons through sympathy for the characters, instead of offering those lessons under the form of intellectual demonstrations:

> Tout ce que Montaigne, Charron, La Rochefoucauld et Nicole ont mis en maximes, Richardson l'a mis en action [...].
> Une maxime est une règle abstraite et générale de conduite, dont on nous laisse l'application à faire. Elle n'imprime par elle-même aucune image sensible dans notre esprit: mais celui qui agit, on le voit, on se met à sa place ou à ses côtés; on se passionne pour ou contre lui; on s'unit à son rôle, s'il est vertueux; on s'en écarte avec indignation, s'il est injuste et vicieux.[23]

Here Diderot reveals the empirical approach taken by sentimental literature, already noted by Janet Todd, and which tightens its connection to reality, 'not through any notion of a mimetic depiction of reality but through the belief that the literary experience can intimately affect the living one'.[24]

The didactic aim in sentimentalist literature is based on the assumption of this possible linkage between fiction and reality. The reader, sympathising with a character, feels the need to intervene so as to defend moral values. However, he finds his good intentions frustrated by the fact that he is confronted with a fictive situation. The bet sentimental literature makes is that the reader will then be all the more keen to act virtuously when facing in reality a situation similar to that presented in the novel. This wager implies that there was no longer a need to rely on intellectual demonstration to pass on to the reader the moral lesson of the text, as in philosophical tales. This was confirmed by the *Encyclopédie* according to which sensibility is much more effective in promoting virtue: 'La réflexion peut faire l'homme de probité; mais la *sensibilité* fait l'homme vertueux'.

The moral lesson provided by sentimental novels depends on the reader's own degree of sensibility. If the reader lacks sensibility, not only will he not be receptive to the novel's didacticism, but he will also be condemned for having a heart of stone.[25] This is why the novel tries as hard as possible to engage the reader, and to force him to participate and react. In *Jacques le fataliste*, insensitive characters are stigmatised. Mme Duquênoi is presented unfavourably as she is described as opportunistic and unrepentant at having tricked the Marquis into marrying her dishonourable daughter. This is increased by the contrast with the burning remorse of Mlle Duquênoi, to whom she speaks curtly: 'L'une montrait la figure du désespoir, l'autre la figure de l'endurcissement' (*JF*, p. 784). Mme de La Pommeraye is another character with a heart of stone. She is insensitive to the desperation of her two *protégées*, who would gladly accept the Marquis's offer. By taking Mlle Duquênoi as his mistress, the Marquis would put an end to the mother and daughter's hardships, and would save them from going deeper in the deception:

> [...] ces deux femmes fondirent en larmes, se jetèrent à ses pieds et lui représentèrent combien il était affreux pour elles de repousser une fortune immense qu'elles pouvaient accepter sans aucune fâcheuse conséquence. (*JF*, pp. 779-80)

The shocked reaction of Jacques exclaiming that 'Cette femme a le diable au corps', intensifies the reader's condemnation of Mme de La Pommeraye, whose insensitivity makes her appear inhuman and unjustifiably immoral.

Sterne and Diderot compelled the reader to abandon passive reception and instead to participate by drawing him in a ludic narrative. In the sentimental novel, the reader is drawn into confusing fiction with reality through the power of sympathy, which does not make the distinction. In the *Eloge de Richardson*, Diderot presents the reader as a puppet in the hands of the author who manipulates him by using sentimental scenes as bait:

> Ô Richardson! on prend, malgré qu'on en ait, un rôle dans tes ouvrages, on se mêle à la conversation, on approuve, on blâme, on admire, on s'irrite, on s'indigne. Combien de fois ne me suis-je pas surpris, comme il est arrivé à des enfants qu'on avait menés au spectacle pour la première fois, criant, *ne le croyez pas, il vous trompe . . . Si vous allez là, vous êtes perdu*.[26]

By its intent focus on the body, dissecting and observing the minutest changes in expression, sentimentalism presents its own particular vision of the human body. The sentimental body is essentially a porous one: emotions and lachrymal fluids cannot be withheld and they reveal a perfect coincidence between what happens inside the body and its external manifestations. This unity allows Bakhtin to distinguish the carnivalesque body from the classical body which is monosemous:

> The body of the new canon is merely one body; no signs of duality have been left. It is self-sufficient and speaks in its name alone. All that happens within it concerns it alone, that is, only the individual, closed sphere. Therefore, all the events taking place within it acquire one single meaning.[27]

The sentimental body may be considered as a classical one in so far as it represents the centre where the conformity between the outside and the inside is accomplished.

The fashion for *tableaux* was born from this aesthetic of conformity, as the perfect coincidence between the signifier and the signified implied that a sentimental scene would be self-explanatory. Literary *tableaux* thus focused on one particular scene held in suspension, isolated from the narrative, as long as was necessary for the description to be completed and for the reader to indulge in his own time in its emotional and aesthetical qualities. Sterne offers such a *tableau*, but makes it deviate from the sentimental line by introducing farcical and grotesque elements. In *Tristram Shandy*, the episode of Maria offers the opportunity for a classical sentimental *tableau*. Having lost her senses because of her thwarted love, 'poor Maria' is placed on the stage, 'sitting upon a bank playing her vespers upon her pipe, with her little goat beside her' (*TS*, IX, xxiii, p. 573). The sentimentalism of this melancholy pastoral scene is then broken by a bawdy comparison Tristram draws between the goat and himself. The author's manipulation of the reader is made here even more noticeable than in the case of Richardson mentioned by Diderot. Indeed, the reader is drawn into the pathetic story of Maria, but his sympathy is brusquely foiled by a grotesque conclusion. Sterne makes use of sentimentalist devices but without necessarily writing a fully sentimental scene. Tristram's feelings for Maria are not untainted empathy: sentimentalism is certainly present, but it is mixed with farce and the grotesque.

In his study of the evolution of laughter in *Rabelais and his World*, Bakhtin remarks that, from the seventeenth century, laughter is directed to what does not fit the classical conception of order, to what is at odds with the prevailing vision of the world.[28] In the *tableau* previously referred to, the superposition of the grotesque on sentimentalism offends the reader's sense of order and cohesion. Bakhtin's remark may be applied to *Tristram Shandy* and *Jacques le fataliste* as the only way to respond to such discrepancy between the two antithetic registers seems to be laughter.

Exposing Inconsistencies in Sentimentalism

Sentimentalism strives to offer a complete system in which sociability, morality and aesthetics are supposed to combine. Yet flaws remain. In *Jacques le fataliste* and *Tristram Shandy*, inconsistencies in sentimentalism are exaggerated and their comical potential is exploited. To expose the failings of sentimentalism, the best method is to dismantle its mechanism. An example of sensibility as pure mechanical reaction to an emotional stimulus, without the necessary distance to reflect upon the process, is given in Diderot's novel, when Jacques takes pity on the woman with the broken oil jar. Jacques's pity has led him to act in a virtuous way, but it is also a mechanical response to signs of anguish. Without thinking, he gives the money he needed to pay the surgeon for his knee operation. When offering her the money to pay back the oil, Jacques is not acting on the basis of a rational judgment. He is responding to a physical feeling the sight of this mother and children has stirred within him and which is a much more convincing rhetorical device than her verbal appeal for help. But because Jacques has acted mechanically and not reasonably, he ends up regretting his 'deux gros écus, qui n'en étaient pas moins donnés' and thus spoils 'par mon regret l'oeuvre que j'avais faite' (*JF*, p. 729). What at first seemed a typical sentimental scene becomes more complex by the introduction of mixed feelings. We do not blindly sympathise alongside Jacques with the woman, we also reflect on the mechanisms triggering our emotions.

When the news of Bobby's death reaches the servants' quarters, it is also a specific effect that mechanically triggers sympathy within the characters. At first, Susannah feels sympathy for her mistress: not for having lost a son but because she will have to go in mourning and renounce 'her red damask, — her orange-tawny, — her white and yellow lutestrings, — her brown taffata, — her bone-laced caps, her bed-gowns, and comfortable under-petticoats' (*TS*, V, vii, p. 325). Obadiah is concerned about 'stubbing the ox-moor', whereas the dim-witted scullion can only come up with the remark that she herself is still living, and Jonathan the coach-man that Bobby 'was alive last *Whitsontide*' (*TS*, V, vii, p. 325). At this point, none of the characters are able to go beyond their concern for the disruption Bobby's death will cause to their daily lives. The dominant feeling is more one of annoyance than sympathy. Sympathy will finally be triggered mechanically by Trim's eloquent hat:

> Are we not here now, continued the corporal, (striking the end of his stick perpendicularly upon the floor, so as to give an idea of health and stability) — and are we not — (dropping his hat upon the ground) gone! In a moment! — 'Twas infinitely striking! *Susannah* burst into a flood of tears. — We are not stocks and stones. — *Jonathan, Obadiah*, the cook-maid, all melted. — The foolish fat scullion herself, who was scouring a fish-kettle upon her knees, was rous'd with it. (*TS*, V, vii, pp. 325-26).

This 'stroke of the corporal's eloquence' (*TS*, V, vii, p. 326) condenses Todd's point on 'sudden reversal' used to increase the dramatic effect of the sentimental, a point I will later come back to.[29] The characters respond to this reversal, as the sight of the dropped hat makes them leave their own private concerns so as to share the awe of death.

The narrator thrice replays the scene of the hat, each time adding a commentary to help the reader appreciate the greatness of Trim's eloquence, but at every repetition forcing him to distance himself from its sentimental nature by considering it rhetorically. The narrator progressively denatures the emotional content of the scene by stressing its rhetorical nature, which slowly slips into being mechanical and finally manipulative:

> Ye who govern this mighty world and its mighty concerns with the *engines* of eloquence, — who heat it, and cool it, and melt it, and mollify it, — and then harden it again to *your purpose* —
> [. . .] Ye, lastly, who drive — and why not, Ye also who are driven, like turkeys to market, with a stick and a red clout — meditate — meditate, I beseech you, upon *Trim*'s hat. (*TS*, VII, p. 327)

The italics of '*engines*' stress the mechanics of sentimentalism where emotions are triggered by a sight, as 'the eye [. . .] gives a smarter stroke, and leaves something more inexpressible upon the fancy, than words can ever convey' (*TS*, V, vii, p. 326). This is demonstrated not only by the Shandy servants, who cry less for Trim's speech than for his dropped hat, but also by Jacques, who is moved to charity not by the woman's plea, but at the sight of her children.

However, the narrator introduces a more disturbing note when he suggests that such visual signs can be mastered through rhetoric, and thus can be just as manipulative as language. Despite his ominous warning, the narrator has not in this case used Trim's eloquent hat to manipulate the reader. Obadiah, Susannah, Jonathan, and the scullion may have been 'driven, like turkeys to market, with a stick and a red clout'. As for the reader, the narrator has prevented him from joining them by forcing him to take a certain distance. The characters' comically divergent thoughts at hearing the sad news prevent the reader from himself emotionally adhering to the scene and sharing sympathy.

As Vila reminds us, the term 'sensibility' replaced that of 'irritability' in the mid eighteenth century to describe the capacity to react to stimuli.[30] It is because I react to external stimuli, because there are points of contact between the world and myself that I am able to be aware of both. Louis Lavelle puts it in terms of a 'point de conjugaison de l'univers et nous'.[31] Sensibility presents a paradox in that it creates a bridge by which the individual can feel the world. This should mean that sensibility implies the discovery of the world by the self. But it can also imply a reflection on how the self senses itself through feeling. Laupies raises the question, 'La sensibilité fait-elle connaître la nature du senti ou la nature du sentant?'[32] Sensibility should maintain the tension of this paradox so as to preserve dialogue and reflection. When the individual fails to do so, sensibility is perverted.

Sentimentalism has often been taxed with measuring the value of a literary scene by the emotions with which it is charged, by the degree of intensity with which it affects its readers. Emotions end up more obscuring than revealing the world to the individual. The individual becomes absent to the world and only receptive to his emotions.

> Le sentimentalisme semble être une inattention aux choses et aux êtres due à une projection de l'émotion sur le monde. Le sujet voit le monde à travers un sentiment récurrent voire obsessionnel. La rêverie l'emporte sur la perception et la déforme: un mot anodin sera prétexte à imagination, prendra une ampleur inattendue. Dans ces conditions, le sujet n'est plus tout à fait partie prenante du sensible, il n'habite plus le monde; loin d'être enraciné dans un 'il y a' sensible, il fragmente le perçu au gré de ses fantasmes. Le sentimentalisme est comme une version élémentaire et inconsciente de la pensée abstraite: le sujet n'est plus ouvert au monde dans sa cohérence perçue mais prélève des éléments en fonction de ses attentes et de ses souhaits.[33]

Uncle Toby provides a perfect illustration to Laupies's comments. In her efforts to kindle an amorous flame in Toby's heart, Widow Wadman asks him to look into her eye under the pretence that dust has been caught in it and is irritating her. It is actually Toby who ends up being caught by that eye which reflects his own innocence, instead of Widow Wadman's flirtatious manipulations:

> [. . .] 'twas an eye full of gentle salutations — and soft responses — speaking — not like the trumpet stop of some ill-made organ, in which many an eye I talk to, holds coarse converse — but whispering soft — like the last low accents of an expiring saint — 'How can you live comfortless, captain

Shandy, and alone, without a bosom to lean your head on — or trust your cares to?' (*TS*, VIII, xxv, p. 525)

Uncle Toby is unable to perceive Widow Wadman's true character; he is blinded by his own expectations he projects on her. Indeed, Widow Wadman is far from interested in engaging in Platonic love: her worries concerning Toby's groin wound are not out of pure sympathy for him.

If Toby is so blind to Widow Wadman's intentions, it is not simply on the account of his innocence; she herself tries to deceive him into believing that she corresponds to his idea of her. If Sterne and Diderot both point to the unreliability of verbal language, they portray body language as just as unreliable. Gestures can be as easily misinterpreted and deceptive as words. A tragic conclusion to deceitful gestures may be found in the story of Mme de La Pommeraye who uses Mlle d'Aisnon as bait to trap the Marquis. In order to disguise her past as a prostitute helping her mother to hold a gambling den, Mme de La Pommeraye commands her to act the *dévote*. Mlle d'Aisnon plays the part so well that the Marquis is convinced that she is as virtuous as she is beautiful:

> C'est la tête d'une *Vierge* de Raphaël sur le corps de sa *Galatée*; et puis une douceur dans la voix! — Une modestie dans le regard! — Une bienséance dans le maintien! — Une décence dans le propos qui ne m'a frappée dans aucune jeune fille comme celle-là. Voilà l'effet de l'éducation. — Lorsqu'il est préparé par un beau naturel. (*JF*, p. 769)

This passage reveals how the Marquis progressively slips from Mlle d'Aisnon's body language to her character, and is tricked into believing that the former is the signifier of the latter. Sincerity of gestures may indeed be questioned by appreciating that which is at stake: in the first case, the opportunity of sexual gratification, but generally the public manifestation of personal virtue made visible through physiognomy.[34] This is true for Mlle d'Aisnon, but also for the reader who must be seen as moved by sentimental novels. Diderot invites the reader not to conclude that only depraved people deceive others by seeming what they are not. Mlle d'Aisnon was brought to lead a depraved existence not out of taste — her mother complains that she has 'aucun esprit de libertinage' — but out of destitution.

If Mlle d'Aisnon knowingly deceives the Marquis by not conforming her behaviour to her true character, she unwittingly taints his sympathy and admiration for her with erotic desire. Sentimentalism carries a certain degree of ambiguity in the way it allows emotions to be expressed. In *Tristram Shandy* and *Jacques le fataliste*, feelings and sexuality are often confused. The scene of the knee rubbing, present in both novels, illustrates this confusion perfectly. Though this is supposed to be a love story, the focus is much more on sensuality than on affection; yet Trim reconciles this by implying that one leads to the other as his feelings increase with the Beguine's rubbing. His overly precise descriptions of the rubbing approach fetishism, as she 'began with the forefinger of her right-hand to rub under [his] knee' and then '[. . .] from rubbing, for some time, with two fingers — proceeded to rub at length, with three — till by little and little she brought down the fourth, and then rubb'd with her whole hand' which was 'white' and 'softer than satin' (*TS*, VIII, xxii, p. 521). Sterne exploits the comical potential of the scene by exaggerating Trim's confusion between love and sex, which in his eyes makes his story perfectly innocent.

Toby seems to share this view as his own chaste conclusion to the story suggests:

> The more she rubb'd, and the longer strokes she took — the more the fire kindled in my veins — till at length, by two or three strokes longer than the rest — my passion rose to the highest pitch — I seiz'd her hand —
> — And then, thou clapped'st it to thy lips, Trim, said my uncle Toby — and madest a speech. (*TS*, VIII, xxii, p. 522)[35]

Toby's ending increases the comical nature of the scene by accentuating the distance between his love version and the more likely erotic one the narrator himself seems to favour by adding 'Whether the corporal's amour terminated precisely in the way my uncle Toby described it, is not material' (*TS*, VIII, xxii, p. 522). Trim's rather delicate disclosure made previously in the course of the conversation to his master, would also make the erotic version a more coherent reading:

> — "*It was not love*" — for during the three weeks she was almost constantly with me, fomenting my knee with her hand, night and day — I can honestly say, an' please your honour — that * * * * * * * * * * * * once.
> That was very odd, Trim, quoth my uncle Toby —
> I think so too — said Mrs. Wadman.
> It never did, said the corporal. (*TS*, VIII, xx, p. 519)

Though not explicitly mentioned, the reader may have a fair idea as to what 'it' refers to. If the reader is indeed right in his assumption, then this passage undermines Tristram's belief in his uncle's complete innocence and modesty when it comes to sexual matters.

We must assume that some readers contemporary to Sterne shared Toby's clean perspective since the episode of the knee rubbing has been included intact in *The beauties of Sterne* supposed to be a compilation of 'chaste' Shandean sentimental scenes. However, this expurgated compilation of passages 'Selected for the heart of sensibility', as the title indicates, strongly encourages the reader to take the sentimental handle, and has carefully left out the more clearly bawdy passage quoted above. The intentions of *The beauties of Sterne* have been to extirpate the grotesque handle so as to ensure that sentimentalism is the authoritative discourse, thus transforming *Tristram Shandy* into a monologic novel.

In his famous plagiarised version of Trim and the Beguine, Diderot reproduces the same confusion between love and sex as, just like for Trim, Jacques's feelings for Denise intensify with her rubbing. The comical effect is also left until the end but this time it resides less in the contrast between the chaste and the probable ending than in the ambiguity of the grammatical construction and of the word *baiser*: 'La passion de Jacques, qui n'avait cessé de la regarder, s'accrut à un tel point que n'y pouvant plus résister, il se précipita sur la main de Denise ... et la baisa' (*JF*, p. 883). The suspension points invite the reader to recognise the possible *double entendre* created by the fact that the female personal pronoun *la* can have as antecedent either 'la main' or Denise. If applied to Denise, *baiser* can easily slip from a chaste meaning to an erotic one.[36]

The ambiguity of sentimentalism is heightened by its relation to money. Goring noticed this when remarking that Harley, the hero of Mackenzie's *The Man of Feeling*, during his tour of Bedlam, gives two guineas to a young woman who particularly moved him, as she had lost her wits after having lost her love. As Goring underlines, this leaves the reader with the impression that Harley is giving money less out of charity than as payment for a touching spectacle.[37] In *Tristram Shandy*, payment for feeling is made explicit. In his encounter with Maria — who bears a striking resemblance to the Bedlam girl both in predicament and attractive appearance — Tristram is so moved by his postilion's description of her that he wants to 'give him a four and twenty sous piece' (*TS*, IX, xxiv, p. 573). Tristram's sympathy for the 'beautiful' Maria who made him feel 'the full-force of an honest heart-ache' takes an eroticised turn when he draws a comparison between himself and her goat (*TS*, IX, xxiv, p. 574).

One may then easily assume that if Tristram pays for being moved, he may also pay to be aroused by a young girl whose distressed looks increase her attraction, especially as this practice is shared by the reader who bought *Tristram Shandy* on its sentimental or bawdy reputation. Anne Vincent-Buffault remarks that in sentimental literature, tears have acquired a commercial value.[38] Vincent-Buffault suggests that the commercialisation of tears enticed authors to write ever more moving sentimental novels to satisfy the demand of the public. The reader's response to sentimental scenes was perceived at first as a sign of morality, but then became ambiguous as it led to a cheapening of sentimentalism itself.[39]

Extreme cases of sympathy appear in *Jacques le fataliste* and *Tristram Shandy*, and their appropriateness is discussed. Diderot brings up the case of people who feel more sympathy for animals than for men. Such cases were discussed by contemporaries of Sterne and Diderot, who commonly viewed sentimentality as misplaced and losing its moral claims when it ceased to be applied to human beings.[40] Such criticism is voiced by the master and Jacques who laugh at 'la passion de l'hôtesse pour les bêtes' (*JF*, p. 747). Fussing over her dog Nicole, who has been maltreated by a customer (who turns out to be the Marquis des Arcis) it was importuning, the landlady is amazed to find in her pet the same moving body language as in humans: 'La pauvre bête! comme cela parle! qui n'en serait touché?' However, her sympathy seems to extend only to her dog, as she seems rather unfeeling towards her maid, who is trying to humour her mistress by showing empathy. Just after having brusquely silenced her maid, threatened that 'au moindre cri qu'elle [the dog] fera je m'en prends à vous', and called her 'sotte', she continues to marvel at dogs:

> Ces chiens, cela est si bon; cela vaut mieux...'
> JACQUES: Que père, mère, frères, sœurs, enfants, valets, époux...
> L'HOTESSE: Mais oui, ne pensez pas à rire, cela est innocent, cela vous est fidèle, cela ne vous fait jamais de mal, au lieu que le reste...
> JACQUES: Vive les chiens! il n'y a rien de plus parfait sous le ciel.
> L'HOTESSE: S'il y a quelque chose de plus parfait, du moins ce n'est pas l'homme. (*JF*, pp. 746–47)

To justify her point, the landlady gives the example of the miller's dog who displays more love and constancy for Nicole than any man for a woman. Later on, the master recalls the landlady's misplaced love for dogs and criticises it as responsible for diverting sympathy from men: 'Ce qu'on donne à ces animaux-là suffirait à la nourriture de deux ou trois malheureux' (*JF*, p. 801).

Amongst the literary scenes considered as displaying misplaced sentimentalism is the episode of the ass eating a macaroon in *Tristram Shandy*. Just like the landlady and her dog in *Jacques le fataliste*, Tristram is amazed by the expressiveness of body language in an ass whose 'patient endurance of sufferings, wrote so unaffectedly in his looks and carriage, which pleads so mightily for him', enables him to engage in a conversation and 'commune for ever' with it (*TS*, VII, xxxii, pp. 470 & 471). Completely uninterested in the owner, who only appears in the text as 'a person' and of whose circumstances we know nothing, Tristram bestows his undivided sympathy on the ass chewing an artichoke:

> God help thee, Jack! said I, thou hast a bitter breakfast on't — and many a bitter day's labour — and many a bitter blow, I fear, for its wages — 'tis all — all bitterness to thee, whatever life is to others. — And now thy mouth, if one knew the truth of it, is as bitter, I dare say, as soot — (for he had cast aside the stem) and thou hast not a friend perhaps in all this world, that will give thee a macaroon. (*TS*, VII, xxxii, p. 471)

To consider this scene as a truly sentimental one and believe that the narrator is in all seriousness full-heartedly sympathising with the ass would be a misreading.

Sterne is yet again mixing the sentimental with the farcical visible in the narrator's self-derision when talking to the ass and the animal's serious and melancholy body language serving as answers. Most tellingly, the narrator does not take his own display of sympathy completely seriously, but considers it more as a lark, as he admits 'that there was more of pleasantry in the conceit, of seeing *how* an ass would eat a macaroon — than of benevolence in giving him one, which presided in the act' (*TS*, VII, xxxii, p. 472). Nevertheless, as the comical conversation sadly ends with the falling of 'a thundering bastinado upon the poor devil's crupper', the reader is left with a feeling of pity for the ass. If Sterne does seem to ridicule misplaced sentimentalism by exaggerating it, he also allows the reader to sympathise truly with an animal.

Impolite Transgressions

Sentimentalism transgresses the external/internal limits through the mingling of tears. Vincent-Buffault mentions the circulation of tears as an internal liquid secretion, spilling out to be exchanged and shared.[41] Yet despite its porosity, the sentimental body is kept under control: the only physical manifestations allowed are those that reveal a complete correlation between what is happening inside and outside the body, and are susceptible to arouse empathy. The carnivalesque body is unfettered by such checks and multiplies external and internal transgressions. Bakhtin gives us a definition of the classical body by setting it against its opposite, the carnivalesque body:

> That which protrudes, bulges, sprouts, or branches off (when a body transgresses its limits and a new one begins) is eliminated, hidden, or moderated. All orifices of the body are closed. The basis of the image is the individual, strictly limited mass, the impenetrable façade. The opaque surface and the body's valleys acquire an essential meaning as the border of a closed individuality that does not merge with other bodies and with the world. [. . .]
>
> In the modern image of the individual body, sexual life, eating, drinking, and defecation have radically changed their meaning: they have been transferred to the private and psychological level where their connotation becomes narrow and specific, torn away from the direct relation to the life of society and to the cosmic whole. In this new connotation they can no longer carry on their former philosophical functions.[42]

When listing the qualities necessary for the governor who will be in charge of the education of his son, Walter is very particular regarding the discipline of the body which must be perfectly controlled:

> There is, continued my father, a certain mien and motion of the body and all its parts, both in acting and speaking, which argues a man *well within* [. . .]
>
> There are a thousand unnoticed openings, continued my father, which let a penetrating eye at once into a man's soul [. . .]
>
> It is for these reasons, continued my father, that the governor I make choice of shall neither lisp, or squint, or wink, or talk loud, or look fierce, or foolish; — or bite his lips, or grind his teeth, or speak through his nose, or pick it, or blow it with his fingers. —
>
> [. . .] — nor (according to *Erasmus*) shall he speak to any one in making water, — nor shall he point to carrion or excrement. (*TS*, VI, v, pp. 373–74)

In this excerpt, Walter negatively portrays the carnivalesque body by opposing it to the polite body. The italics, original to the text, emphasise the closure of the polite body and what is transgressed by the carnivalesque, especially in its farcical scatological manifestations. According to Walter, impropriety of bodily behaviour creates 'a thousand unnoticed openings', indiscreet in that they expose the soul to the 'penetrating eye'.

Unlike the sentimental body, the carnivalesque body is inherently grotesque in the way it transgresses the external/internal limits. Sentimentalism uses these transgressions to provoke sympathy within the reader with the intention to strengthen his sense of morality and virtue. The carnivalesque transgresses with the purpose of turning upside-down established values and thus taking the reader out of his comfort zone:

> It is looking for that which protrudes from the body, all that seeks to go out beyond the body's confines. Special attention is given to the shoots and branches, to all that prolongs the body and links it to other bodies or to the world outside.[43]

Such farcical transgressions keep recurring in *Tristram Shandy* and *Jacques le fataliste*. In volume I, the farcical nature of the Sorbonne treatise on intra-uterine baptism is based on the transgressive intrusion of holy water in both female and male genitalia to ensure the christening of the foetus or, in the other case, of the homunculi. In volume III, the excommunication edict also transgresses the external and internal limits in damnation: 'Maledictus sit intus et exterius' (*TS*, III, xi, p. 158). Its obsessive list of body parts, grotesque by the minutiae and progressing towards scatology, parallels the list drawn by Walter for his son's governor:

> Maledictus sit viviendo, moriendo, — [...] — manducando, bibendo, esuriendo, sitiendo, jejunando, dormitando, dormiendo, vigilando, ambulando, stando, sedendo, jacendo, operando, quiescendo, mingendo, cacando, flebotomando.
> [...]
> Maledictus sit in capillis; maledictus sit in cerebro. Maledictus sit in vertice, in temporibus, in fronte, in auriculis, in superciliis, in oculis, in genis, in maxiliis, in naribus, in dentibus, mordacibus sive molaribus, in labiis, in gutture, in humeris, in harmis, in brachiis, in manibus, in digitis, in pectore, in corde, et in omnibus interioribus stomacho tenus, in renibus, in inguinibus, in femore, in genitalibus, in coxis, in genubus, in cruribus, in pedibus, et in unguibus. (*TS*, III, xi, p. 158)

In volume IV, 'Slawkenbergius's tale' plays on the reversal of what is acceptably visible and what must remain hidden, as the 'protruding' nose of huge dimensions stands as a signifier for the genitals. In the course of his travels, Slawkenbergius enters the town of Strasburg where the sight of his enormous nose stirs an uproar amongst the population, making the men jealous, the women longing to touch it, and tormenting the nuns who lose their sleep. Diderot uses a similar device when Jacques, whose room 'n'était séparée [...] que par des planches à claire-voie sur lesquelles on avait collé du papier gris' (*JF*, p. 682), cannot help but follow his hostess reaching orgasm through the increasing tingling of her ear.

This episode illustrates Bakhtin's remark on the transgression of the carnivalesque where taboo body-parts are exhibited, in the case of Slawkenbergius and the peasant woman by taking the place of inoffensive ones. It also intertextually refers to Rabelais, Bakhtin's primary source for the elaboration of the notion of the carnivalesque: the episode of Gargantua's birth through Gargamelle's ear, her womb having been obstructed by a vast quantity of tripe on which she had feasted. These three examples illustrate what Goring refers to as 'Sterne's knowing and often wry treatment of both polite and exuberantly impolite aspects of embodiment'.[44] They are also impolite towards Catholicism, which they turn to ridicule, and yet there is more to them than simply the expression of anti-popish sentiments. They obey the true medieval carnivalesque style. Indeed, carnival plunges deeply its roots in Catholicism as the celebration before Lent, but also as a counterbalance to the sternness of some of its religious demands.

Far from attacking Catholicism, carnival celebrates it through parody, which explains why members of the clergy participated in the festivities by making a travestied use of sacred objects and texts, such as a farcical rewriting of Latin prayers. Sterne appears to be familiar with such aspects of medieval carnival as he includes the Latin version of the excommunication edict and Slawkenbergius' tale, and places it next to his English translation. In volume I, the reader has already learned to distrust the Shandean translations: '*Amicus Plato*, my father would say, construing the words to my uncle *Toby*, as he went along, *Amicus Plato*; that is, DINAH was my aunt; — *sed magis amica veritas* — but TRUTH is my sister' (*TS*, I, xxi, 61). And indeed, by closely comparing the Latin text of the excommunication to its English counterpart, additions increasing the farcical nature of the text become apparent, such as 'capillis', meaning hair, but translated as 'the hair of his head', and 'unguibus', meaning nails, but translated as 'toe-nails' (*TS*, III, xi, p. 158). Tristram's translation further exaggerates the exactness of the edict in the naming of the various body parts by being even more punctilious than the original. Catholicism and philosophy are mocked in the same way that Plato ends up by being embodied by the infamous aunt Dinah.

In the carnivalesque, the reversal of classical order is not limited to the body. As Bakhtin points out, it is generalised to every aspect of daily life:

> All the symbols of the carnival idiom are filled with this pathos of change and renewal, with the sense of the gay relativity of prevailing truths and authorities. We find here a characteristic logic, the peculiar logic of the "inside out"

(*à l'envers*), of the "turnabout", of a continual shifting from top to bottom, from front to rear, of numerous parodies and travesties, humiliations, profanations, comic crownings and uncrownings. A second life, a second world of folk culture is thus constructed; it is to a certain extent a parody of the extracarnival life, a 'world inside out'.[45]

The characters in both Sterne's and Diderot's novels are submitted to such movements. A peasant girl is accidentally pushed off horse and lands in an embarrassing posture because the rider, a pedantic country doctor, got over-excited in trying to prove his point. Elsewhere, the master falls off his horse into the arms of his servant anticipating the accident as he intentionally attached his saddle badly. This is particularly humiliating as he brutally passes from a dominant position to a debasing one, at the mercy of his servant who is the one in control of the situation. However, Jacques is not exempt from such 'uncrownings', which he accepts as he is prepared to share the fate of Thales, whose philosophy was based more on the elaboration of abstract systems than on the exploration of what reality has to offer. The penalty for this is the reversal of situation, the 'comic crownings and uncrownings' described by Bakhtin, where the philosopher tumbles down from his lofty spheres onto hard reality.

Jacques does indeed suffer a similar uncrowning to Thales. After having ominously rushed towards every gibbet along the road, Jacques's horse gallops with all speed into a house, the rider's head violently colliding against the doorframe, thus knocking him unconscious. Jacques is well taken care of by the master of the house; and the next day, when it is time for him to pursue his travels, brimming with gratitude, he heartily thanks his host with many caresses and calling him a 'citoyen officieux' and 'honnête' (*JF*, p. 722). Still ignoring the identity of his benefactor, who seemed rather embarrassed, he praises him to his master, saying that 'n'attachant aucune importance aux services qu'il rend, il faut qu'il soit naturellement officieux et qu'il ait une longue habitude de bienfaisance' (*JF*, p. 722). The master confounds Jacques, who is discredited as a judge of character, when he tells him that the man whose praises he has been singing is in fact the hangman who owned the whimsical horse. Such reversals contribute to the revelation of 'The essence of the grotesque [which] is precisely to present a contradictory and double-faced fullness of life'.[46]

In *Tristram Shandy* and *Jacques le fataliste*, the coincidence of opposites extends to novelistic registers, thus strangely combining sentimentalism and the grotesque in the same episode. For example, the landlady of the Grand-Cerf keeps being interrupted in her story of Mme de La Pommeraye's revenge on the Marquis des Arcis by trivial questions and calls concerning the daily running of the inn. In *Tristram Shandy*, the confusion of interlocutors also leads to a confusion of registers. In Slawkenbergius' tale, the stranger mixes his sentimental discourse to his love, the absent Julia, with his remarks to his mule:

> O Julia, my lovely Julia! — nay I cannot stop to let thee bite that thistle — that ever the suspected tongue of a rival should have robbed me of enjoyment when I was upon the point of tasting it. —
> — Pugh! — 'tis nothing but a thistle — never mind it — thou shalt have a better supper at night. —
> — Banish'd from my country — my friends — from thee. —
> Poor devil, thou'rt sadly tired with thy journey! — come — get on a little faster — (*TS*, IV, Slawkenbergius's Tale, p. 228)

The result is a farcical muddle where the reader mistakes the discourse addressed to Julia and that directed to the mule. Both interlocutors, though complete opposites, end up being fused. Such disruptions act as palimpsests as they superpose meaning.

In the article 'Yorick's Sentimental Journey: A comic "Pilgrim's Progress" for the man of feeling', Stout summarises perfectly the incapacity of the critics to analyse *A Sentimental Journey* as a whole, by taking into account both the sentimental and the grotesque aspects of the novel. Stout's remarks on *A Sentimental Journey* can just as easily be applied to *Tristram Shandy*:

> In the course of his journey, Yorick displays with manifest self-approval all the benevolent sentiments widely regarded during the eighteenth century as the essence of virtue, particularly by those who shared the credo of the 'man of feeling'. On the other hand, his sentimental travels consistently exhibit the comic incongruities between his exalted impulses and the situations which occasion them, expose their instability and radical impurity, and reveal his susceptibility to all the venial imperfections of human nature, including pruriency, concupiscence, selfishness, and vanity.[47]

Critics contemporary with Sterne and Diderot preferred to ignore the grotesque side of the novel, while critics contemporary with Stout have opted for its more comical elements, sentimentalism having fallen into disrepute. As Vincent-Buffault remarks in *The History of Tears*, comedy was no longer fashionable in the second half of the eighteenth century, and instead the public demanded 'tears', untainted by laughter, to be found in the *drame bourgeois*.[48] Both Sterne and Diderot went against the current by heartily mixing tears and laughter, and that sometimes in the same episode. Critics contemporary with Sterne and Diderot were unable to understand the coincidence of sentimental and grotesque registers. Naigeon, Diderot's publisher, preferred the story of Mme de la Pommeraye, and regretted it did not constitute the entirety of the book. Critics contemporary with Sterne praised *Tristram Shandy* for its sentimental scenes. The great favourites were the story of Yorick's death, of Maria, and most of all of Le Fevre (probably because it was the one where the comical aspects were the least obvious). Many eighteenth-century critics' commendations have been recorded by Mullan.[49]

The fashion for sentimentalism automatically made the grotesque unpopular. Jacques's various love stories, similar to the medieval *fabliaux*, shocked readers, who considered them as gratuitous bawdiness, without any literary value. However, one may say that they are a more realistic depiction of man and woman relationships than the sentimental episodes. The same problem arose with *Tristram Shandy*. As Mullan underlines, the success of Sterne in sentimental compilations is explained by the fact that readers could thus have access to the 'clean' and 'safe' expurgated version of the text. *The beauties of Sterne [...] selected for the heart of sensibility*, which had reached its thirteenth edition in 1799, compiles the sentimental passages of *Tristram Shandy* and *A Sentimental Journey* for the aesthetical pleasure and moral instruction of the '*chaste* lovers of literature'.

The beauties of Sterne include many carnivalesque scenes, such as Walter choosing a governor for his son, the story of Le Fever and Maria, the beguine rubbing Trim's wounded knee, Trim dropping his hat. But as the preface announces, these extracts were rid of any devious allusion, since the grotesque was felt as a corruption of the supposedly sentimental novel:

> The *chaste* part of the world complained so loudly of the obscenity which taints the writings of *Sterne*, (and, indeed, with some reason), that those readers under their immediate inspection were not suffered to penetrate beyond the title-page of his *Tristram Shandy* [....].[50]

Looking at the eighteenth-century reviews of *Tristram Shandy* collected by Mullan, it becomes apparent that contemporaries of Sterne were unable to understand the coincidence of sentimental and grotesque registers, which they could only attribute to bad writing and the author's irrepressible lewdness.[51] Some of the expressions used to describe this coincidence point towards farce without appreciating it. The phrase 'interlarded with obscenity', quoted by both Mullan and Goring from the *Monthly Review* and referring to Sterne's volumes, pinpoints the farcical nature of the text.[52] Just as in the traditional farce where religious texts were 'interlarded' with buffoonish additions, grotesque elements are interspersed within the sentimental scenes in *Tristram Shandy*. Goring joins Mullan's conclusions on the reception of the novel by its contemporaries who desired to see the grotesque completely replaced by sentimentalism.[53]

> With its sentimental moments thus mixed with moderated but enduring Rabelaisianism, *Tristram Shandy* appeared to some early readers to offer jewels buried in mud: moral and affecting passages surrounded by lewdness, but not totally compromised or contaminated by it.[54]

Goring suggests that the difficulty resides in the fact that the grotesque does not annul the text's sentimental character, and *vice versa*, thus making a Manichean reading unsatisfying.

Yet the challenge of analysing the grotesque and the sentimental conjointly remains, and such wavering between the two registers may be the true reason for the readers' discontent. In the article 'Garrick and Tristram Shandy', Hafter suggests that by making sentimentalism and the grotesque coincide, Sterne is borrowing from Garrick the technique of 'creating striking contrasts' so as to make the public experience the shock of running through emotional extremes.[55] Yet Hafter's explanation seems unsatisfactory since the reader, unlike Garrick's audience, has difficulty in emotionally following the narrator from one register to the other, and has a tendency to exclude one from the other. Stout himself is unsatisfied with having to choose between the grotesque and sentimentalism, and goes back to the didactic quality of the novel to find an answer. According to him, Sterne's purpose was to increase a sense of philanthropy in the reader. Philanthropy here should be taken in the sense of love for one's fellow brethren, and is characterised by 'an ability to share sympathetically the joys and sorrows of our fellow-creatures, and a faculty for good-humored cheerfulness enabling man to participate in all the God-given pleasures and joys of a benign universe.'[56]

This must however be accompanied by the 'comic proof of the incongruities between his [the man of feeling] faith in his benevolent impulses — and the realities of acting on imperfect motives in an imperfect, though beneficent, world.'[57] Consequently, the grotesque enables the reader to avoid self-complacency in witnessing with satisfaction his own virtue, which is one of the dangers of sentimentalism. However, Stout warns us not to misinterpret the use of the grotesque as a way to negate sentimentalism, the virtues of which Sterne believed in. Both can only function jointly, hence revealing man's own contradictions and ambiguity, instead of the single version sentimentalism offers. Stout thus views the coincidence of sentimentalism and the grotesque as part of the Socratic 'know yourself' principle. Stout's views on the coincidence of sentimentalism and the grotesque as an inner dialogue as opposed to a single dominant vision of the self can be furthered by Bakhtin's notion of the carnivalesque developed in *Rabelais and his World*.

The Carnivalesque

The answer as to what motivated Sterne's and Diderot's decision to combine opposites may be found in Bakhtin's notion of the carnivalesque he developed in his study on Rabelais. Bakhtin himself invites us to make use of the carnivalesque for *Tristram Shandy* and *Jacques le fataliste* by presenting them as direct descendants of Rabelais.[58] In the same way that carnival takes its meaning from its opposition to everyday life, the grotesque must not be dissociated from sentimentalism, and my aim is to demonstrate that the coincidence of these two registers constitutes a true carnivalesque transgression, furthering the sociable exchange of sympathy eventually shut out by sentimentalism. Sterne and

Diderot use the carnivalesque so as to prevent sentimentalism from becoming the dominant discourse of their novels. As Todd briefly remarks, sentimental novels 'discourage multiple readings', which in other words means they favour a single, authoritative discourse. This is far from being the case in our two texts, renowned for their complexity and their multi-layered readings.

The subjective nature of sensibility is problematic, especially when it comes to communication, as my experience of the world differs from that of another person. But this does not mean that sensibility brings dialogue to a close. On the contrary, it is because of those inexorable divergences that the endlessness of dialogue is guaranteed, and that there is no place for a dominant discourse. Mullan opposes *Tristram Shandy* to traditional sentimental novels on similar grounds to Bakhtin. Sterne refuses to enclose his work in any moral system through a didactic purpose:

> The suggestiveness of parts of *Tristram Shandy* binds the discriminating, private reader more thoroughly to the text's 'sociality' and parodies debates about how to read a narrative morally. It also enacts that avoidance of completion or fulfilment whose larger patterns run through the novel (from mis-conception to misconception). The novel that tried to be utterly, exhaustively moral (*Clarissa* is the model) was always striving for completion. Its ideal was that of the achievement of instructive intent, the reader who had been taught to read properly. Sterne, on the contrary, exploits the incompleteness that demands the reader's inferences.[59]

Closed, complete discourse is what draws us away from an appreciation of the world, itself incomplete and open. The complete discourse is reassuring in that it can be fully understood, unlike the world which will always offer the resistance of its otherness. Neither Sterne nor Diderot engages in the free will *versus* fatalism debate. Unlike philosophical tales, *Tristram Shandy* and *Jacques le fataliste* side with neither camp and do not try to convince the reader of one stance or the other. Diderot offers a parody of these debates going round in circles and which must eventually be put to an end without reaching a conclusion by the narrator's interruption.

Refusal to systematise does not solely depend on the narrator's direct intervention. According to Bakhtin, 'the essence of grotesque is [...] to present a contradictory and double-faced fullness of life', and its principle is the 'degradation, [...] the lowering of all that is high, ideal, abstract'.[60] The grotesque represents one of the two facets of the Janus carnivalesque, its counterpart being the 'high, ideal, abstract', or in the case of *Tristram Shandy* and *Jacques le fataliste*, sentimentalism. Yet the grotesque does not annul sentimentalism, and *vice versa*: each 'revives and renews' the other.[61] This joins Mullan's own interpretation of Sterne's 'coexistence of sentimentalism and suggestiveness' which furthers the sociability between the text and the reader. The reader is 'flattered to be segregated from "the *herd* of the *world*"' as the novel presumes he is intelligent enough to make sense of this coexistence of opposites. This point is part of Mullan's focus on how the text *Tristram Shandy* socialises with its reader by translating the characters' strange behaviour and body language into feelings, thus enabling him to comprehend their eccentricities.[62] But more important here is Mullan's claim that 'This reader was capable of a private act of inference which would discover the 'humour', the insinuations, of the text, but which would also enliven its pathos into an intense, because visceral, experience'.[63] Though Mullan does not refer to the carnivalesque, the term 'enliven' is but a synonym for Bakhtin's 'revives and renews'.

The 'enlivening' of sentimentalism does not necessarily lead to a strengthening of its moral aim. Mullan claims that 'Sterne has shrugged off the usual duty of sentimentalism: the teaching of virtue'.[64] Indeed, in the episode of the donkey eating a macaroon, the narrator humorously acknowledges misplaced sentimentalism. Yet this does not prevent the reader, encouraged by the text, to feel sympathy for the beaten animal. Morality here does not enter the reader's and the narrator's pity, and humour does not serve as a deterrent, as it does in classical laughter, to guide the reader in recognising what is worthy of sympathy and what is not. By not being morally charged, humour enlivens sympathy by allowing it to enter the domain of simple 'experience', unburdened by any didactic intention. This complements Todd's remark that 'a plot of sudden reversal' creating emotional contrasts between scenes, enhances the vividness of sentimental tableaux.[65]

Sterne and Diderot do indeed employ this technique of 'sudden reversal', but displace it from the plot to the registers so as to create quite a different effect. The grotesque does, as expected, make the sentimental scenes very striking by contrast. Nevertheless, it does not valorise them, in the sense that it invites the reader to question their appropriateness; nor does it invalidate or annul them in the process. The function of the carnivalesque is to undermine the authority and dominance of established discourse, but it does not negate the discourse itself. It is interesting to note that Bakhtin links this rejection of a totalitarian discourse to the vision of cosmic order of Tristram Shandy's namesake, Hermes Trismegistes, who describes 'the sphere, whose centre is everywhere, whose circumference is nowhere'.[66]

In his definition of carnivalesque laughter, Bakhtin places the emphasis on its ability to undermine the supremacy of a dominant and established discourse:

> True ambivalent and universal laughter does not deny seriousness but purifies and completes it. Laughter purifies from dogmatism, from the intolerant and the petrified; it liberates from fanaticism and pedantry, from fear and intimidation, from didacticism, naïveté and illusion, from the single meaning, the single level, from sentimentality. Laughter does not permit seriousness to atrophy and to be torn away from the one being, forever incomplete. It restores this ambivalent wholeness.[67]

Bakhtin opposes carnivalesque laughter to that of classical aesthetics confined to the role of 'a light amusement or a form of salutary social punishment of corrupt and low persons'.[68] Classical laughter, directed at what does not conform to a given order, is likely to be found in sentimental literature to mock individual vices and offer a contrast to the virtuous characters. Far from policing for a particular order and asserting its authority, carnivalesque laughter questions and challenges it by turning it 'upside down'. It thus creates a 'peculiar view relative to the world' of its own. For this reason, according to Bakhtin, it carries 'deep philosophical meaning'.[69] On that account, Bordeu's advice to put sensibility at a distance, as opposed to Mlle de L'Espinasse who lets herself be engulfed by emotions and as a result leaves no space for thought, must not be misunderstood for deactivation.[70] On the contrary, such distance allows one to feel sensibility and to learn to be more receptive to it and to refine it, instead of being governed by it.

Diderot used this distancing as a way to discriminate between great men, who turn sensibility into an active principle, and ordinary men, who are unable to reflect on the emotions which are thrust upon them. Diderot is here adapting one of the rules of conduct of the *honnête homme* who distances himself from his actions so as to reflect upon them and assure that they do not discord with his will. The *malhonnêtes*, on the contrary, are unable to distance themselves from their passions and they are forced to hide the fact that they are governed by them.[71]

For Adam Smith in *The Theory of Moral Sentiments* (1759), distance is an unconditional criterion of sympathy. Sympathy can only be felt when one is placed in the position of a spectator: it is because the spectator is not pressed by the immediacy of the feeling and is able to understand it by being aware of the context that he will truly be able to sympathise. When Jacques explains how he is able to sympathise with a woman in the pangs of labour, he explains that it is because he is witnessing the visible signs of her pains. By taking the place of the spectator, Jacques can imagine a type of suffering that is foreign to him, and with which he would have been incapable of sympathising if he had not taken the necessary distance. Distance does not negate the self-reflexive power of sympathy; if anything, it strengthens it. Through the grotesque, Sterne and Diderot provide the reader with the means to take the necessary distance from sentimentalism. However, many readers did not recognise this.

Bakhtin claims that, by no longer recognising a dominant order and by questioning its laws, carnival suspended its hierarchy and consequently barriers to sociability:

> [...] free, familiar contacts were deeply felt and formed an essential element of the carnival spirit. People were, so to speak, reborn for new, purely human relations. These truly human relations were not only a fruit of imagination or abstract thought; they were experienced.[72]

Paradoxically, the carnivalesque furthers sociability by restoring polite conversation. When a conversation is governed by a dominant point of view, it keeps in check diverging opinions and prevents full participation. By refusing such hierarchy and presenting every opinion as equally valid, the carnivalesque is at heart polite, though rude in its form, in the sense that it promotes the respect of diverging views. In her portrait of polite conversation, Martine Lucchesi-Belzane underlines the fact that it must not be limited to the simple reiteration of a received idea. On the contrary, polite conversation should liberate the participants from authoritative views by offering a free area where one may follow one's own train of thought:

> [. . .] elle apparaît dépourvue de toute finalité comme de tout enjeu et de toute urgence; calme et insouciante, elle pratique la suspension de jugement, la mise entre parenthèses des intérêts théoriques et pratiques. Dénuée de parti pris, de violence et d'inquiétude, elle paraît vouloir nous délivrer du souci de définir, de signifier et de prouver.[73]

By substituting an object/individual for emotion, exacerbated sensibility gives the illusion that, because we are embracing emotion, we are embracing the object/individual itself in its entirety. Such an illusion marks the desire to annul the singularity of the object/individual, and to appropriate it. Such domination is profoundly impolite. Martine Lucchesi-Belzane considers that to tear away subjectivity so as to realise 'un idéal de communion et de transparence des âmes', would mean destroying 'ces mêmes voiles [qui] délimitent et protègent à la fois le territoire de l'intime'. She defends politeness on the grounds that, even though it impedes an anyway utopian 'fusion des âmes', it creates the means for sociability while at the same time acknowledging and respecting otherness.[74] Following Laupies's comment, politeness agrees with sensibility's teaching on how to perceive otherness and to appreciate its resistance as the proof of its reality:

> La sensibilité est aptitude à saisir la différence: elle est constituée par cela même; je suis sensible, en effet, à proportion de ma capacité à appréhender l'indicible, l'arrière-plan, le jeu de distinctions qui donnent sens. La volonté de jouir immédiatement du 'spectacle' annule la résistance des choses, les difficultés qu'il peut y avoir à les appréhender, leur altérité: le produit culturel recycle ainsi les œuvres sous formes d'extraits, de digests ou de 'remake' pour rendre consommable ce qui demanderait un effort . . . on oublie toutefois qu'il n'y a de vraie sensibilité que dans l'effort.[75]

Laupies's remarks are particularly appropriate for *Tristram Shandy*, transformed in *The beauties of Sterne* into a collection of sentimental scenes, purged from the grotesque and enabling the reader '[de] jouir immédiatement du spectacle'. Following Laupies's argument, the dislike for the mixing of registers lies less in the moral infringements than in the effort it requires from the reader to reconcile the two, to make sense of the 'jeu de distinctions', and which leads to 'vraie sensibilité'.

The transgression of limits prompts openness and helps establish the dialogue of contraries. This fulfils the communication desired by sentimentalism in its quest for sociability:

> The object transgresses its own confines, ceases to be itself. The limits between the body and the world are erased, leading to the fusion of the one with the other and with surrounding objects. [...]
> All these convexities and orifices have a common characteristic; it is within them that the confines between bodies and between the body and the world are overcome: there is an interchange and an interorientation.[76]

Lavelle's remark on sensibility as being a 'point de conjugaison de l'univers et nous' suggests that transgression of the external and internal limits constitutes a point of contact between sensibility and the carnivalesque.[77] Whereas sentimentalism offers to individuals an interaction limited by politeness, the carnivalesque proves to be much better suited to prolong and strengthen sensibility's 'point de conjugaison'.

Conclusion

The closing words of *Tristram Shandy*, 'A COCK and a BULL' (*TS*, IX, xxxiii, p. 588), have often served to describe Sterne's novel. *Tristram Shandy* may indeed be regarded as a 'cock and bull story', in the sense that it is 'long rambling' and 'disconnected' (*OED*). This idiomatic expression has its French counterpart in the phrase *passer du coq à l'âne*, which shares the same meaning and may be applied equally well to *Jacques le fataliste*, also full of disjointed discourses. The cock-and-bull, or *coq-à-l'âne* quality of both novels points towards their carnivalesque nature. Bakhtin was interested in *coq-à-l'âne* in literature and its relation to the carnivalesque. In *Rabelais and his World*, he describes it thus:

> One of the popular forms of comic speech was the so-called *coq-à-l'âne*, "from rooster to ass." This is a genre of intentionally absurd verbal combinations, a form of completely liberated speech that ignores all norms, even those of elementary logic.[78]

Bakhtin presents the *coq-à-l'âne* as a representative form of the carnivalesque in that it flaunts its disrespect for any form of rule and offers a space where all types of discourse may freely combine.

By offering a space where associations are created without following any given pattern, the *coq-à-l'âne* is diametrically opposed to '"classic" aesthetics, that is, the aesthetics of the ready-made and the completed.'[79] For Bakhtin, the *coq-à-l'âne* constitutes a form of speech used as a means to induce the most extreme digressions, whereas classic aesthetics offer a linear progression guaranteeing completion. These diverging aesthetic qualities are accompanied by their corresponding ideologies. According to Bakhtin, the *coq-à-l'âne* conveys the 'artistic and ideological meaning' of the carnivalesque, which leads him to consider it as 'the carnivalization of speech' 'which freed it from the gloomy seriousness of official philosophy as well as from the truisms and commonplace ideas.'[80]

The *coq-à-l'âne*, or cock and bull, has been recognised by many as one of the defining features of *Jacques le fataliste* and *Tristram Shandy*.[81] It is also representative of the carnivalesque dimension present in both novels, and which has participated in their aesthetic and ideological shaping. By allowing conflicting registers and genres to combine, the carnivalesque questions the dominance of the established canon of beauty and places it at an equal level with its own unconventional model. The aesthetics of the carnivalesque have ideological implications as this questioning is extended to the ideas expressed in the novels. Just as it challenges classic aesthetics, the carnivalesque disputes the dominance of established discourses and annuls hierarchy between diverging philosophical views, thus dethroning authoritative order.

Notes to Chapter 4

1. McMorran has studied in depth the impact of travel writing on the narrative in *Tristram Shandy* and *Jacques le fataliste*. See chapters 6 and 7.
2. Gardner D. Stout, Jr, 'Yorick's Sentimental Journey: A comic "Pilgrim's Progress" for the man of Feeling' *ELH*, 30 (1963), 395–412, p. 396.
3. For further reading on the carnivalesque in the English Enlightenment, see Terry Castle, *Masquerade and Civilisation: The Carnivalesque in Eighteenth-Century English Culture and Fiction* (London: Methuen, 1986). Castle applies Bakhtin's concept of the carnivalesque with regard to masquerades in eighteenth-century English society and their literary representation.
4. John Mullan, *Sentiment and Sociability, The Language of Feeling in the Eighteenth Century* (Oxford: Clarendon Press, 1988), p. 2.
5. See James Beattie, *The Theory of Language* (Menston: The Scholar Press Limited, 1968), and Locke, *An Essay concerning Human Understanding*.
6. In *A Treatise of Human Nature*, ed. L.A. Selby-Bigge (Oxford: Clarendon Press, 1978), p. 318, quoted by Mullan, p. 29, David Hume marvelled at the universality of feeling confirming the inherently sociable nature of man: 'Nature has preserv'd a great resemblance among all human creatures, and that we never remark any passion or principle in others, of which, in some degree or other, we may not find a parallel in ourselves'. On the universality of body language, see also chapter 1 of Paul Goring, *The Rhetoric of Sensibility in Eighteenth-Century Culture* (Cambridge: Cambridge University Press, 2005).
7. Anne C. Vila, *Enlightenment and Pathology, Sensibility in the Literature and Medicine of Eighteenth-Century France* (Baltimore, London: John Hopkins University Press, 1998), p. 155.
8. The reader might remember how quickly Walter recovered from the death of his eldest son, Bobby, which may seem unnatural in comparison with the great grief displayed at Tristram's crushed nose. One possible explanation for this could be that Walter's distress is linked to the upsetting of his theories rather than to his son's death. Bobby's death does

not disturb his ideas; on the contrary, it actually nourishes them, which makes up for his loss and offers a form of compensation. On the other hand, in the episode of the crushed nose, Walter grieves not so much for the mutilation of his newborn son than for the fact that according to his theory on noses, the worst-case scenario has come to pass.

9. Janet Todd, *Sensibility, an Introduction* (London: Methuen, 1986), p. 2.
10. Diderot, *L'Eloge de Richardson*, in *Contes et romans*, p. 908.
11. Diderot, *La Religieuse*, in *Contes et romans*, pp. 384-85. Quoting this passage, Connon warns us that '[this] is not, as the narrative would have us believe, Grimm reporting d'Alainville observing Diderot, but Diderot writing about himself. This change of perspective certainly modifies our attitude to this tale — what is intended to seem an affectionate tribute begins to look like mere self-indulgence, and we may also be inclined to be less convinced of the veracity of the anecdote. Surely, though, the real point of this incident is that it provides another illustration of the power of fiction — what better proof of the fact that a lack of literal belief is no obstacle to the impact of a story than that it can have the power to produce such a strong emotional reaction even in its creator.' In Connon, pp. 209-10.
12. Goring, p. 29.
13. See on the *mise en abyme* Anne Vincent-Buffault, *The History of Tears, Sensibility and Sentimentality*, trans. by Teresa Bridgeman (London: Macmillan, 1991), p. 6.
14. 'Translation' is the word Mullan employs to describe how 'narrative (...) has to make "plain words" mediate the natural articulacy of feeling', p. 160.
15. Sterne, *A Sentimental Journey*, pp. 54-55.
16. Goring, p. 153.
17. Adam Smith, *Theory of Moral Sentiments* (Amherst, N.Y.: Prometheus Books, 2000), p. 466.
18. Vila, p. 182.
19. Jean-Jacques Rousseau, *Les Confessions* (Paris: Gallimard, 1973), I, p. 36.
20. David Hume, *A Treatise of Human Nature*, ed. by David Fate Norton and Mary J. Norton (Oxford, New York: Oxford University Press, 2000), p. 302; on Hume's treatment of passions see Mullan, pp. 18-19.
21. Vincent-Buffault, p. 4.
22. Diderot, *Discours de la poésie dramatique*, in *Œuvres complètes*, ed. Lewinter, III, pp. 417-18.
23. Diderot, *Contes et romans*, p. 897.
24. Todd, p. 4.
25. Diderot thus gives the example of a lady who put an end to her friendship with another woman untouched and even rather cynical at the reading of *Clarissa*. This lady pushes her aversion for insensitive people to the point that she would prefer 'que ma fille mourût entre mes bras que de l'en savoir frappée.' Diderot, *Contes et romans*, p. 908)
26. Diderot, *Contes et romans*, p. 898.
27. Bakhtin, *Rabelais and his World*, p. 321.
28. See Bakhtin, *Rabelais and his World*, p. 67.
29. Todd, p. 4.
30. Vila, p. 2.
31. Louis Lavelle, *L'Erreur de Narcisse* (Paris: Grasset, 1939), p. 88, quoted by Frédéric Laupies, *Leçon philosophique sur la sensibilité* (Paris: Presses Universitaires de France, 1998), p. 7.
32. Laupies, p. 28.
33. Laupies, p. 74.
34. See Goring, p. 29.
35. Also in Laurence Sterne, *The beauties of Sterne: including all his pathetic tales, and most*

distinguished observations on life. Selected for the heart of sensibility (London: C. Etherington, 1782), p. 88.
36. See '1.Baiser' in *Dictionnaire historique de la langue française*, vol. I, pp. 298–99.
37. See Goring, pp. 163–64.
38. See Vincent-Buffault, p. 17; see also Markman Ellis, *The Politics of Sensibility, Race, Gender and Commerce in the Sentimental Novel* (Cambridge: Cambridge University Press, 1996), chapter 4,
39. See Vincent-Buffault, p. 5.
40. See Ellis, pp. 195–96.
41. See Vincent-Buffault, p. 17.
42. Bakhtin, *Rabelais and his World*, pp. 320–21.
43. Bakhtin, *Rabelais and his World*, pp. 316–17.
44. Goring, p. 29.
45. Bakhtin, *Rabelais and his World*, p. 11.
46. Bakhtin, *Rabelais and his World*, p. 62.
47. Stout, p. 397.
48. Vincent-Buffault, p. 65.
49. See Mullan, pp. 153–55.
50. Sterne, *The beauties of Sterne: including all his pathetic tales, and most distinguished observations on life. Selected for the heart of sensibility* (London: C. Etherington, 1782), p. vii.
51. See chapter 4 'Laurence Sterne and the "Sociability" of the Novel', by Mullan.
52. Mullan, p. 152.
53. Goring, pp. 195–96
54. Ibid., p. 194.
55. Ronald Hafter, 'Garrick and Tristram Shandy', *SEL 1500–1900*, 7 (1967), 475–89, p. 486.
56. Stout, p. 398.
57. Ibid., p. 407.
58. See Bakhtin, *Rabelais and his World*, pp. 34, 36–37.
59. Mullan, p. 188.
60. Bakhtin, *Rabelais and his World*, pp. 62, 19.
61. Ibid., p.11.
62. Mullan, p. 158, and see pp. 160–72.
63. Ibid., p. 158.
64. Mullan, pp. 171–72.
65. Todd, p. 4.
66. Bakhtin, *Rabelais and his World*, p. 369.
67. Bakhtin, *Rabelais and his World*, pp. 122–23.
68. Ibid., p. 67; on the moralising aim of classical laughter, see Emmanuel Bury, *Littérature et politesse, l'invention de l'honnête homme 1580–1750* (Paris: Presses Universitaires de France, 1996), pp. 164–65.
69. Bakhtin, *Rabelais and his World*, p. 66.
70. See *Le Rêve de d'Alembert*, in Diderot, *Le Neveu de Rameau et autres dialogues philosophiques*, ed. by Jean Varloot (Paris: Gallimard, 1972), pp. 227–28.
71. See Bury, pp. 187–88.
72. Bakhtin, *Rabelais and his World*, p. 10.
73. Martine Lucchesi-Belzane, 'Un vide essentiel', in *La Politesse, vertu des apparences*, ed. by Régine Dhoquois (Paris: Autrement, 1991), p. 42.
74. Lucchesi-Belzane, pp. 29–32.
75. Laupies, pp. 73–74.
76. Bakhtin, *Rabelais and his World*, pp. 310, 317.

77. Lavelle, p. 88.
78. Bakhtin, *Rabelais and his World*, p. 422.
79. Bakhtin, *Rabelais and his World*, p. 25.
80. Bakhtin, *Rabelais and his World*, pp. 423, 426.
81. The title of the film *Tristram Shandy: a Cock and Bull Story*, directed by Michael Winterbottom, is clear evidence of this.

CONCLUSION

I have explored the ways in which the narrative structure of *Tristram Shandy* and *Jacques le fataliste* alters and renews the meaning of the philosophical debates inside the two novels. Those philosophical debates are profoundly contradictory, and do not provide an authorial discourse with a didactic content for the reader to follow: no philosophical system is imposed. The narrative structure continually prevents one discourse from becoming the dominant voice of the novel. On the other hand, what Sterne and Diderot do offer is a philosophical approach to truth, reached through a multiplicity of diverging voices, instead of through a unifying system. I argue that this is what, in *Tristram Shandy*, appealed to Diderot and what he wanted to put into practice in *Jacques le fataliste*. A comparative study has allowed me to highlight this fundamental connection between the two novels.

One of the main problems in the study of *Jacques le fataliste* and *Tristram Shandy* is the temptation to focus on a single angle, either aesthetically or philosophically, and to disregard and ignore all inconvenient contradictions. In the course of this book, I have maintained the necessity of analysing these contradictions as a whole instead of teasing them out from each other. In this approach, I have followed Bakhtin, who called for a new reading of Dostoevsky's works, on the same grounds as I have for Sterne's and Diderot's:

> [The tendency to monologize Dostoevsky's novels] is expressed in a striving, through analysis, to give finalizing definitions to the heroes, to find without fail a definite monologic authorial idea, to seek everywhere a superficial real-life verisimilitude, and so forth. The rigorous unfinalizability and dialogic openness of Dostoevsky's artistic world, that is, its very essence, is ignored or rejected.[1]

Similarly, to monologise *Jacques le fataliste* and *Tristram Shandy* would prevent the reader from assessing their aesthetic and philosophical qualities at their correct value. The two novels correspond far more to the dialogic than the monologic model, as defined by Bakhtin.

The first and second chapters have underlined the presence of a multiplicity of independent and divergent voices, each carrier of its own particular view. These voices, embodied by the characters of the novel, are not isolated from each other but enter into a dialogue in which they are confronted with their differences, without one voice dominating or invalidating another. This means that a particular voice cannot 'serve as a vehicle for the author's own ideological position'.² In the dialogic novel, the characters are not the mouthpieces of the author. If the views of Tristram Shandy and the narrator of *Jacques le fataliste* are heard, they remain alongside the other, sometimes contradictory, voices which are also present in the novel. The narrator's, or author's, position does not prevail; it is but one voice amongst many others: '[alongside] and in front of itself [the author's consciousness] senses others' equally valid consciousnesses, just as infinite and open-ended as itself.'³ Sterne and Diderot do not impose their own discourse by giving authority to one voice, but create a literary space where diverging voices, their own amongst them, engage in dialogue.

In order to preserve the dialogue and to prevent one voice from taking the ascendancy, it is necessary to introduce distance. The fourth chapter explored the way Diderot and Sterne introduced the grotesque register so as to create a distance from sentimentalism and prevent it from becoming the dominant tone of their novels. Bakhtin was attentive to this combination of registers in Sterne's work, as he draws a parallel between the eighteenth-century English author and Dostoevsky in their use of literary parody to preserve and even heighten dialogism:

> To introduce a parodic and polemical element into the narration is to make it more multi-voiced, more interruption-prone, no longer gravitating toward itself or its referential object. [. . .] [Literary] conventionality, in Dostoevsky's overall plan, not only did not reduce the signifying- and idea-content of his novels, but on the contrary could only increase it (as was also the case, incidentally, with Jean Paul and even with Sterne). Dostoevsky's destruction in his works of the usual monologic orientation led him to exclude altogether from his construction certain elements of this monologic orientation, and conscientiously to neutralize others. One means of neutralization was literary conventionality, that is, introducing into the narration or into the principles of construction a conventionalized discourse, stylized or parodic.⁴

In *Jacques le fataliste* and *Tristram Shandy*, the combination of the grotesque and the sentimental registers maintains the dialogue between the characters' diverging voices, but also brings it to an aesthetic level.

One of the key terms Bakhtin associates with dialogism is the notion of 'unfinalisability': a dialogue ends only when a dominant voice has brought it to a conclusion. The aim of the dialogic novel is to keep the dialogue going. In the dialogic novel, dialogue stands 'not as a means but as an end in itself.' 'When dialogue ends, everything ends. Thus dialogue, by its very essence, cannot and must not come to an end.'⁵ Through the study of outsideness, the third chapter argued that this unfinalisability starts at the characters' level. Indeed, Sterne's and Diderot's characters are particularly difficult to define with regard to their description, their biographies, and their views. The second chapter emphasised the fact that a character, though he stands for an idea, is not without his contradictions. As a consequence of what Bakhtin refers to as 'a *dialogic* penetration of

[a] personality', distance is created even within the character, and dialogue on the idea he stands for remains open.[6]

Unfinalisability carries consequences for the narrative. The centre of the dialogic novel cannot be the unfolding of the plot, as the novel does not progress towards a predefined conclusion, which would put an end to the dialogue. The plot provides opportunities for a dialogue to be initiated, but it does not constitute the main structure of the dialogic novel:

> The potential endlessness of dialogue in Dostoevsky's design already in itself answers the question why such dialogue cannot be plot-dependent in the strict sense of the word, for a plot-dependent dialogue strives toward conclusion just as inevitably as does the plot of which it is in fact a component. Therefore dialogue in Dostoevsky is, as we have said, always external to the plot, that is, internally independent of the plot-related interrelationships of the speakers — although, of course, dialogue is prepared for by the plot.[7]

Bakhtin's remarks may be equally well applied to *Tristram Shandy* and *Jacques le fataliste* where digressions have taken over the main narrative and where the conclusion is either rushed through or even non-existent, and the dialogue simply interrupted.

Bakhtin perceived aesthetics and ideology as inextricably linked, and varying depending on whether the novel follows the monologic or the dialogic model. The literary structure of the dialogic novel carries with it a specific ideological approach, which is radically opposed to the monologic model. By this, I do not mean a particular philosophical content, but rather a philosophical method and a representation of truth. In the monologic novel, there is only one truth, that is the one expressed by the authorial voice, and all other ideas are erroneous. In *Toward a Philosophy of the Act*, Bakhtin expressed his reservations with regard to a representation of truth as a universalising force.[8] Bakhtin's reservations complement Diderot's manner of apprehending truth. In *Le Bizarre et le Décousu*, Barbara Abrams argues that, in Diderot's philosophical approach, truth is not reached through a systematic methodology. On the contrary, '[truth] can be found in an imperfect state', 'in the state of being "unravelled"'.[9] This 'unravelling' is present in the dialogue, as diverging ideas are made to confront each other, without a dominant discourse to unify them. Diderot's approach appears remarkably close to the Bakhtinian dialogue. In *Problems of Dostoevsky's Poetics*, Bakhtin emphasises the necessity for an idea to enter into a dialogue with other ideas so as to fulfil its potential:

> The idea begins to live, that is, to take shape, to develop, to find and renew its verbal expression, to give birth to new ideas, only when it enters into genuine dialogic relationships with other ideas, with the ideas of *others*. Human thought becomes genuine thought, that is, an idea, only under conditions of living contact with another and alien thought, a thought embodied in someone else's voice, that is, in someone else's consciousness expressed in

discourse. At that point of contact between voice-consciousnesses the idea is born and lives.[10]

Bakhtin's remarks are echoed in *Pensées sur l'interprétation de la nature*, where Diderot also mentions the need for opinions to be confronted by external elements in order to develop: 'Tant que les choses ne sont que dans notre entendement, ce sont nos opinions; ce sont des notions qui peuvent être vraies ou fausses, accordées ou contredites. Elles ne prennent de la consistance qu'en se liant aux êtres extérieurs.'[11] The connection between Bakhtin and Diderot is tightened by Roland Mortier who defines the Diderotian dialogue as a space 'où l'affrontement des points de vue vise avant tout à un approfondissement philosophique des opinions et à la prise en compte de leur diversité.'[12]

For Bakhtin, as for Diderot and Sterne, dialogue constitutes a philosophical method in which the confrontation of contradictory ideas creates a dynamic for the pursuit of truth. The first chapter demonstrated that both novels invite the reader to contribute to this dynamic by offering his own diverging voice. The part played by the reader in Sterne's and Diderot's novels tallies with that of the reader of a dialogic text. According to Bakhtin, the reader of a dialogic novel cannot be a 'viewer who would objectify an entire event' according to a dominant system, but a 'participant' who takes part in the dialogue.[13] In this conclusion, I have said that at the end of *Tristram Shandy* and *Jacques le fataliste*, dialogue is interrupted. This is not entirely correct: it is pursued by the reader who is a participant in the dialogic novel, and ultimately represents the last 'être extérieur' with whom the plurality of opposing voices is confronted.

Notes to the Conclusion

1. Mikhail Bakhtin, *Problems of Dostoevsky's Poetics*, trans. by Caryl Emerson (Minneapolis, London: University of Minnesota Press, 1984), p. 272.
2. Bakhtin, *Problems of Dostoevsky's Poetics*, p. 7.
3. Bakhtin, *Problems of Dostoevsky's Poetics*, p. 68.
4. Bakhtin, *Problems of Dostoevsky's Poetics*, pp. 226–27.
5. Bakhtin, *Problems of Dostoevsky's Poetics*, p. 252.
6. Bakhtin, *Problems of Dostoevsky's Poetics*, p. 59. Author's italics.
7. Bakhtin, *Problems of Dostoevsky's Poetics*, p. 252.
8. 'It is an unfortunate misunderstanding (a legacy of rationalism) to think that truth *[pravda]* can only be the truth *[istina]* that is composed of universal moments; that the truth of a situation is precisely that which is repeatable and constant in it. Moreover, that which is universal and identical (logically identical) is fundamental and essential, whereas individual truth *[pravda]* is artistic and irresponsible, i.e., it isolates the given individuality.' Mikhail Bakhtin, *Toward a Philosophy of the Act*, trans. by Vadim Liapunov (Austin: University of Texas Press, 1999), p. 37.
9. The term 'unravelled' serves to translate the word 'décousu' used by Diderot. Barbara Lise Abrams, *Le Bizarre and le Décousu in the Novels and Theoretical Works of Denis Diderot: How the Idea of Marginality Originated in Eighteenth-Century France* (Lampeter: Edwin Mellen Press, 2009), p. 96.

10. Bakhtin, *Problems of Dostoevsky's Poetics*, p. 88.
11. Pensée VII, in *Pensées sur l'interprétation de la nature* in Denis Diderot, *Œuvres complètes*, ed. Roger Lewinter (Paris: le Club français du livre, 1969), II, p. 720; also quoted by Abrams, p. 104.
12. *Dictionnaire de Diderot*, ed. Roland Mortier and Raymond Trousson (Paris: Honoré Champion, 1999), p. 140; quoted by Abrams p. 30.
13. Bakhtin, Problems of Dostoevsky's Poetics, p. 18.

BIBLIOGRAPHY

Primary Works

BEATTIE, JAMES, *The Theory of Language* (Menston: The Scholar Press Limited, 1968)
DIDEROT, DENIS, *Contes et romans*, ed. by Michel Delon (Paris: Gallimard, 2004)
—— *Correspondance de Diderot*, ed. by Laurent Versini (Paris: Robert Laffont, 1997)
—— *Œuvres complètes*, ed. Roger Lewinter, 15 vols (Paris: le Club français du livre, 1969–73)
—— *Le Neveu de Rameau et autres dialogues philosophiques*, ed. by Jean Varloot (Paris: Gallimard, 1972)
DU BOIS, PHILIPPE, *Avertissement en tête de sa traduction des sermons de Saint Augustin*, ed. by Thomas Carr (Geneva: Droz, 1992)
HUET, PIERRE-DANIEL, *Lettre-traité sur l'origine des romans* (Paris: A.-G. Nizet, 1971)
HUME, DAVID, *A Treatise of Human Nature*, ed. by David Fate Norton and Mary J. Norton (Oxford, New York: Oxford University Press, 2000)
—— *A Treatise of Human Nature*, ed. by L. A. Selby-Bigge (Oxford: Clarendon Press, 1978)
LOCKE, JOHN, *An Essay concerning Human Understanding* (London: Penguin Books, 1997)
MONTAIGNE, MICHEL DE, *Les Essais* (Paris: Le Livre de Poche, 2001)
ROUSSEAU, JEAN-JACQUES, *Les Confessions*, 2 vols (Paris: Gallimard, 1973)
SMITH, ADAM, *Theory of Moral Sentiments* (Amherst, N.Y.: Prometheus Books, 2000)
STAËL, GERMAINE DE, *Lettres inédites de Mme de Staël à Henri Meister*, ed. by Paul Usteri and Eugène Ritter (Paris: Hachette, 1903)
STEELE, RICHARD and JOSEPH ADDISON, *Selections from* The Tatler *and* The Spectator (Harmondsworth: Penguin, 1988)
STERNE, LAURENCE, *The Life and Opinions of Tristram Shandy, Gentleman*, ed. by Melvyn New and Joan New (London: Penguin Classics, 1997)
—— *A Sentimental Journey through France and Italy by Mr. Yorick*, ed. by Paul Goring (London: Penguin Books, 2001)
—— *The Beauties of Sterne: Including all His Pathetic Tales, and Most Distinguished Observations on Life. Selected for the Heart of Sensibility* (London: C. Etherington, 1782)

Secondary Works

ABRAMS, BARBARA LISE, *Le Bizarre and le Décousu in the Novels and Theoretical Works of Denis Diderot: How the Idea of Marginality Originated in Eighteenth-Century France* (Lampeter: Edwin Mellen Press, 2009)

ASFOUR, LANA, *Laurence Sterne in France* (London: Continuum, 2008)
BAKHTIN, MIKHAÏL, *Art and Answerability: Early Philosophical Essays by M. M. Bakhtin*, ed. by Michael Holquist and Vadim Liapunov, trans. by Vadim Liapunov (Austin: University of Texas Press, 1990)
—— *The Dialogic Imagination, Four Essays*, trans. by Caryl Emerson and Michael Holquist (Austin: University of Texas Press, 2008)
—— *Esthétique de la création verbale*, trans. by Alfreda Aucouturier (Paris: Gallimard, 1984)
—— *Rabelais and his World*, trans. by Helene Iswolsky (Cambridge, Mass.: MIT Press, 1968)
—— *Toward a Philosophy of the Act*, trans. by Vadim Liapunov (Austin: University of Texas Press, 1999)
—— *Problems of Dostoevsky's Poetics*, trans. by Caryl Emerson (Minneapolis, London: University of Minnesota Press, 1984)
BALDWIN, CHARLES SEARS, 'The Literary Influence of Sterne in France', *PMLA*, 17 (1902), 221–36
BARTHES, ROLAND, *S/Z* (Paris: Editions du Seuil, 1970)
—— *S/Z*, trans. by Richard Miller (Oxford: Blackwell, 1990)
BARTON, FRANCIS B., *Etude sur l'influence de Laurence Sterne en France au dix-huitième siècle* (Paris: Hachette, 1911)
BERCHTOLD, JACQUES, *Les Prisons du roman (XVII°–XVIII° siècle), lectures plurielles et intertextuelles de Guzman d'Alfarache à Jacques le fataliste* (Geneva: Droz, 2000)
BURCKHARDT, SIGURD, 'Tristram Shandy's Law of Gravity', *ELH*, 28 (1961), 70–88
BURKE, RUTH E., *The Games of Poetic, Ludic Criticism and Postmodern Fiction* (New York: Peter Lang, 1994)
BURY, EMMANUEL, *Littérature et politesse, l'invention de l'honnête homme 1580–1750* (Paris: Presses Universitaires de France, 1996)
CASH, ARTHUR H. and JOHN M. STEDMOND, ed., *The Winged Skull, papers from the Laurence Sterne Bicentary Conference* (London: Methuen, 1971)
CASTLE, TERRY, *Masquerade and Civilisation: The Carnivalesque in Eighteenth-Century English Culture and Fiction* (London: Methuen, 1986)
CATRYSSE, JEAN, *Diderot et la mystification* (Paris: A.-G. Nizet, 1970)
CONNON, DEREK, *Diderot's Endgames* (Berne: Peter Lang, 2002)
CRU, R. LOYALTY, *Diderot as a Disciple of English Thought* (New York: AMS Press, 1966)
DHOQUOIS, RÉGINE, ed., *La Politesse, vertu des apparences* (Paris: Autrement, 1991)
EHRMANN, JACQUES, ed., *Game, Play, Literature* (New Haven: Eastern Press, 1968)
ELLIS, MARKMAN, *The Politics of Sensibility, Race, Gender and Commerce in the Sentimental Novel* (Cambridge: Cambridge University Press, 1996)
FEDERMAN, RAYMOND, ed., *Surfiction: Fiction Now . . . and Tomorrow* (Chicago: The Swallow Press, 1975)
FREDMAN, ALICE GREEN, *Diderot and Sterne* (New York: Columbia University Press, 1955)
GADAMER, HANS-GEORG, *Truth and Method*, trans. by William Glen-Doepel (London: Sheed and Ward, 1979)

GASCOIGNE, DAVID, *The Games of Fiction, Georges Perec and Modern French Ludic Literature* (Oxford, Berlin: Peter Lang, 2006)
GENETTE, GÉRARD, *Figures III* (Paris: Editions du Seuil, 1972)
GIFFORD, HENRY, *Comparative Literature* (London: Routledge & Kegan Paul, 1969)
GOMEZ-GÉRAUD, CHRISINE and PHILIPPE ANTOINE, eds, *Roman et récit de voyage* (Paris: Presses de l'Université de Paris-Sorbonne, 2001)
GORING, PAUL, *The Rhetoric of Sensibility in Eighteenth-Century Culture* (Cambridge: Cambridge University Press, 2005)
HAFTER, RONALD, 'Garrick and Tristram Shandy', *SEL 1500–1900*, 7 (1967), 475–89
HOBSON, MARIAN, *The Object of Art: the Theory of Illusion in Eighteenth-Century France* (Cambridge: Cambridge University Press, 2009)
—— 'Jacques le fataliste: l'art du probable', in *Diderot: les Dernières Années 1770–1784*, ed. by Peter France and Anthony Strugnell (Edinburgh: Edinburgh University Press, 1985), pp. 180–96
HOWELLS, ROBIN, *Playing Simplicity, Polemical Stupidity in the Writing of the French Enlightenment* (Oxford: Peter Lang, 2002)
HUIZINGA, JOHAN, *Homo Ludens: A Study of the Play-Element in Culture* (London: Paladin, 1970)
HUTCHINSON, PETER, *Games Authors Play* (London and New York: Methuen, 1983)
ISER, WOLFGANG, *Laurence Sterne: Tristram Shandy*, trans. by David Henry Wilson (Cambridge: Cambridge University Press, 1988)
LAMB, JONATHAN, *Sterne's Fiction and the Double Principle* (Cambridge: Cambridge University Press, 1989)
LAMY, BERNARD, *La Rhétorique ou l'art de parler* (Paris: PUF, 1998)
LANHAM, RICHARD A., *Tristram Shandy: The Games of Pleasure* (Christchurch, New Zealand: Cybereditions, 2001)
LAUPIES, FRÉDÉRIC, *Leçon philosophique sur la sensibilité* (Paris: Presses Universitaires de France, 1998)
LAVELLE, LOUIS, *L'Erreur de Narcisse* (Paris: Grasset, 1939)
LEMON, LEE T. and MARION J. REIS, eds and trans., *Russian Formalist Criticism, Four Essays* (Lincoln, London: University of Nebraska Press, 1965)
LOEB, ARTHUR L., *Space Structures: Their Harmony and Counterpoint* (Reading, Mass.: Addison-Wesley, 1976)
LOY, J. ROBERT, *Diderot's Determined Fatalist: A Critical Appreciation of* Jacques le fataliste (New York: King's Crown Press, Columbia University, 1950)
MCMORRAN, WILL, *The Inn and the Traveller: Digressive Topographies in the Early Modern European Novel* (Oxford: Legenda, 2002)
MEINER, CARSTEN, *Les Mutations de la clarté, exemple, induction et schématismes dans l'oeuvre de Marivaux* (Paris: Honoré Champion, 2007)
MONTANDON, ALAIN, *Sociopoétique de la promenade* (Clermont-Ferrand: Presses Universitaires Blaise Pascal, 2000)
MORTIER, ROLAND and RAYMOND TROUSSON, eds, *Dictionnaire de Diderot* (Paris: Honoré Champion, 1999)
MULLAN, JOHN, *Sentiment and Sociability: The Language of Feeling in the Eighteenth Century* (Oxford: Clarendon Press, 1988)
OGÉE, FRÉDÉRIC, ed., *"Better in France?": The Circulation of Ideas Across the Channel in the Eighteenth Century* (Lewisburg: Bucknell University Press, 2005)

PLANTIÉ, JAQUELINE, *La Mode du portrait littéraire en France (1641-1681)* (Paris: Champion, 1994)

PRUNER, FRANCIS, *L'Unité secrète de* Jacques le Fataliste (Paris: Minard, 1970)

RACAULT, JEAN-MICHEL, *Nulle part et ses environs, Voyage aux confins de l'utopie littéraire classique (1657-1802)* (Paris: Presses de l'Université de Paris-Sorbonne, 2003)

RAYMOND, A.G., *La Genèse de* Jacques le fataliste *de Diderot, quelques clefs nouvelles* (Paris: Archives des Lettres Modernes, 1977)

REY, ALAIN, ed., *Dictionnaire historique de la Langue française* (Paris: Dictionnaires Le Robert, 1998)

SMIETANSKI, JACQUES, *Le Réalisme dans* Jacques le Fataliste (Paris: A. G. Nizet, 1965)

SOUD, STEPHEN, '"Weavers, Gardeners, and Gladiators": Labyrinths in *Tristram Shandy*', *ECS*, 28 (1995), 397-411

STOUT, GARDNER D., JR, 'Yorick's Sentimental Journey: A comic "Pilgrim's Progress" for the man of Feeling' *ELH*, 30 (1963), 395-412

TODD, JANET, *Sensibility, an Introduction* (London: Methuen, 1986)

TODOROV, TZVETAN, *Nous et les autres. La réflexion française sur la diversité humaine* (Paris: Editions du Seuil, 1989)

VILA, ANNE C., *Enlightenment and Pathology, Sensibility in the Literature and Medicine of Eighteenth-Century France* (Baltimore, London: John Hopkins University Press, 1998)

VINCENT-BUFFAULT, ANNE, *The History of Tears, Sensibility and Sentimentality*, trans. Teresa Bridgeman (London: Macmillan, 1991)

WALLACE, ANNE D., *Walking, Literature, and English Culture: The Origins and Uses of Peripatetic in the Nineteenth Century* (Oxford: Clarendon Press, 1994)

WARNING, RAINER, *Illusion und Wirklichkeit in "Tristram Shandy" und "Jacques le Fataliste"* (Munich: Wilhelm Fink Verlag, 1965)

WEBER, SAMUEL, 'Reading: "To the Very End of the World"', *MLN*, 111 (1996), 819-34

WEISGERBER, JEAN, *L'Espace romanesque* (Lausanne: Editions de l'Age d'Homme, 1978)

WOODHOUSE, ANNE F., 'Eighteenth-Century English Visitors to France in Fiction and Fact', *MLS*, 6 (1976), 37-41

Lightning Source UK Ltd.
Milton Keynes UK
UKOW05n1531220317
297097UK00011BA/59/P